LEARN
Adobe InDesign CC
for **Print** and **Digital Media Publication**

SECOND EDITION

Adobe Certified Associate Exam Preparation

Jonathan Gordon
and Conrad Chavez
with Rob Schwartz

Adobe

LEARN ADOBE INDESIGN CC FOR PRINT AND DIGITAL MEDIA PUBLICATION, SECOND EDITION
ADOBE CERTIFIED ASSOCIATE EXAM PREPARATION
Jonathan Gordon (video)
Conrad Chavez (book)
with **Rob Schwartz**

Adobe Press books is an imprint of Pearson Education, Inc.
For the latest on Adobe Press books, go to www.adobepress.com.
To report errors, please send a note to errata@peachpit.com. For information regarding permissions, request forms and the appropriate contacts within the Pearson Education Global Rights & Permissions department, please visit www.pearsoned.com/permissions/.

Adobe Press Editor: Laura Norman	**Proofreader:** Elizabeth Welch
Development Editor: Robyn G. Thomas	**Compositor:** Kim Scott, Bumpy Design
Technical Reviewer: Chad Chelius	**Indexer:** Valerie Haynes Perry
Senior Production Editor: Tracey Croom	**Cover & Interior Design:** Mimi Heft
Production Editor: Becky Winter	**Cover Illustration:** Markovka/ShutterStock
Copyeditor: Scout Festa	

ISBN-13: 978-0-13-487839-3
ISBN-10:   0-13-487839-6

4 2023

To Jennifer, my wife and best friend. You make me want to do my best at everything I do.

To Jacob, my son and Bubba. I love your curiosity and desire to learn. Though I have been a teacher for over two decades, you inspire me to be the eternal student.

To Juliana, my daughter and baby girl. Your humor and laughter can always put a smile on my face.

—Jonathan Gordon

To my niece Kiki, who has an entire wonderful lifetime of learning and creativity ahead of her.

—Conrad Chavez

Acknowledgments

This journey would not have been possible without my family. Jacob and Juliana, you are my Captain Toothless and Princess Sourpuss, my Bubba and my baby girl. Jennifer, I know you were just as stressed as I was with the book. I have wanted only the best for you and the kids. Whenever I am with you I feel safe. Like I am home. I am glad I am home. I love you so much.

I also have to thank my parents for all the support and encouragement over the years. I appreciated it more than you know.

Thanks goes to Robyn Thomas, my editor, without whose insight and motivation I could not have gotten through video after video after video after video.

To Rob Schwartz, the brains behind brainbuffet.com and this book series. Thanks for involving me in this endeavor. I owe you a lot—going all the way back to Rickards and McFatter. I admire your tenacity, brilliance, and modesty.

—Jonathan Gordon

Thanks go to editor Robyn Thomas, who kept the project together; and to Chad Chelius, whose deep knowledge of InDesign helped ensure the technical accuracy of this book. And a mountain of thanks to Sarah, who patiently supported me during the long hours of writing this book.

—Conrad Chavez

About the Authors

Jonathan Gordon (video author) is a prominent InDesign instructor who has trained students and adults in Adobe products for over 20 years. Jonathan has lectured at various conventions and media workshops across the United States. An award-winning instructor, he was named Broward County Journalism Adviser of the Year by the *Sun Sentinel* and was awarded the same distinction by the Florida Scholastic Press Association. Jonathan has taught digital media technology (Adobe InDesign, Photoshop, Illustrator, and Dreamweaver) through McFatter Technical College. He has provided video content and material for Brainbuffet.com and has also consulted for Certiport as a subject matter expert. Jonathan earned a master's degree in mass communication from the University of Florida, specializing in online communication and web design. Several of his former journalist students have gone on to be published in the *Columbia Spectator*, the *Miami Herald*, the *New York Times*, and *Sports Illustrated*.

Conrad Chavez (primary book author) is an author and photographer. His experience with digital media workflows extends back to the birth of desktop publishing with Aldus PageMaker, the precursor to Adobe InDesign. During his time at Adobe Systems, Inc., Conrad helped write the user guide for Adobe InDesign. He is the author of several titles in the Adobe Classroom in a Book and Real World Adobe Photoshop series, and he writes articles for CreativePro.com and *InDesign Magazine*. Visit his website at conradchavez.com.

Rob Schwartz (author of Chapters 7 and 8) is an award-winning teacher (currently at Sheridan Technical College in Hollywood, Florida) with over 15 years of experience in technical education. Rob holds several Adobe Certified Associate certifications and is an Adobe Certified Instructor. As an Adobe Education Leader, Rob won the prestigious Impact Award from Adobe, and in 2010, Rob was the first winner of the Worldwide Certiport Adobe Certified Associate Championship.

Find out more about Rob at his online curriculum website at brainbuffet.com.

Contents

Getting Started

Welcome to *Learn Adobe InDesign CC for Print and Digital Media Publication (2018 release)*. We use a combination of text and video to help you learn the basics of design with Adobe InDesign CC along with other skills that you will need to get your first job in graphic design. The industry-leading page design and layout program, Adobe InDesign CC lets you create and publish anything from printed books and brochures to digital magazines, eBooks, and interactive online documents.

About This Book and Video

Learn Adobe InDesign CC for Print and Digital Media Publication, Second Edition was created by a team of expert instructors, writers, and editors with years of experience in helping beginning learners get their start with the cool creative tools from Adobe Systems. Our aim is not only to teach you the basics of graphic design with InDesign, but to give you an introduction to the associated skills (like design principles and project management) that you'll need for your first job.

We've built the training around the objectives for the Print and Digital Media Publication Using Adobe InDesign CC Adobe Certified Associate (ACA) Exam, and if you master the topics covered in this book and videos, you'll be in good shape to take the exam. But even if certification isn't your goal, you'll still find that this training will give you an excellent foundation for your future work in graphic design. To that end, we've structured the material in the order that makes most sense for beginning learners (as determined by experienced classroom teachers), rather than following the more arbitrary grouping of topics in the ACA Objectives.

To aid you in your quest, we've created a unique learning system that uses video and text in partnership. You'll experience this partnership in action in the Web Edition, which lives on your Account page at *peachpit.com*. The Web Edition contains more than 11 hours of video—the heart of the training—embedded in an online eBook that supports the video training and provides background material. The eBook material is also available separately for offline reading as a printed book or as an eBook in a variety of formats. The Web Edition also includes interactive review questions you can use to evaluate your progress. Purchase of the book in any format entitles you to free access to the Web Edition (instructions for accessing it follow).

Most chapters provide step-by-step instructions for learning specific techniques. Many chapters include several optional tasks that let you further explore the features you've already learned. Don't stop exploring when you reach the end of the print book. Two additional online chapters acquaint you with other skills and concepts that you'll come to depend on as you use the software in your everyday work. Here is where you'll find coverage of Domains 1 and 2 of the ACA Objectives, which don't specifically relate to features of InDesign but are important components of the complete skill set that the ACA exam seeks to evaluate. Along with those chapters you'll find an appendix that covers using InDesign to build an index for a book. You'll find all three online items posted at peachpit.com along with the Web Edition and lesson files.

Each chapter opens with two lists of objectives. One list lays out the learning objectives: the specific tasks you'll learn in the chapter. The second list shows the ACA Objectives that are covered in the chapter. A printable table you can download along with the lesson files (see instructions below) guides you to coverage of all the exam objectives in the book and videos.

Conventions Used in This Book

This book uses several elements styled in ways to help you as you work through the projects.

Terms that are defined in the glossary appear in bold and in color, such as:

Kerning increases or decreases the amount of space between two characters.

Links to videos that cover the topics in depth appear in the margins.

▶ Video 5.1

The ACA Objectives covered in the chapters are called out in the margins beside the sections that address them.

★ ACA Objective 2.1

Notes and tips give additional information about a topic. The information they contain is not essential to accomplishing a task but provides a more in-depth understanding of the topic.

NOTE

The default behavior for background images is to tile across and down the container where they are set.

TIP

You can also show or hide panels by choosing them from the Window menu.

Working in InDesign means you'll sometimes need to enter code-like text; this text is listed in a bold monospaced font:

Enter **mailto:** immediately followed by the email address.

Other text that you should enter appears in **bold**.

OPERATING SYSTEM DIFFERENCES

In most cases, InDesign CC works the same in both Windows and macOS. Minor differences exist between the two versions, mostly due to platform-specific issues. Most of these are simply differences in keyboard shortcuts, how dialogs are displayed, and how buttons are named. Where specific commands differ, they are noted within the text. Windows commands are listed first, followed by the macOS equivalent, such as Ctrl+C/Command+C. In general, the Windows Ctrl key is equivalent to the Command (or Cmd) key in macOS, and the Windows Alt key is equivalent to the macOS Option (or Opt) key.

In most cases, screen shots were made in the macOS version of InDesign and may appear somewhat different from your own screen. The screen shots in this book show a Light interface, to allow for higher contrast in the print version of the book. Interface elements such as panels and dialogs will be darker on your screen.

As chapters proceed, instructions may be shortened with the assumption that you picked up the essential concepts earlier in the chapter. For example, at the beginning of a chapter you may be instructed to "press Ctrl+C/Command+C." Later, you may be told to "copy" text. These should be considered identical instructions. If you find you have difficulties in any particular task, review earlier steps or techniques in that chapter. In some cases when a technique is based on concepts covered earlier, you will be referred back to the specific chapter.

Installing the Software

Before you begin using *Learn Adobe InDesign CC for Print and Digital*, make sure that your system is set up correctly and that you've installed the proper software and hardware. This material is based on the original 2018 release of Adobe InDesign CC (version 13.0) and is designed to cover the objectives of the Adobe Certified Associate Exam for that version of the software.

The Adobe InDesign CC software is not included with this book; it is available only with an Adobe Creative Cloud membership, which you must purchase or which must be supplied by your school or another organization. To install applications from Adobe Creative Cloud onto your computer, follow the instructions provided at *helpx.adobe.com/creative-cloud/help/download-install-app.html*.

ADOBE CREATIVE CLOUD DESKTOP APP

In addition to Adobe InDesign CC, some extended activities suggested in the text require the Adobe Creative Cloud desktop application, which provides a central location for managing the dozens of apps and services that are included in a Creative Cloud membership. Although the central lessons in this book and the videos do not require a Creative Cloud subscription, you should explore the ways the Creative Cloud desktop application can be used to sync and share files, manage fonts, access libraries of stock photography and design assets, and showcase and discover creative work in the design community.

The Creative Cloud desktop application is installed automatically when you download your first Creative Cloud product. If you have Adobe Application Manager installed, it auto-updates to the Creative Cloud desktop application.

If the Creative Cloud desktop application is not installed on your computer, you can download it from the Creative Desktop Apps page on the Adobe website (*adobe.com/creativecloud/catalog/desktop.html*). If you are using software on classroom machines, be sure to check with your instructor before making any changes to the installed software or system configuration.

Accessing the Free Web Edition and Project Files

Your purchase of this book in any format includes access to the corresponding Web Edition hosted on *peachpit.com*. The Web Edition contains the complete text of the book augmented with hours of video and interactive quizzes, as well as online chapters and other bonus content.

If you purchased an eBook from *peachpit.com* or *adobepress.com*, the Web Edition will automatically appear on the Digital Purchases tab on your Account page. Click the Launch link to access the product. Continue reading to learn how to register your product to get access to the lesson files.

If you purchased an eBook from a different vendor or you bought a print book, you must register your purchase on *peachpit.com*:

1 Go to *www.peachpit.com/register*.

2 Sign in or create a new account.

NOTE

Adobe periodically provides updates to software. You can easily obtain these updates through Creative Cloud. If these updates include new features that affect the content of this training or the objectives of the ACA exam in any way, we will post updated material to peachpit.com.

NOTE

When opening any of the project files, a warning dialog may inform you that your document contains links to sources that have been modified; click Update Links. A Missing Fonts dialog may also appear. Click Sync Fonts to install missing fonts from Adobe Typekit. For information on Adobe Typekit, see Chapter 2.

3   Enter the ISBN: **9780134878393**.

4   Answer the questions as proof of purchase.

5   The Web Edition will appear under the Digital Purchases tab on your Account page. Click the Launch link to access the product.

NOTE

You'll find a video walkthrough of these instructions at www.peachpit.com/ LearnACAindesign.

To work through the projects in this product, you will first need to download the lesson files from peachpit.com. You can download the files for individual lessons or download them all in a single file.

The Lesson Files can be accessed through the Registered Products tab on your Account page. Click the Access Bonus Content link below the title of your product to proceed to the download page. Click the lesson file links to download them to your computer.

Additional Resources

Learn Adobe InDesign CC for Print and Digital Media Publication is not meant to replace the documentation that comes with the program or to be a comprehensive reference for every feature. For comprehensive information about program features and tutorials, refer to these resources:

Adobe InDesign Learn & Support: *helpx.adobe.com/support/indesign.html* is where you can find and browse Help and Support content on *Adobe.com*. Adobe InDesign Help is accessible from the Help menu in InDesign. Help is also available as a printable PDF document. Download the document at *helpx.adobe. com/pdf/indesign_reference.pdf*.

Adobe Forums: *forums.adobe.com/community/indesign* lets you tap into peer-to-peer discussions, questions, and answers on Adobe products.

Adobe InDesign CC product home page: *adobe.com/products/indesign* provides information about new features and intuitive ways to create responsive web page layouts that display beautifully on any screen.

Adobe Exchange: *adobeexchange.com/creativecloud.html* is a central resource for finding tools, services, extensions, code samples, and more to extend your Adobe products.

Resources for educators: *adobe.com/education* and *edex.adobe.com* offer information for instructors who teach classes on Adobe software at all levels.

Adobe Certification

The Adobe training and certification programs are designed to help designers and other creative professionals improve and promote their product-proficiency skills. Adobe Certified Associate (ACA) is an industry-recognized credential that demonstrates proficiency in Adobe digital skills. Whether you're just starting out in your career or planning to switch jobs, the Adobe Certified Associate program is for you! For more information, visit *edex.adobe.com/aca*.

Resetting the Preferences to Their Defaults

InDesign lets you determine how the program looks and behaves (such as tool settings and the default unit of measurement) using the extensive options in Edit > Preferences (Windows) or InDesign CC > Preferences (macOS). To ensure that the preferences of your copy of InDesign match those used in this book, you can reset your preference settings to their defaults. If you are using software installed on computers in a classroom, don't make any changes to the system without checking with your instructor.

To reset your preferences to their default settings, follow these steps:

1 Quit Adobe InDesign.

2 Hold down the Shift+Ctrl+Alt keys (Windows) or the Shift+Control+Option+Command keys (macOS) as you start up InDesign.

3 Continue to hold down the keys until the Delete InDesign Preference Files dialog appears.

4 In the Startup Alert dialog box, click Yes.

5 The file containing your preferences will be deleted.

CHAPTER OBJECTIVES

Chapter Learning Objectives

- Identify and understand different elements of the InDesign CC interface.

- Define common panels and clarify their usage.

- Identify tools and their functionality.

- Navigate through an InDesign document and change zoom levels.

- Organize and customize the InDesign workspace.

Chapter ACA Objectives

For full descriptions of the objectives, see the table on pages 270–276.

DOMAIN 2.0
PROJECT SETUP AND INTERFACE
2.2, 2.3

CHAPTER 1

Getting Started with InDesign

You are about to start your Adobe InDesign CC journey. As an industry-standard layout application, InDesign is a powerhouse used by graphic designers worldwide to design and produce print and digital media publications.

You probably saw something today that was created with InDesign. People use InDesign to create printed newspapers, magazines, yearbooks, reports, newsletters, and flyers. On your tablet or smartphone, eBooks, digital magazines, and PDF documents and forms might have been created in InDesign. A single InDesign document can be the source for all of those types of printed and digital media.

Whether you end up working as a graphic designer for a design studio in communications, marketing, advertising, public relations, or elsewhere, there is a high probability that InDesign experience will be a required criterion for the job.

Let's step into InDesign so that you can start to find your way around the program. In this chapter, you'll learn to recognize and identify commonly used tools and panels, and to customize the look and feel of InDesign based on what works best for your project.

▶ *Video 1.1 Learn Adobe InDesign CC for Print and Digital Media Publication*

Starting InDesign

You start InDesign just as you start any other application you use. Whether you're using Windows or a Mac, there are many ways to start InDesign. Choose the way that's easiest and fastest for you in your day-to-day work.

Why are there so many ways to open an application? People have different preferences for how they like to work. One person might be used to opening applications from the Taskbar (Windows) or Dock (macOS), another likes to open applications from shortcuts on the desktop, and so on. You don't have to memorize every way; just use the way that you're most comfortable with.

NOTE

*This chapter supports
the project created in
Video Project 1. Go to
the Project 1 page in
the book's Web Edition
to watch the entire
video from beginning
to end.*

To start InDesign, do one of the following:

- In Windows, click the Adobe InDesign CC application icon on the Start menu, Start screen, or Taskbar—if it's there. If a shortcut icon for InDesign exists on the desktop or in a folder window, you can double-click that.

  You can also type **InDesign** into Cortana (the Windows search feature), and when the InDesign application appears in the search results, double-click it or press Enter.

- In macOS, click the Adobe InDesign CC application icon in the Launchpad or Dock—if it's there. If an alias icon for InDesign exists on the desktop or in a folder window, you can double-click that.

  You can also type **InDesign** into Spotlight (the macOS search feature), and when the InDesign application appears in the search results, double-click it or press Enter.

TIP

*You can also start
InDesign by clicking it
in the Creative Cloud
desktop application.*

The Start workspace appears. We'll take a closer look at that in the next section.

Using the Start Workspace

In many applications, starting up puts you in an empty workspace. But that's not very useful, is it? When you start InDesign, something better appears: a Start workspace (**Figure 1.1**). The Start workspace is designed to help you get right to working or learning about InDesign.

NOTE

*Earlier versions of
InDesign will show
a Welcome screen
instead of the Start
workspace.*

NOTE

*In this book, you may notice that the InDesign user interface is light, while
in the videos it is dark. The light interface is easier to see in print. You can
change this: In the Interface panel in the Preferences dialog, select a Color
Theme setting.*

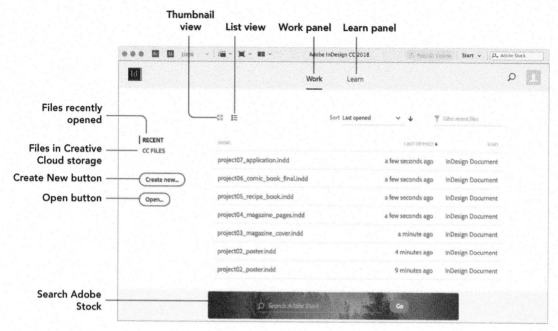

Thumbnail view · **List view** · **Work panel** · **Learn panel**

Files recently opened

Files in Creative Cloud storage

Create New button

Open button

Search Adobe Stock

Figure 1.1 The Start workspace in InDesign

Because you're a beginner, consider clicking the Learn tab to watch tutorials that teach you how to make different kinds of InDesign documents.

When you're ready to make a new InDesign document, the Start workspace's Work tab gives you a couple of ways to get started. The main way is to click the Create New button, which is a shortcut for the File > New > Document command. That opens the New Document dialog, which presents several presets you can use as starting points. We'll look more closely at the New Document dialog later.

 TIP

As in other applications, you can use keyboard shortcuts. You can create a new file by pressing the keyboard shortcut for the File > New > Document command, which is Ctrl+N (Windows) or Command+N (macOS). You can open a file by pressing the keyboard shortcut for File > Open, which is Ctrl+O (Windows) or Command+O (macOS).

If you'd like to start from a template, type what you're looking for into the Adobe Stock search field at the bottom of the Start workspace and click Go, which will take you to an Adobe Stock web page of InDesign document templates. (Adobe Stock may not be available on computers in some schools and businesses.)

NOTE

As useful as the Start workspace is, if for some reason you prefer not to see the Start workspace when InDesign starts up, you can disable it: Open InDesign Preferences, and in the General pane, deselect Show "Start" Workspace When No Documents Are Open.

In day-to-day use, the first thing you'll often want to do after starting InDesign is to continue working on your current projects. When the Start workspace appears, click Recent, which displays a list of InDesign documents that were opened recently. (The Recent list may be empty if this is your first time using InDesign on this computer or if InDesign preferences were reset.) The Recent list is a shortcut for the File > Open Recent command.

NOTE

If you're using a shared computer where you can't sign in with your own Adobe ID, Creative Cloud Files storage might not be available to you.

If you're keeping InDesign documents in Creative Cloud Files online storage, you can see them by clicking CC Files. Creative Cloud Files is cloud storage associated with the Adobe ID that's signed in to the computer. If you've used cloud storage services such as Dropbox, Google Drive, Microsoft OneDrive, or iCloud Files, Creative Cloud Files works much the same way: You can transfer files to and from Creative Cloud Files storage using a web browser, folders on your Windows or Mac desktop, or a mobile app on your phone or tablet.

Getting to Know the InDesign Workspace

★ *ACA Objective 2.2*

▶ *Video 1.4*
The InDesign Workspace

Once you've opened an InDesign document, you find yourself in the InDesign document workspace (**Figure 1.2**), which is designed to present the options that are most relevant to what you're currently working on. Beyond that, you can customize the InDesign workspace with the controls you'd like to see up front, and free up screen space by hiding options you don't want to see.

Let's tour some areas of the InDesign workspace that you'll use most often.

Looking at the Control Panel

Professional applications such as InDesign offer hundreds of features and options spread out across menus, panels, and dialogs. It could be a major challenge to navigate back and forth across so many places in the application while you're working, and especially while you're still learning.

The Control panel (**Figure 1.3**) takes a big step toward solving that problem by automatically adapting to what you're doing. When you choose a tool, the Control panel shows options for that specific tool. When you select something, the Control panel changes to focus on the options that are useful for the selected object in

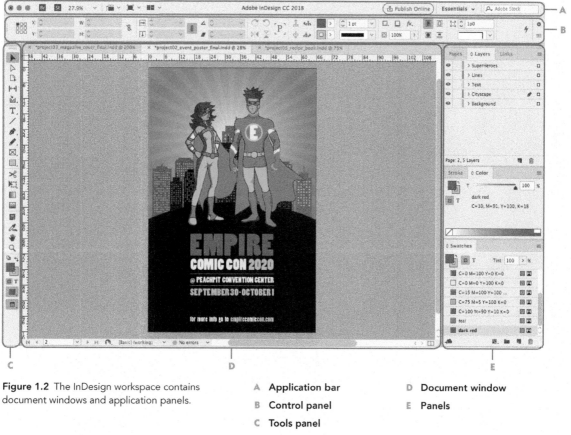

Figure 1.2 The InDesign workspace contains document windows and application panels.

A Application bar
B Control panel
C Tools panel
D Document window
E Panels

the document. For example, if you select a graphic object, the Control panel shows graphics options. If you select text, the Control panel offers type controls. If you select multiple objects, the Control panel adds options for aligning them.

The options on the Control panel don't exist only there. For example, while the Control panel shows you type-related options for a selected text frame, if you also have the Character panel open (**Figure 1.4**) you'll see many of the same options displayed there too. The point is that just because you're going to work with text for 30 seconds, you won't need to go to the trouble of opening the Character panel if the type options you want are already showing in the Control panel.

Figure 1.3 The Control panel shows commonly used options for the currently active object.

Figure 1.4 Options on the Control panel are taken from more specialized panels, so that you can do more work with fewer panels open.

The options you see in the Control panel may differ from what's shown in the book. The Control panel shows fewer options when it's within a smaller InDesign application frame or on a narrower computer display.

Changing the Tools Panel Layout

After a fresh installation of InDesign, the Tools panel is always a single column along the left side of the workspace. But as you can see in the video, the Tools panel may be too tall for some smaller screens. When that happens, you can click the double arrows at the top of the Tools panel to switch it to one of its other modes (**Figure 1.5**), which may fit the Tools panel better on your screen and make it easier to see some of the useful buttons within the Tools panel.

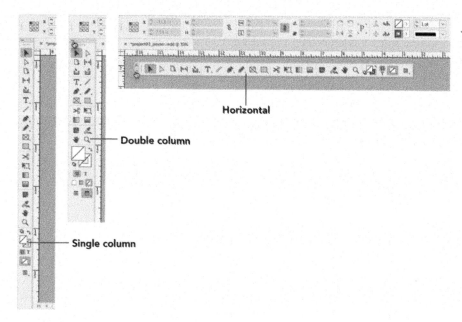

Horizontal

Double column

Single column

Figure 1.5 To try different Tools panel layouts, click the double arrows at the top of the panel.

Switching Workspaces

So far we've talked about the InDesign workspace as the overall presentation of tools and options on your screen. And we've mentioned how they're customizable, because you can expand, collapse, and rearrange the panels you see onscreen. But there are a lot of those panels, so you don't want to be fiddling with them all day long. That's why you can save different panel configurations as your own named workspaces.

You can change workspaces near the right side of the *application bar* at the top of the InDesign workspace, just to the left of the search field. Click the *workspace switcher* (**Figure 1.6**) to see a menu of the preset workspaces installed with InDesign. If you create your own workspaces, they'll appear at the top of that menu.

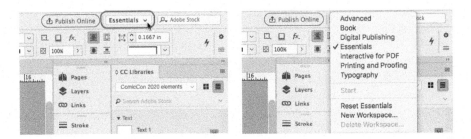

Figure 1.6 The workspace switcher lets you change the active workspace.

The list of workspaces also appears under the Window > Workspaces submenu.

Here are some more tips for using workspaces:

- If you've created an arrangement of panels that you like and you want to save it, choose New Workspace from the workspace switcher menu.

- If you're using one of your own named workspaces and you want to update it, choose New Workspace again and give it the same name as the workspace you want to update; InDesign will ask you if you want to replace the existing one.

- If you rearranged some panels in one of your named workspaces, choose Reset [name of workspace] from the workspace switcher menu. The workspace will be restored to the way you saved it.

Looking at Screen Modes

One of the great things about the InDesign document window is that it shows you all kinds of visual aids to help you understand what you're looking at and to help you lay out your document efficiently. Objects have indicators and controls on them. Pages have margins, guides, and grids to help your layout meet production requirements. But none of these visual aids are going to be on the final document, and they can get in the way and be distracting when you just want to see what your design looks like on its own. For this reason, InDesign provides multiple screen modes (**Figure 1.7**) so that you can hide or show different types of elements on the workspace.

- **Normal.** The Normal screen mode will usually be your daily working mode, because you can see all objects and guides, even those on the nonprinting pasteboard area outside the page edges.

- **Preview.** The Preview mode is a great way to see how the document design looks on its own if it were to be printed or exported at that moment, without the distracting clutter of the pasteboard, various guides, and onscreen indicators.

- **Bleed** and **Slug**. You probably won't be using the Bleed and Slug modes right away, but they're useful for some print-oriented projects where the document has bleed and slug values found in the File > Document Setup dialog. A bleed is an area around a page for elements that will be trimmed after printing, and a slug is extra space to print document information (which will also be trimmed). The Bleed and Slug modes show these areas that are outside the page edge.

Normal

Presentation

Preview

Bleed

Slug

Figure 1.7 Screen modes in InDesign

- **Presentation.** If you ever want to show an InDesign document as an onscreen slide show, this is the way. It hides everything but the design, trims everything outside the page edges, and shows the page on a black background. You can turn pages using the arrow keys or the Page Up and Page Down keys.

You can change the screen mode in more than one place. Use the method that works best for you:

- In the application bar, click the Screen Mode button (**Figure 1.8**) and choose a mode.

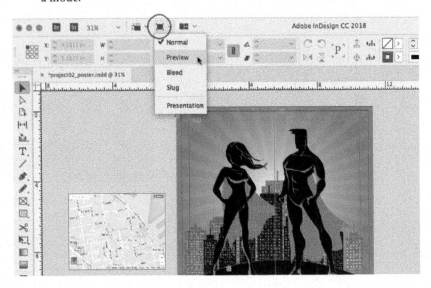

- In the Tools panel, click the Screen Mode button (**Figure 1.9**) and choose a mode. Note that if the Tools panel is in two-column mode, there are two Screen Mode buttons: The left button is a one-click reset to Normal, and the right button lets you switch to any mode except Normal by pressing and holding the button.

- Choose View > Screen Mode, and choose a mode from the submenu.

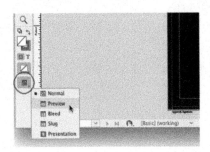

Figure 1.9 There's also a Screen Mode button in the Tools panel.

TIP

Want to quickly switch between Normal and Preview screen modes, just to get a sense of the final document? Press W on your keyboard to toggle between those two modes. That's a single-key shortcut, so press it only when you don't have an active text cursor.

Managing Document Window Tabs

When you open documents in InDesign, they open as a series of tabs along the top edge of the document windows (**Figure 1.10**). If you've worked with tabbed documents in other applications, such as web browsers, you already have some idea of how document window tabs work in InDesign:

- To switch to a different document, click its tab.
- To rearrange the tabs, drag a tab to the left or right.

Figure 1.10 Multiple InDesign documents appear as tabs that you can arrange.

TIP

To switch document tabs with a keyboard shortcut, press Ctrl+` (Windows) or Command+` (macOS). The ` key is the grave accent key at the upper-left corner of a US English keyboard. This is sometimes called the tilde key, by those who name it after the tilde character (~), which is the uppercase form of the key on a US English keyboard.

You don't have to use tabbed documents. If you want an InDesign document window to float free from the rest of the workspace, you can undock it from the tabs. Drag the document's tab up or down, make sure there is no blue line within the application frame (or it will become a tab when you release the mouse button), and then release the mouse button.

A disadvantage of tabbed documents is that you can see only one document at a time, the one in front of the stack of tabs. Want to see documents side by side instead? InDesign has that covered too. In the application bar, click the Arrange Documents icon (**Figure 1.11**) and in the grid of icons, choose the window arrangement you want:

- The top row of icons show tiling options, where all open documents are given the same amount of space.
- The center grid of icons shows various arrangements that can use unequal areas. Some of them may be unavailable. For example, if you have only two documents open, you can't choose the arrangements that involve three or

four documents. You may see pop-up tool tips with names like "4-up." The "-up" is a printing term for when a sheet of paper has multiple pages on it; 4-up means printing four pages on a sheet, but of course, this feature isn't about printing.

- **Float All in Windows** breaks out all documents from the workspace and makes them independent floating windows. The opposite of this is **Consolidate All**, which puts any floating windows back into the row of tabbed documents.

- **New Window** creates a second window for the currently active document (the one in front). This is useful when you want to see two different views of the same document—if, for example, you want to check something on both page 24 and page 186 at the same time.

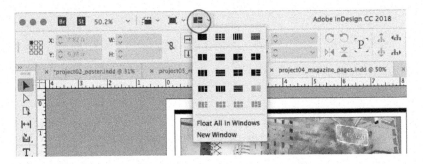

Figure 1.11 The Arrange Documents icon lets you instantly organize open document windows.

Adjusting the Application Frame

As with many applications today, the InDesign workspace is contained in a single application window, also called the application frame. At first, the application frame may seem to block out everything else on the screen. But it's possible to arrange the InDesign application frame (**Figure 1.12**) along with other windows you're using.

- To see or get to items behind the application frame, just drag a corner to make it smaller.

- To reposition the application frame, drag the application bar.

If you're a Mac user who prefers the older way, where document windows float without an application frame, click the Window menu and deselect Application Frame. The lessons in this course are presented with the application frame on. Also, be aware that the InDesign application frame and document windows don't support the native Mac full-screen mode; they can be maximized but cannot go full screen. The only way to view an InDesign document full screen is to use the Presentation screen mode; however, you can't edit the document in this mode, because it's only for presenting an InDesign document as a slide show.

Figure 1.12 You can resize the InDesign application frame from any corner, letting you see other programs and windows on your computer.

Getting to Know the Tools Panel

★ ACA Objective 2.2

★ ACA Objective 4.1

▶ **Video 1.5** The Tools Panel

Once a tool is selected in the Tools panel, it remains the active tool until you click a different one. To learn the names of various tools and the shortcuts for quick access, move your pointer over each tool in the Tools panel and pause. A tool tip appears with the name and the tool's single-letter shortcut (**Figure 1.13**).

Figure 1.13 The tool tip for the Type tool shows the tool name and shortcut.

There are so many tools that they can't all be visible at once. Some tools are grouped, with one of the group's tools visible at a time. When you see a small triangle at the lower-right corner of a tool, that triangle indicates that it's a group with hidden tools (**Figure 1.14**). To see the entire tool group, press and hold the tool, and the rest of the tools will appear in a pop-up menu.

Earlier you learned that the Tools panel can appear as a single column, a single row, or a double column, switchable by clicking the double arrows at the top corner of the panel. In Video 1.5 you see an example of where this is useful. The screen mode options at the bottom of the Tools panel are not originally visible because the single-column Tools panel is too tall for the video screen. To reveal the bottom of the Tools panel, Jonathan switches the Tools panel to double-column mode, and the Screen Mode buttons become visible.

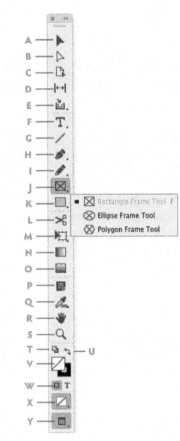

A Selection tool

B Direct Selection tool

C Page tool

D Gap tool

E Content Collector tool (grouped with the Content Placer tool)

F Type tool (grouped with the Type on a Path tool)

G Line tool

H Pen tool (grouped with the Add Anchor Point tool, Delete Anchor Point tool, and Convert Direction Point tool)

I Pencil tool (grouped with Smooth tool and Erase tool)

J Rectangle Frame tool (grouped with Ellipse Frame tool and Polygon Frame tool)

K Rectangle tool (grouped with Ellipse tool and Polygon tool)

L Scissors tool

M Free Transform tool (grouped with Rotate tool, Scale tool, and Shear tool)

N Gradient Swatch tool

O Gradient Feather tool

P Note tool

Q Color Theme tool (grouped with Eyedropper tool and Measure tool)

R Hand tool

S Zoom tool

T Default Fill and Stroke

U Swap Fill and Stroke

V Fill and Stroke icons for applying colors

W Container and Text icons for applying colors

X Apply Color/Gradient/None icon

Y Screen Mode icon

Figure 1.14 The Tools panel contains different kinds of tools, with some hidden in tool groups.

This chapter presents the most commonly used tools, but InDesign offers many more. If you ever forget what a tool does or are curious about a particular tool, select the tool in the Tools panel and display the Tool Hints panel (Window > Utilities) for more information (**Figure 1.15**).

You can also consult InDesign Help (Help > InDesign Help).

> **NOTE**
>
> *When the Tools panel is docked (attached to the workspace), it toggles only between single-column and double-column modes. When the Tools panel is floating (detached from the workspace), it also toggles through the single-row mode.*

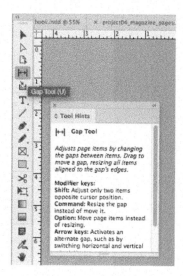

Figure 1.15 The Tool Hints panel provides a short description of each tool's function as well as handy modifier keys and shortcuts.

Understanding the Selection Tools

Of all the tools in the Tools panel, you'll probably use the Selection tool most. At the simplest level, you can use the Selection tool to select most types of objects in an InDesign document. Once an object is selected, you can edit it. Also, selecting an object displays its attributes in open panels—for example, in the Control panel—so that you can apply or adjust its attributes. For example, when you click an object to select it, the Control panel reports the object's width and height, and you can change those values.

Just below the Selection tool is the Direct Selection tool. It comes in handy when you want to work with an object that's complex or made up of multiple objects—such as a group or an image inside a frame. You won't use it right away, but you'll realize its value when you start working with more advanced types of objects.

SELECTING AN OBJECT

To select an object (**Figure 1.16**):

1 Click the Selection tool ( ) in the Tools panel to select it.

2 Position the pointer over an object on the page and click. A bounding box with eight handles appears around the object.

3 Move the object you selected by dragging it into a new position (**Figure 1.17**).

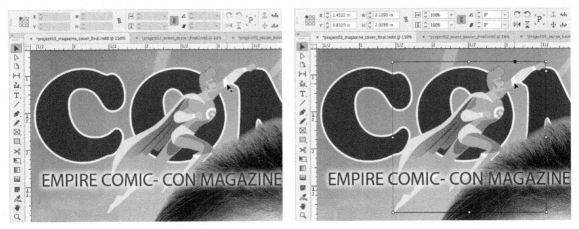

Figure 1.16 After you click to select an object with the Selection tool, selection handles appear around the object, and the object's attributes appear in the Control panel.

Figure 1.17 Selecting (left) and moving an object with the Selection tool

Keep an eye on the pointer—did you notice that it changed appearance as you selected the object and moved it? From a pointer, to a pointer with a dot (for selecting the object), to a small triangle (for moving an object)? Yup, the Selection tool is a multipurpose tool and the pointer will always tell you what it's up to.

ROTATING AN OBJECT

To rotate a selected object (**Figure 1.18**):

1 Move the pointer just outside the object's bounding box, near one of the corners. The pointer indicates when you can rotate.

2 Drag in a large circular motion to rotate the object.

Figure 1.18 Rotating an object with the Selection tool

RESIZING AN OBJECT

To resize a selected object (**Figure 1.19**):

1 Move the pointer over one of the handles on the bounding box.

2 Drag the handle.

You can temporarily change any tool to the last-used selection tool by holding down the Ctrl key (Windows) or the Command key (macOS). When you release the key, InDesign switches back to the tool you were previously using.

An imported graphic always exists inside a frame, but dragging a bounding box handle resizes the frame, not the graphics content. To resize both, drag a bounding box handle while holding down Ctrl+Shift (Windows) or Command+Shift (macOS). The Shift key ensures that the original proportions are maintained.

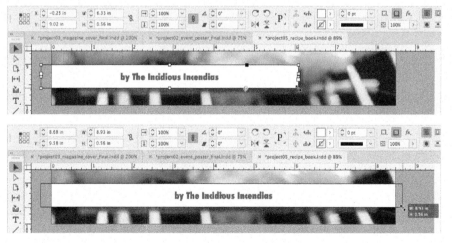

Figure 1.19 Resizing an object with the Selection tool

Understanding Frame Tools

The primary way of creating InDesign layout elements is to draw frames. An empty frame can be a placeholder for text or graphics that you add later, or it can be a simple object on its own, such as a circle with a solid blue fill color. You create frames using the frame tools in the Tools panel (**Figure 1.20**).

Figure 1.20 The frame tools are next to each other in the Tools panel.

CREATING A FRAME

To create a frame with one of these tools (for example, a rectangle) (**Figure 1.21**):

1 Select the Rectangle Frame tool (▭).

2 Drag diagonally across the page and release the mouse button.

Figure 1.21 Drawing a rectangle with the Rectangle Frame tool

 TIP

To create a frame at an exact size, click (don't drag) a frame tool on the page. In the dialog that appears, type the dimensions you want and click OK.

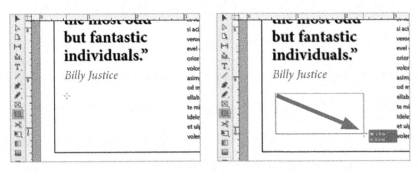

RECOGNIZING A FRAME TYPE

It's easy to recognize the kind of frame you're looking at (**Figure 1.22**):

- An empty graphics frame has an X through it.
- An empty text frame has in and out ports on the upper-left and lower-right sides; these are used to link a single text story across multiple frames.
- An unassigned frame is just an outline.

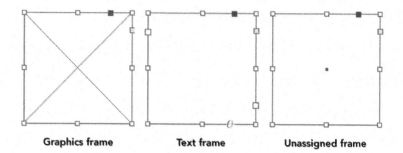

Figure 1.22 From left: a graphics frame, a text frame, and an unassigned frame

Graphics frame   **Text frame**   **Unassigned frame**

SHOWING HIDDEN FRAME EDGES

If you're sure a frame is supposed to be a placeholder but you don't see the visual indicators for a graphic or text frame, they might be hidden. Choose View > Extras, and if the first command says Show Frame Edges, choose that. (Hide Frame Edges means they're set to be visible.) Also, remember that frame edges are hidden in Preview screen mode.

CHOOSING THE RIGHT FRAME TYPE

If you want to lay out a multicolumn page for a printed magazine, you'd use the Rectangle Frame tool to draw the columns using text frames as placeholders for the story text that's coming later. To lay out space for graphics and ads on the page, you'd use the Rectangle Frame tool to draw frames for them and then set them as graphics frames.

Although you can see tools for creating rectangular, circular, and polygonal frames, frames aren't limited to those shapes. You can use other tools, such as the Pen tool, to draw frames of any shape. Any frame can contain text or graphics, and you can customize the look of any frame by setting attributes such as its stroke (outline) color, fill color, and visual effect, such as a drop shadow.

When you're experimenting with layout ideas, you don't have to be too precise about which frame tool you use because you can easily change it later. If you want to change the type of an empty selected frame, choose Object > Content and then choose the kind of frame you want it to be. You can't change a frame's type when it already contains something.

Setting Basic Frame Attributes

Whether or not you put anything inside a frame, you can edit its attributes, such as size, position, and color. The two main parts of a frame are its **stroke**, or outline, and its **fill**, or interior. While you can do this with a mouse, if you need numerical precision you can also use the Control panel. As long as an object is selected, you can adjust its width, height, and other settings.

MOVING AN OBJECT

To move a selected object (**Figure 1.23**), do one of the following:

- Position the Selection tool over an object (avoid the edges and the center), and drag. You used this method earlier.
- Select the object, and in the Control panel adjust the X and Y values.

Figure 1.23 Changing the position of a rectangle using the Control panel

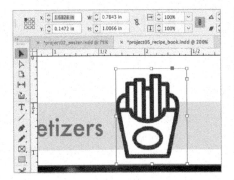
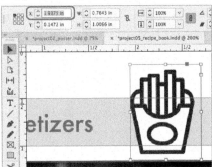

CHANGING THE WIDTH AND HEIGHT

To change the width and height (**Figure 1.24**), do one of the following:

- With the Selection tool, drag any of the bounding box handles.
- Enter Width and Height settings in the Control panel.

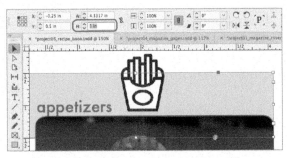

Figure 1.24 Changing the width and height of a rectangle using the Control panel

CHANGING THE FILL COLOR

To change the fill color (**Figure 1.25**):

1 Select an object.

2 Double-click the Fill box in the Control panel, pick a color, and then click OK.

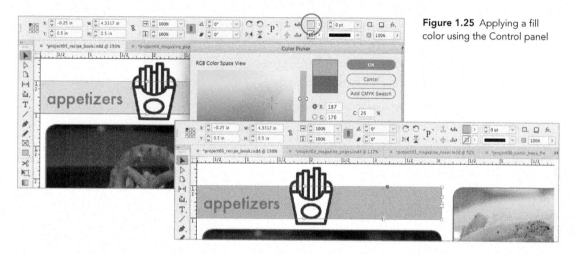

Figure 1.25 Applying a fill color using the Control panel

ADJUSTING STROKE SETTINGS

To adjust stroke settings (**Figure 1.26**):

1 Select the object.

2 Double-click the Stroke box in the Control panel, pick a color, and then click OK.

3 Select a width from the Weight menu in the Control panel.

4 Select a stroke type from the Type menu in the Control panel.

Stroke box for color   Stroke weight   Stroke type

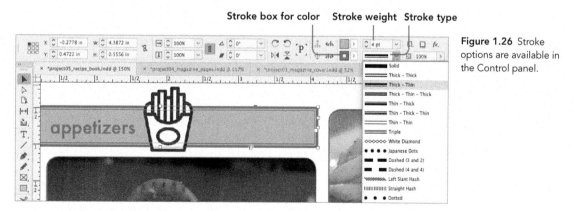

Figure 1.26 Stroke options are available in the Control panel.

USING SPECIALIZED PANELS

While the Control panel is a convenient place to adjust attributes, be aware that many of the options are also available in more specialized panels:

- Position and size options are also available in the Transform panel (choose View > Object & Layout > Transform).

- Fill and stroke color options are also available in the Tools panel, the Color panel (choose Window > Color > Color), and the Swatches panel (choose Window > Color > Swatches).

- Stroke options are also available in the Stroke panel (choose Window > Stroke).

We'll discuss various frame and shape tools, as well as work with color, in more detail in the following chapters.

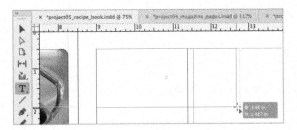

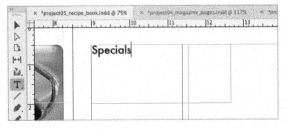

Figure 1.27 You can type text into a text frame that you draw on the layout.

Adding Text to a Layout by Typing

Now that you've got the hang of selecting an object and adjusting its options, you can carry those skills over to creating and editing text frames. There will be many times in InDesign when you'll import text into an existing text frame placeholder, but when you want to type text right away, you can draw a quick text frame and start typing (**Figure 1.27**):

1. Select the Type tool (T), and drag a rectangle on the page. This creates a text frame with a blinking text cursor, indicating that it's ready for you to start typing.

2. Type your text.

After you type, the insertion point will still be blinking in the text frame, so if you're done typing you should exit text-editing mode so that you can press keys for shortcuts without accidentally typing text. These are some of the many ways to exit text-editing mode (**Figure 1.28**):

- Hold down the Ctrl key (Windows) or Command key (macOS) to temporarily switch to the Selection tool, and click an empty area of the page.

- Press the Esc key.

- Choose Edit > Deselect All.

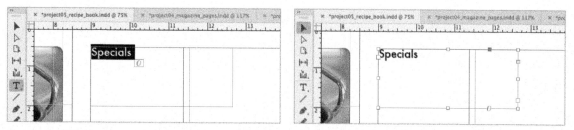

Figure 1.28 When you deselect text by pressing the Esc key, you can no longer edit text, but the text frame remains selected so you can edit it as an object. (If you use the Deselect All command, nothing is selected afterward.)

Setting Basic Text Attributes

As with the fill and stroke color options you changed earlier, you can change type attributes using the Control panel when text within a frame is selected (**Figure 1.29**):

1   With the Type tool, drag to highlight the text you want to change.

2   To change the font, click the drop-down arrow at the right side of the font list and select a font from the list.

    If you know the name of the font you want, you can simply type it into the font search field. Notice that InDesign provides a preview of how each font looks, along the right edge of the font drop-down menu.

3   To change the size, click the size drop-down arrow at the right side of the font list and select a size from the list. (You can also type a size into the size field and then press Enter or Return.)

4   Exit text-editing mode, using any of the methods described earlier.

TIP

If a selection tool is active, you can edit text in a frame by double-clicking the text frame. This saves you the trouble of switching to the Type tool.

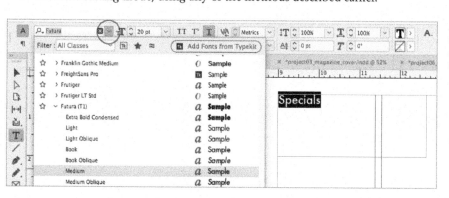

Figure 1.29 You can apply a font and size to selected text using the Control panel.

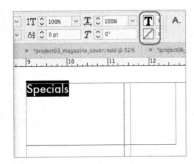

Figure 1.30 If you see a T in the fill or stroke box, applying a color will affect text, not its containing frame.

Want to change the color of text (**Figure 1.30**)? It's similar to changing the fill or stroke color of a shape, which you did earlier, but with a twist that's important to pay attention to. Text always exists inside a text frame, and the frame itself has a stroke and fill, so how do you tell InDesign that you want to change the color of the text and not the frame around it? It's easy: Look for the T icon in the fill or stroke box. If you select something and you see a T in the fill or stroke box, that means you'll change the color of the text. If you don't see a T in the fill or stroke box, you'll change the color of the text frame.

The type options you just tried in the Control panel are also available in the Character panel (choose Window > Type & Tables > Character).

Working with Panels

▶ *Video 1.6*
Managing Panels

To provide a professional range of design and production features, InDesign has more than 50 panels that present various sets of options; they're listed in the middle section of the Window menu. That number of panels can be a little overwhelming (**Figure 1.31**), especially if you're new to InDesign. But there are ways to think about panels that can keep things simple, organized, and manageable for you.

Figure 1.31 InDesign organizes many of its features into a large number of task-specific panels. But don't panic...

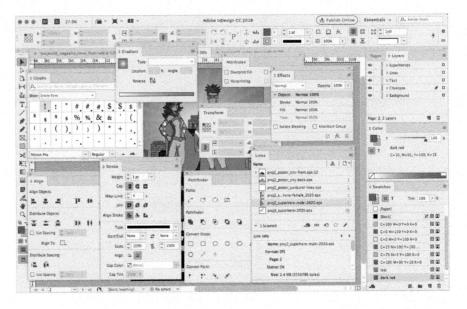

First, you probably don't need to use every last panel. Many panels are used only for specific workflows, so there may be some panels that you'll never need to see. If you aren't an indexer, you might never use the Index panel. If you design only for print, you might never touch the 11 Interactive panels.

Second, the majority of general work in InDesign happens in just a few panels. Those are the panels that Adobe has gathered into the preset workspaces. Furthermore, the most commonly used options appear in the Control panel, so in many cases the options you need might already be there. For example, if you want to change the width of an object, you can do it in the Control panel instead of opening the Transform panel.

But some panels are so essential that you will inevitably work with those panels. For example, an InDesign professional will spend a lot of time managing pages in the Pages panel, color swatches in the Swatches panel, and maintaining text style standards in the Paragraph Styles panel.

Having many panels open lets you keep a wide range of tools immediately available. But there's a catch: The more panels you have open, the less space is left onscreen to see your layout. That's why InDesign panels are resizable and have multiple size modes. A panel can be fully expanded, have just its title visible, or be collapsed down to an icon. This flexibility lets you keep your favorite panels onscreen but collapsed to stay out of your way until you need them (**Figure 1.32**).

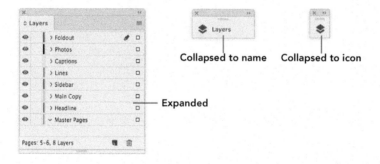

Collapsed to name   Collapsed to icon

— Expanded

Figure 1.32 You can display panels fully expanded or collapsed to two sizes.

What you don't want is a loose collection of panels strewn across the screen, so InDesign makes it easy to keep panels together. You can attach panels together as a group, so you can drag the panel group in one move. You can also dock panels and panel groups to the sides of the workspace. Unlike non-docked (floating) panels, docked panels are attached to the InDesign workspace. If you move the InDesign application window, all docked panels and windows move with it.

Expanding and Collapsing Panels

To expand and collapse docked panels (**Figure 1.33**), click the double arrow at the top of the panel stack.

Figure 1.33 Click the double arrow at the top of the panel stack to expand or collapse a stack of docked panels.

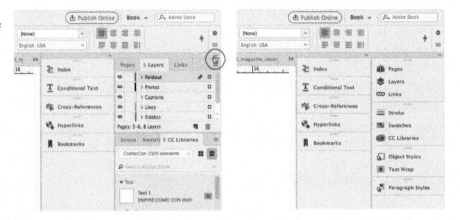

To expand and collapse one docked panel (**Figure 1.34**), click the icon or name of the panel.

To collapse a panel stack to icons, drag a panel stack's left edge to the right (to make the stack narrower) until it displays just an icon. Icon view can save a lot of space on a smaller screen, such as on a laptop computer.

Figure 1.34 Click the panel icon or name to expand or collapse one docked panel.

To expand and collapse one floating or docked panel (**Figure 1.35**), double-click the panel tab. Many panels have two expanded states and will cycle to the next one when you double-click the panel tab.

Adjusting Panel Height

To adjust the width or height of a panel or panel stack, position the pointer over any edge of a panel until a double-headed arrow appears, then drag (**Figure 1.36**).

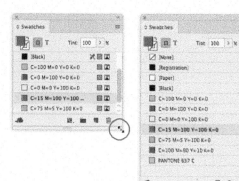

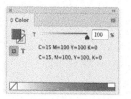

Expanded

Compact

Collapsed

Figure 1.36 Drag an edge to resize a panel.

Figure 1.35 Double-click the tab of a floating panel to expand or collapse it.

Combining and Rearranging Panel Groups

To combine or rearrange panel groups (**Figure 1.37**):

1 Drag a panel's icon or tab.

2 As you drag, position the pointer over another panel or group. Pay attention to the blue line that appears:

- If the blue line appears around a panel, the panel you're dragging will be grouped with that panel.

- If the line appears above or below the panel, the panel you're dragging will be stacked with that panel.

- If the line appears to the side of a panel, the panel you're dragging will be docked alongside that panel.

3 Release the mouse to drop the panel, adding it to the other panel.

TIP

Looking for a panel but can't find it anywhere? Click the Window menu and choose the name of the panel; that will either open the panel or, if it's already open, bring it forward.

Figure 1.37 When rearranging panels, pay attention to the blue line—it tells you where the panel will land.

The panel will stack between others.

The panel will be grouped with others.

The panel will be docked alongside others.

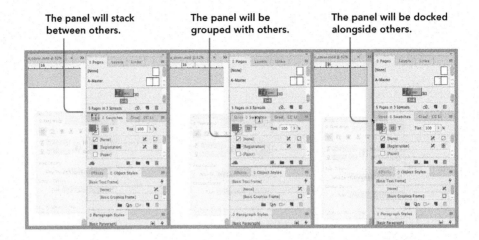

Undocking a Panel

To undock a panel (**Figure 1.38**), drag its icon or name away from a panel stack. As long as you drop it away from any other panel, it becomes a floating panel.

Figure 1.38 Drag a panel away from other panels to undock it.

SHORTCUT *To view your design without seeing all the panels or to eliminate any panel clutter, press Tab. Every panel that was visible onscreen is hidden. Press Tab again to bring the panels back. To show and hide all panels except for the Tools panel and Control panel, press Shift+Tab. (Note that this does not work when the text insertion point is active in text.)*

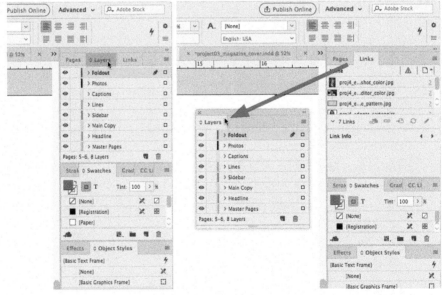

Many panels have a `panel menu` that provides a list of commands specific to the features in that panel. When you see the panel menu symbol (**Figure 1.39**), click to see the menu.

Some commands also appear at the bottom of a panel as a clickable button. A lot of these buttons are similar across panels. For example, the button that looks like a flipping page or notepad ( ) is found in panels such as the Swatches, Layers, and Paragraph Styles panels. In each of these panels, the button does something similar: It makes something new. It creates a new color swatch, a new layer, or a new style when clicked.

Exploring Buttons in Different Panels

To see what these buttons do in different panels (**Figure 1.40**):

1 Show the panel.

2 Position the pointer over the button.

A tool tip appears.

Hiding Panels

To hide a floating panel, click its close box (**Figure 1.41**).

If you want to save a panel arrangement as your own workspace...that's coming up in the next section.

Figure 1.39 The Layers panel menu contains many layer-specific commands in one place.

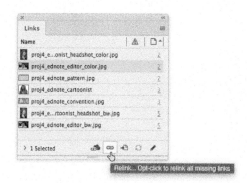

Figure 1.40 Use tool tips to learn about unknown buttons.

Figure 1.41 Click the close box to hide a floating panel.

▶ **Video 1.7**
Creating a Custom Workspace

Using Workspaces

Because the panels in InDesign are so task specific, some panels are useful only for specific tasks or workflows. For example, you could be using InDesign to create an interactive PDF or an eBook with animations, which requires the use of specific panels, such as the Buttons and Forms panel or the Animation panel. Adobe created a number of preset InDesign workspaces for common workflows; you can select them from the workspace switcher you saw earlier.

Switching Workspaces

To switch the workspace, do either of the following:

- Click the workspace switcher and select a workspace (**Figure 1.42**).
- Choose Window > Workspace and select a workspace.

Try switching between the available workspaces. Notice that the available panels change as you switch workspaces.

Figure 1.42 Using the workspace switcher in the application bar to change workspaces

The InDesign default workspaces include:

- **Start:** When no documents are open in InDesign, the Start workspace is the only workspace available, and it appears automatically. When one or more documents are open, the Start workspace is not available.
- **Essentials:** This is the default workspace. You can use it for a wide range of basic projects.
- **Advanced:** This workspace includes the panels in the Essentials workspace, while adding panels that help you maintain graphics and typographical standards through InDesign style lists (the Object Styles, Paragraph Styles, and Character Styles panels).

- **Book:** The panel layout in this workspace is optimized for creating and managing long documents. That's why it adds panels for long-document features such as cross-references, conditional text, index, and bookmarks.

- **Digital Publishing:** This workspace focuses on the panels needed to create interactive digital documents, such as the Animation, Timing, Media, Buttons, and Hyperlinks panels.

- **Interactive for PDF:** This workspace emphasizes the panels that support the creation of interactive PDF files, such as the Page Transitions, Buttons and Forms, and Media panels.

- **Printing and Proofing:** The panels in this workspace are focused on a prepress workflow for commercial printing, such as the Separations Preview, Trap Presets, and Preflight panels.

- **Typography:** This workspace emphasizes panels containing the powerful text and typography features in InDesign, such as the Character, Character Styles, Paragraph, Paragraph Styles, Glyphs, and Story panels.

The preset workspaces are just suggestions. You're free to use any workspace at any time. For example, if you're working on a catalog, you might use the Advanced workspace to do the general layout of the pages, switch to the Typography workspace to fine-tune text, switch to the Printing and Proofing workspace to get the catalog ready for the press, and then switch to the Interactive for PDF workspace to prepare a downloadable PDF version of the catalog.

As you gain experience in InDesign, you may find yourself preferring a panel arrangement that's different than any of the presets. That's when you want to save your own custom workspace.

Creating Custom Workspaces

To create a custom workspace (**Figure 1.43**):

1 Close any panels you don't want.

2 Open and arrange panels in the way you want your workspace to be saved.

3 In the workspace switcher, choose New Workspace.

4 Name your workspace, ensure that Panel Locations is selected, and then click OK.

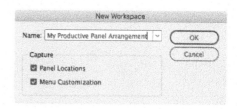

Figure 1.43 After you create a custom workspace, it appears at the top of the workspace switcher.

You may want to create the Learn workspace as demonstrated in Video 1.7, because it can be used in chapters later in this book. Creating the Learn workspace isn't required, because you can always open any panel from the Window menu. You might also prefer to create a workspace with your own panel arrangement. The best workspace is the one that works most efficiently for you, on the display size that you work with. If you work on both desktop and laptop computers, you might even create one workspace for the large desktop screen and another designed to better fit a small laptop screen.

★ *ACA Objective 2.3*

▶ *Video 1.8* *Using Zoom to View a Document*

Getting Around on a Page

The process of design and production naturally involves switching between layout details and a "big picture" view of an entire page or spread, and constantly moving around pages and spreads. InDesign provides quite a few ways to pan and zoom around a document.

Changing the Magnification of the Current View

By now, it probably won't surprise you to know that you have a number of ways to change the magnification of an InDesign document window, from tools to commands and shortcuts. As usual, you have all these choices so that you can pick the methods that best fit your working style.

To change the document magnification with the Zoom tool:

1 Select the Zoom tool ().

2 Click an object you want to zoom in to.

    With each click, the magnification level increases. It might take several clicks to zoom in to a section of the page.

3 To zoom back out, Alt-click (Windows) or Option-click (macOS) the Zoom tool.

To magnify by filling the document window with a specific area (**Figure 1.44**):

1 Select the Zoom tool.

2 Drag a marquee rectangle around the area of the page you want to magnify.

    The area you surrounded now fills the document window.

Figure 1.44 Zoom in to a section of a page by dragging a marquee around the area with the Zoom tool.

Two of the most useful preset magnification levels are Actual Size (100%) and Fit Page In Window. While both magnification levels have convenient menu commands, you may want to memorize their keyboard shortcuts so that you can instantly go to either view at any time:

- To zoom back out and center the active page in the document window, choose View > Fit Page In Window or press or Ctrl+0 (zero) (Windows) or Command+0 (zero) (macOS).

- To set the zoom level to 100%, choose View > Actual Size, or press Ctrl+1 (Windows) or Command+1 (macOS).

When you design reports, books, or magazines destined for print, viewing facing pages (with the right- and left-page designs side by side) will help with the placement of design elements and obtaining rhythm, balance, and harmony in your design. Pages that face each other are referred to as a **spread**.

> **SHORTCUT** *To temporarily access the Zoom tool when another tool is selected, press Ctrl+spacebar (Windows) or Command+spacebar (macOS). Add the Alt (Windows) or Option (macOS) key to zoom out.*

To center the active spread in the document window (**Figure 1.45**), choose View > Fit Spread In Window or press Ctrl+Alt+0 (Windows) or Command+Option+0 (macOS).

Figure 1.45 When you work with multipage spreads, you can center an entire spread in the document window.

SHORTCUT *To quickly zoom out to 50% zoom level, press Ctrl+5 (Windows) or Command+5 (macOS). To quickly zoom to 200%, press Ctrl+2 (Windows) or Command+2 (macOS).*

The View menu contains an entire section of magnification commands and their keyboard shortcuts (**Figure 1.46**). The Zoom In and Zoom Out commands magnify in preset increments.

Another place to change the document magnification is in the Zoom Level menu in the application bar (**Figure 1.47**). Simply select from any of the preset zoom levels, or enter a custom zoom level.

When using the commands or shortcuts for zooming, keep in mind that if nothing is selected on the page, the zoom centers on the current view. If objects are selected or the insertion point is in text, the zoom level centers on that element.

Figure 1.46 You'll find preset zoom levels, and the Zoom In and Zoom Out commands, on the View menu.

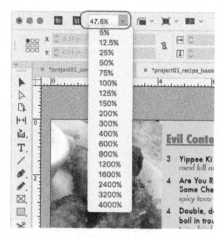

Figure 1.47 The Zoom Level menu in the application bar

Using Animated Zoom

You've used the Zoom tool by clicking and by dragging, but on certain Mac computers you get one more way to use the Zoom tool: animated zoom (also known as scrubby zoom).

Earlier, you magnified a specific area of a page by dragging the Zoom tool around that area. Animated zoom is a different way of dragging the Zoom tool; it's more like an invisible horizontal zoom slider.

One benefit of animated zoom is that you don't have to switch modes to zoom in or out; you drag left to zoom out and drag right to zoom in. Another benefit is that you aren't locked to preset magnification increments—zooming is smooth and continuous.

Animated zoom is a side benefit of graphics acceleration, which is currently supported only on some Macs. For the complete system requirements, see https://helpx.adobe.com/indesign/using/gpu_performance.html.

Because graphics acceleration support became available in InDesign only recently, it's possible that in the future more Macs and Windows PCs may be able to use it.

To set up animated zoom (**Figure 1.48**):

1 On a computer that InDesign supports for graphics acceleration, choose InDesign CC > Preferences > GPU Performance.

2 Make sure the GPU Performance option is enabled.

3 Click OK.

Figure 1.48 Set up animated zoom in the GPU Performance pane of the Preferences dialog.

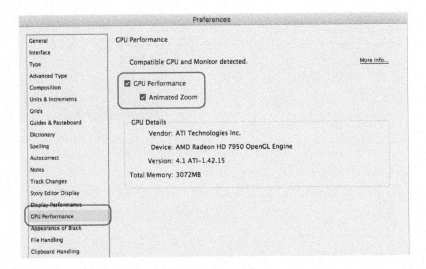

To use animated zoom, position the Zoom tool over the point you want to magnify or reduce, and then do either of the following (**Figure 1.49**):

■ To reduce the magnification, drag left until you get the magnification you want.

■ To increase the magnification, drag right until you get the magnification you want.

Because animated zoom is interactive and continuous, zooming starts immediately; stop as soon as you see the magnification you want.

NOTE

If you're used to dragging a magnification rectangle with the Zoom tool, turning on Animated Zoom radically changes what the Zoom tool does when you drag it, and this can initially be confusing. If you want to be able to use both methods, leave Animated Zoom enabled, and when you use a magnification rectangle, hold down the Shift key as you drag the Zoom tool.

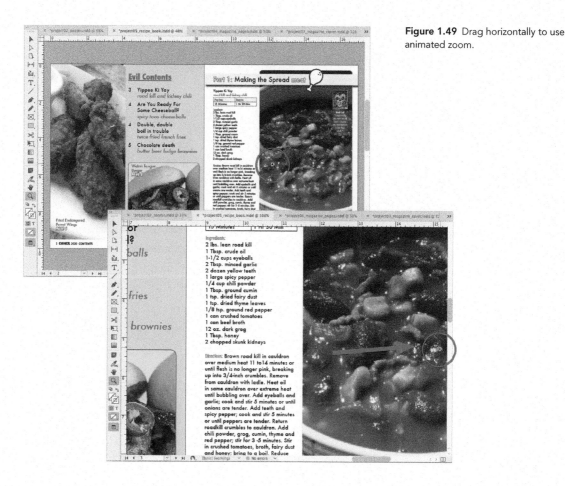

Figure 1.49 Drag horizontally to use animated zoom.

Using the Hand Tool

Once you've zoomed in to a small section of a page, you can use the Hand tool (✋) to pan to other sections of the page. The Hand tool is an alternative to using the scroll bars in a document window.

To see the areas of a page that are beyond the edges of the document window (**Figure 1.50**), select the Hand tool, position it inside a document window, and drag.

> **SHORTCUT** *You can temporarily change any tool to the Hand tool by holding down the spacebar. When you release the spacebar, InDesign switches back to the tool you were previously using. If you happen to be editing text with the Type tool, press Alt+spacebar (Windows) or Option+spacebar (macOS) instead.*

Figure 1.50 Drag with the Hand tool to navigate to a different area on the page.

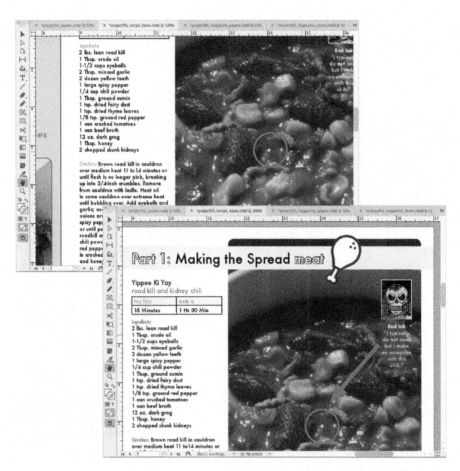

★ ACA Objective 2.3

Getting Around in a Document

You'll work more efficiently in InDesign by understanding how to trade off display speed and display quality, how to quickly move from page to page, and how to jump to any page in an InDesign document.

▶ Video 1.9
Choosing Options for Displaying a Document

Using Display Performance Settings

As you zoom in to graphics, they might appear to be jagged or pixelated instead of at full sharpness. This may be due to a display setting, and it's not necessarily evidence of a technical problem. On slower or older computers, displaying full-resolution graphics may make it take longer for InDesign to draw a page, so by default InDesign displays graphics at a lower resolution that draws faster but is still good enough for many purposes. If you need absolute visual precision or have a fast computer, you can set InDesign to display graphics at full resolution.

Display quality is set by the View > Display Performance setting, which is set to Typical Display by default. You can change the Display Performance to High Quality, but keep in mind that this might slow the screen redraw as you move from page to page.

You have three choices for Display Performance (**Figure 1.51**):

- **Fast Display:** Graphics and images are shown as gray boxes, and transparency effects are not shown. This is the fastest mode and is useful for work on which it isn't necessary to see the graphics, such as copyediting, spell checking, or indexing.

- **Typical Display:** Graphics, images, and transparency effects are displayed at low resolution. As the default, this display performance works well while you are busy with your designs. It gives you fast previews for placement and image cropping, as well as a faster screen redraw than High Quality Display.

| Fast | Typical | High Quality |

Figure 1.51 Display Performance settings manage display speed by changing the level of detail you see.

- **High Quality Display:** Images are shown at their full resolution. Vector graphics appear sharp and detailed, allowing you to position them with more precision in your design. When showing the onscreen design to your client, this display performance provides the best-quality view.

As you'll see with many InDesign features, the display performance setting exists at three levels: the default for new InDesign documents, the document level, and the object level.

To change the display performance:

- **For a document:** Choose an option from the View > Display Performance menu.

- **For a selected object:** Choose an option from the Object > Display Performance menu.

Moving Around in a Multipage Document

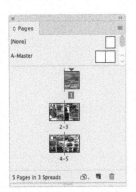

Figure 1.52 The Pages panel

When working with longer documents, such as newsletters, reports, books, or digital magazines, you can use the Pages panel (**Figure 1.52**) to insert new pages, move pages around, or quickly display a page in the document window.

Use the Pages panel to go to pages and spreads:

- To go to a page, double-click a page thumbnail.

- To go to a multipage spread and fit both pages in the document window, double-click the number below a spread.

In Chapter 4, you'll use the Pages panel to manage master pages and apply them to document pages. Master pages add to pages common design elements, such as page numbers, headers, and footers.

Aside from the Pages panel, InDesign offers several other ways to navigate to different pages in the document.

To go to another page:

- Drag the vertical and horizontal scroll bars on the document window.

- In the status bar near the lower-left corner of the document window, either click the drop-down arrow and choose a page number, or enter a page number into the page number field and press Enter or Return (**Figure 1.53**).

- Choose Layout > Go To Page, enter the page number, and click OK.

- Choose one of the commands in the middle of the Layout menu (**Figure 1.54**).

  SHORTCUT *You can press the Page Up and Page Down keys to move to the previous and next pages in a document, respectively. You can press the Home key to go to the first page, and press the End key to go to the last page. If you're using a keyboard that doesn't have those keys, such as a laptop computer, you may be able to use the up arrow, down arrow, left arrow, and right arrow keys as Page Up, Page Down, Home, and End keys, respectively, by also holding down the Fn key.*

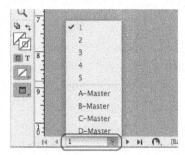

Figure 1.53 The status bar is another way to go to different pages.

Figure 1.54 The middle of the Layout menu provides commands for navigating a multipage document.

Working Faster with Keyboard Shortcuts

★ *ACA Objective 2.2*

▶ *Video 1.10*
Learning Keyboard Shortcuts

In a professional application such as InDesign, many features are buried deep inside menus and dialogs, or are used so frequently that if you use the mouse alone, you'll be moving frequently and repetitively between the controls around the edge of the workspace and the design you're actually working on. Keyboard shortcuts are a way to cut through all of that extra labor and make something happen immediately.

You may already be familiar with the keyboard shortcuts for the Copy, Cut, and Paste commands, which are demonstrated in the video, because those shortcuts work in many applications, not just InDesign:

- **Cut:** Ctrl+X (Windows) or Command+X (macOS).
- **Copy:** Ctrl+C (Windows) or Command+C (macOS).
- **Paste:** Ctrl+V (Windows) or Command+V (macOS).

Learning InDesign Keyboard Shortcuts

Of course, InDesign has a large number of its own keyboard shortcuts. The next question you might have is whether it is necessary to memorize every InDesign key-board shortcut to be productive. The answer to that is no, for a couple of reasons.

Using and memorizing keyboard shortcuts is not required. Although keyboard shortcuts can boost productivity, not everyone enjoys using them or wants to learn them. This is one reason InDesign often offers multiple ways to accomplish a task; if a person is more mouse oriented, they may prefer to use menu commands and point-and-click methods to get their work done. If a person is more keyboard oriented, they may eagerly teach themselves more keyboard shortcuts so that they can use the mouse less often.

Also, keyboard shortcuts are available for quick reference in several places, includ-ing inside InDesign itself:

Figure 1.55 On menus, keyboard shortcuts are shown to the right of their commands.

- When you click a menu, if a command has a keyboard shortcut it's listed with that command, at the right edge of the menu (**Figure 1.55**).

- When you hover the mouse over a tool or option in a panel or window, if a tool tip pops up it often contains the shortcut for that item.

- Adobe maintains a web page listing the default InDesign keyboard shortcuts. Go to https://helpx.adobe.com/indesign/using/default-keyboard-shortcuts.html.

- Choose Edit > Keyboard Shortcuts and explore the Product Area menus. Under each product area is a list of features, and if a feature has a keyboard shortcut assigned to it, it's shown there. You can use the Keyboard Shortcuts dialog to edit the existing shortcuts, or add your own, and save them as a keyboard shortcuts set.

When you use a Tools panel shortcut such as pressing the V key to switch to the Selection tool, you're using an example of a single-key shortcut: You press that key alone, without pressing any other keys. With single-key shortcuts, you do have to be careful to use them only when you're not editing text; otherwise, typing F will enter an F character into text instead of switching tools.

Using Modifier Keys

So far, the keyboard shortcuts in this section do something directly when you press the shortcut. But there's another category of keyboard shortcut—one that when you press it, it doesn't do anything on its own. Instead, it modifies something that's already happening. Naturally, this type of shortcut is called a modifier key. Each modifier key tends to be used consistently so that you can use it in a wide range of situations and be reasonably confident in how that key is going to change the tool or feature you're using (**Figure 1.56**).

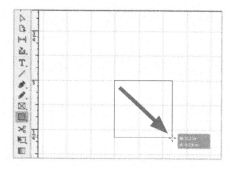 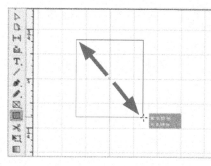

Figure 1.56 Normally, a shape is drawn from the upper-left corner. When you hold down Shift+Alt (Windows) or Shift+Option (macOS), a shape is drawn out from the center.

The Shift key is generally used to constrain actions. For example:

- When drawing a shape, pressing the Shift key constrains the shape to a square.
- When resizing an object, pressing the Shift key constrains the shape to the original proportions so it doesn't get distorted.
- When moving or rotating an object, or drawing a line, the Shift key constrains angles to 45 degrees.

The Alt key (Windows) or Option key (macOS) is often used for centering or copying. For example:

- When drawing or resizing a frame or line, pressing the Alt/Option key sizes the frame from the center.
- When moving or rotating an object, pressing the Alt/Option key creates a copy.

As the name implies, in some cases the Alt/Option key switches the tool or feature you're using to an alternate mode or option of that feature.

These modifier keys often work when you're entering values in panels. For example, if you enter a new X,Y position in the Control panel when an object is selected, and you finish by pressing Alt+Enter (Windows) or Option+Return (macOS), it creates a copy at the new position, just as if you had Alt-dragged (Windows) or Option-dragged (macOS) the object using the mouse.

You can combine modifier keys. If you Alt-Shift-drag (Windows) or Option-Shift-drag (macOS) a corner handle of a shape, it will both resize from the center (because you're pressing the Alt/Option key) and maintain proportions (because you're pressing the Shift key).

Using Other System Shortcuts

Some keys can save you steps throughout InDesign, as well as in other application you use:

- The Enter key (Windows) or Return key (macOS) is a shortcut for confirming the current action. For example, in a dialog, pressing Enter or Return is the same as clicking OK. You can also use it to confirm values you enter into panels such as the Control panel.

- The Esc key is usually a shortcut for canceling the current action. For example, in a dialog, pressing Esc is the same as clicking the Cancel button.

- The Tab key is a handy way to move among the entry fields of a dialog or panel. For example, if you want to edit most of the value fields in the Character panel, you don't have to enter a value, then click the next field, then enter a value, then click in the next field. That's a lot of switching between mouse and keyboard. Instead, type a value and then press Tab and InDesign will move to the next field. That way, you can stay on the keyboard while editing the values in that panel.

Challenge

Now that you've been introduced to the InDesign workspace and tools, try them out on your own.

Open any of the finished InDesign project files that you downloaded for this lesson, immediately choose File > Save As to make a test copy that you can delete later, change the filename, and click Save.

Practice the concepts taught in this chapter, such as:

- Customizing panels and saving your own workspace
- Becoming more familiar with the Selection tool and using it for basic edits to an object, such as moving, scaling, and rotating
- Moving among pages in a multipage document

A little practice will go a long way when you build a ready-to-print InDesign document in the next lesson.

CHAPTER OBJECTIVES

Chapter Learning Objectives

- Create a new project, and identify the correct document setup settings to use for different publishing projects.

- Add ruler guides to a document.

- Create shapes through drawing, and combine common shapes, such as ellipses, rectangles, and lines.

- Understand basic document viewing options, such as using screen modes and window arrangements.

- Organize the stacking order of objects by using layers.

- Add and resize images.

- Add and format text.

- Create color swatches and gradients, and apply them to objects and text.

- Package a finished document for final output at a commercial printing service.

Chapter ACA Objectives

For full descriptions of the objectives, see the table on pages 270–276.

DOMAIN 2.0
PROJECT SETUP AND INTERFACE
2.1, 2.3

DOMAIN 3.0
ORGANIZATION OF DOCUMENTS
3.1

DOMAIN 4.0
CREATE AND MODIFY VISUAL ELEMENTS
4.2, 4.4, 4.5

DOMAIN 5.0
PUBLISHING DIGITAL MEDIA
5.2

CHAPTER 2

Designing an Event Poster

In this first hands-on project, you'll design an event poster that is going to be printed commercially. As part of this project, you'll learn how to create a new document in InDesign CC; add various visual elements, images, and text; and apply color to objects.

You'll also learn how to submit your design as a Portable Document Format (PDF) proof to your client for review and as a press-ready PDF to your printer for production.

Starting the Project

As you start working in graphic design, you will likely create many different InDesign documents. You may need to design documents for print, such as a poster, report, or newsletter. Or perhaps you'll be working on a magazine that contains interactive slide shows or videos and that is destined to be viewed on tablets or mobile devices. Or maybe you need to design eBooks that will be read in an interactive form. You can create all these designs with InDesign, but you'll start with a printed event poster, such as the one in this chapter (**Figure 2.1**).

Figure 2.1 The finished poster design

Planning a New Document

When creating a new document, first ask yourself where you intend to publish this document. To give you a head start in setting the right options for how a document will be published, InDesign gives you the choice of three document *intents*: print, web, and mobile. By choosing the correct intent as you set up a document, several document specifications are set in a way that's appropriate for your intended delivery platform.

NOTE

This chapter supports the project created in video lesson 2. Go to the Project 2 page in the book's Web Edition to watch the entire lesson from beginning to end.

You set up a new InDesign publication in the New Document dialog, which you'll work with soon. The Print, Web, and Mobile publishing intents are listed at the top to the right (**Figure 2.2**). You can easily see the effects of choosing each intent by clicking one; for example:

- **Print.** When you select the Print intent, the presets offer standard print page sizes, defined using picas—the traditional print publishing unit of measure. The document initially defines colors using the CMYK (cyan, magenta, yellow, and black) color mode used by printers and presses.

- **Web.** The Web intent displays presets for standard web page sizes, defined using pixels—the web design unit of measure. The document initially defines colors using the RGB (red, green, blue) color mode used in web design.

- **Mobile.** For documents intended primarily for mobile devices, the Mobile intent shows presets for common display sizes on mobile devices, such as smartphones and tablets, defined in pixels. This intent also uses the RGB color mode by default, since device displays are based on RGB.

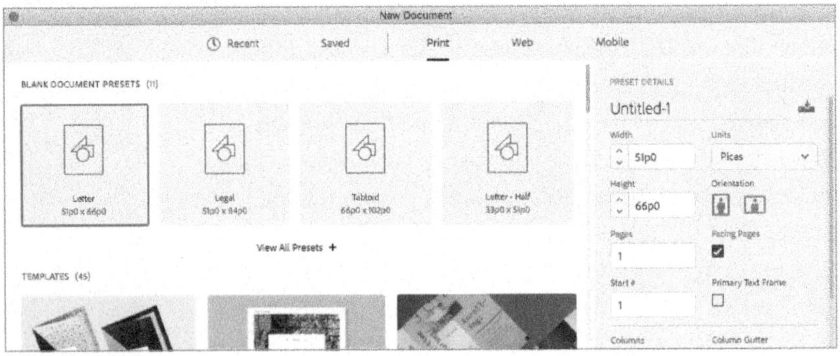

Figure 2.2 Document intents at the top of the New Document dialog

The event poster that you'll create in this lesson will be posted in shop windows or on notice boards, so the intent that applies is Print. Even if you aren't going to print the document yourself but you plan to distribute an Adobe PDF file on a website intending to have others print and post it, the intention is print.

When setting up a new InDesign document for print, be sure to ask yourself some key questions before you jump into the program:

- What will the finished page size for the print publication be, after trimming?

- Will any design elements, such as background graphics and photos, be printed all the way to the edges of the page?

- Will the pages of multipage documents be bound? Smaller newsletters might use saddle-stitch binding, which binds folded sheets by putting staples through the spine.

- Will the document be printed using process color inks, spot color inks, or both?

If you're not sure of the answers to any of those questions, talk to someone at the company that will print your document, show them your design (if you haven't started yet, just a sketch is fine), and discuss it with them. They can sometimes spot potential production issues before they turn into problems, or they might suggest ways to set up your document so that you save time or money when printing.

Creating a New Document

When you've finalized the production specifications for your document, you're ready to create a new document for your project in InDesign. For a single-page poster design destined for print, the new document setup is relatively simple:

1 Choose File > New > Document (**Figure 2.3**).

2 Click the Print intent at the top of the New Document dialog.

3 In the name field under Preset Details, enter the filename **project02_event_poster**.

4 Select Tabloid from the Page Size menu and click the portrait (tall) icon for Orientation.

5 Choose Inches from the Units pop-up menu.

   Although picas are a traditional unit of measure for print publishing, many designers, such as Jonathan, use a mix of inches and picas, which InDesign handles easily.

6 Deselect Facing Pages, because there's only one page.

   Posters or flyers are designed as standalone pages. In contrast, publications such as books or magazines use facing pages. Facing pages are placed on either side of the spine or fold. Creating a new document with Facing Pages selected displays the left and right pages of the document side by side, with the spine in the middle.

▶ **Video 2.1** Introducing the Poster Project

▶ **Video 2.2** Creating and Saving a New Document

NOTE

Even though you're entering a document name in the New Document dialog, the file is not actually saved until you click Create and then choose File > Save. The icon next to the name field is for saving a new document preset, not for saving the document.

TIP

To see how your settings will affect the document page, select the Preview check box in the New Document dialog.

Figure 2.3 New Document dialog and upper Preset Details options

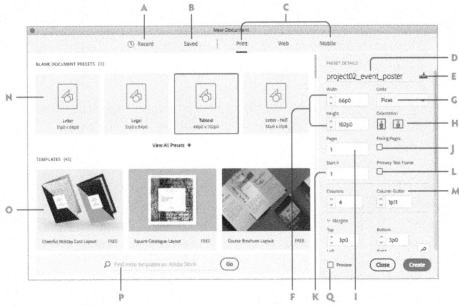

A **Recently used presets and templates**

B **Presets and templates you customized and saved**

C **Document intents**

D **Document name**

E **Save Document Preset button**

F **Document dimensions**

G **Document unit of measure**

H **Page orientation**

I **Number of pages**

J **Facing pages option**

K **Starting page number**

L **Primary Text Frame option**

M **Column settings**

N **Blank document presets**

O **Templates**

P **Search Adobe Stock for more InDesign document templates**

Q **Preview settings in document window**

TIP

If a preset or a template will work for you, select it before you change the Preset Details options in the New Document dialog, because the preset or template will fill in a lot of the details for you.

7   Leave Pages and Start # set to 1.

8   Deselect Primary Text Frame.

This setting adds a text frame to every page so that you can easily add text to every page, so it's useful for long documents such as books. But a primary text frame isn't useful in a single-page poster such as this one, which will have only a few lines of display type.

9   For Columns, enter **4**.

The poster doesn't actually have four columns of text, but columns are often used as a vertical composition unit in some types of grid-based graphic design.

10 For Column Gutter, enter **1p11**.

"1p11" means one pica, eleven points. According to traditional print industry practices, when expressing units smaller than a pica, points are used instead of decimal picas. There are 12 points in a pica, so picas are the large unit and points are used for smaller units.

COLUMNS AND MARGINS

Column and margin settings add helpful nonprinting guides to your document, making it easier for you to consistently position design elements. Aligning them with top, right, bottom, and left margin guides or column guides creates balance and harmony in your design.

Margins define the image area on the page. The image area is the rectangular area on the page marked by the margin guides; it holds most of the content, such as text and images. When setting margins, keep in mind that headers and footers often fall outside this image area. Headers and footers are positioned in the top and bottom margin area between the page edge and the margin guides. The image area, once defined by the margins, can be divided into columns. The *gutter* value sets the spacing between the columns.

Note that when the Facing Pages option is on, the Left and Right options for margin, bleed, and slug settings become the Inside (toward the spine) and Outside (the trim edge, away from the spine) options.

Notice that it's possible to add letters to a measurement value to override the current unit of measure. In other words, even though Unit of Measure was set to Inches, you are able to specify picas and points here using the notation that InDesign recognizes: a number, followed by "p" to indicate picas, and then a second number that InDesign will interpret as points.

11 Expand the Margins section if needed (**Figure 2.4**), make sure the link icon to the right of the values is closed (meaning all Margins fields are linked), enter **3p** (3 picas, no points) into any of the Margins fields, and press Tab to apply it. Because the fields are linked, all fields will now show the value you entered.

Figure 2.4 The lower part of the Preset Details panel in the New Document dialog. To see it, you may need to scroll down.

A Margin settings

B Link icon for making all values in that section the same

C Bleed settings

D Slug settings

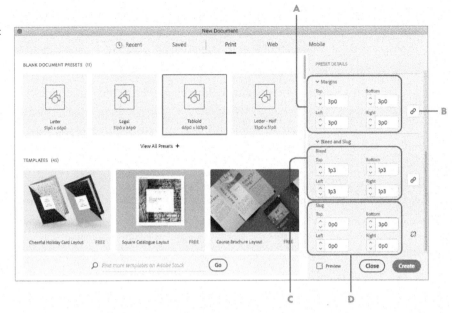

NOTE

The amount of bleed you'll need always depends on the printing equipment that will be used, so don't guess how much you need—always ask the printing company.

TIP

You can spend less time scrolling in the New Document dialog if you make it bigger, by dragging any corner or side.

Video 2.2 demonstrates another example of overriding the unit of measure, where ".75 in" is entered to make sure InDesign interprets that value as inches.

12 Expand the Bleed and Slug section if needed, and in the Bleed section, make sure the link icon to the right of the values is closed, enter **1p3** (1 pica, 3 points) into any of the Bleed fields, and press Tab to apply it. All Bleed fields should now show the value you entered.

13 In the Slug section, make sure the link icon to the right of the values is open (unlinked), enter **3p** in the Bottom slug option, and press Tab to apply it. Because the link icon is open, the four Slug values are not linked and can be set independently. That's why entering 3p for the Bottom slug option did not change the other three Slug values.

The three picas for a slug were added to the bottom edge only, because that's the only side where we want to set aside space for an approval signature.

14 Click Create to close the New Document dialog. When it closes, InDesign creates the new document with the settings you applied.

15 Choose File > Save. The Save As dialog appears with the filename you entered back in the New Document dialog.

16 Navigate to the project02_event_poster folder, and click Save.

You can compare how your new document looks before and after trimming (that is, with and without the bleed and slug areas) by switching between Normal and Preview screen modes using any of the methods you learned in Chapter 1:

- Use the Screen Modes menu in the application bar.
- Use the Screen Mode button in the Tools panel.
- Press W on the keyboard.
- Choose View > Screen Mode, and choose a screen mode from the submenu.

Adding a Slug

You've set aside room for a slug outside the bottom edge of the poster. Let's add the text that goes there for this project.

1 Make sure the screen mode is set to Normal so that you can see the slug area below the page (**Figure 2.5**).

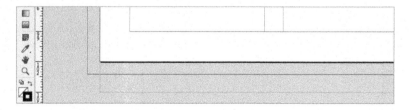

Figure 2.5 Viewing the slug area below the page in Normal screen mode

2   Magnify and scroll the document window so that you're looking at the lower-left corner of the document, including the slug area marked by a blue line extending past the bottom page edge.

3   In the Tools panel, select the Type tool (**T**).

4   Within the slug area, drag to create a text frame wide enough for several words.

5   Type **Approval signature**, then exit text editing mode by clicking the Selection tool in the Tools panel (**Figure 2.6**).

6   Save the document.

Figure 2.6 The text that will print in the slug area, outside the page area

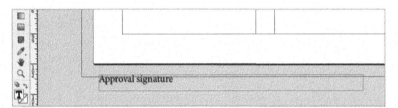

BLEEDS AND SLUGS...
WHAT DO THOSE STRANGE NAMES MEAN?

Bleed and *slug* are traditional printing terminology for two types of areas outside the page edge.

Bleed is important when you have an object that must be printed all the way to the edge of a page. This is because the printing press and the machines that trim the printing sheet down to the final size are sometimes off by a tiny bit, and if the blade cuts slightly outside the intended page edge, there would be a visible gap of blank paper where the ink stopped at the page edge. The solution is to make sure all objects that meet the page edge actually extend slightly past the page edge into what is called the *bleed area*. When the ink extends past the page edge, all edge objects are still fully printed to the page edge even if the cut is imprecise.

A *slug* is an extra area intended for printing job information, instructions, or handwritten notes outside the page. The reason you can't just use the bleed area for this is that the bleed area is likely to have colors or images in it; the slug area should extend past the bleed area so that anything displayed there can be easily read.

Using Layers to Organize Document Elements

★ ACA Objective 3.1

▶ **Video 2.3** Using Layers to Organize Document Elements

Layers are like clear sheets of plastic in a stack. Each layer can contain its own objects. Layers are great for organizing related design elements and controlling the stacking order of objects. Using layers, you can more easily isolate the design elements you are working on without accidentally changing other, nonrelated objects. For example, when working on a magazine, you might work with separate layers for text, images, and background textures or colors. You manage layers using the Layers panel (Window > Layers) (**Figure 2.7**).

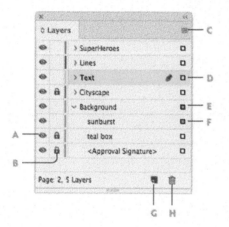

A **Show/hide layer on layout (eye icon)**

B **Lock layer**

C **Panel menu**

D **Current drawing layer**

E **Select all objects on layer**

F **Select individual object**

G **Create New Layer button**

H **Delete Selected Layer button**

Figure 2.7 The Layers panel contains features that help you manage layers and the objects on them.

Looking at Layers in the Finished Document

Layers are useful for keeping a document organized, and for maintaining consistency in which page elements are in front of or behind other page elements.

Each layer can contain objects. Objects on the topmost layer are in front of the stacking order on the page.

Let's examine how layers can be used to structure the poster you're about to create. First, open the Layers panel:

1 If you haven't already opened the finished version of the document, open it: Choose File > Open. Navigate to the project02_event_poster_final folder, select project02_event_poster_final.indd, and click Open.

2   Open the Layers panel by clicking its tab or button; if you can't see either, choose Window > Layers.

In the Layers panel, you see a list of names such as Superheroes, Lines, Text, Cityscape, and Background. Each of those names represents a layer.

Now hide some layers so that it's easier to work with the Sunburst graphic (**Figure 2.8**). That graphic is on the Background layer, so it's currently obstructed by other layers.

Figure 2.8 The Layers panel shown with some layers hidden and the Sunburst graphic selected

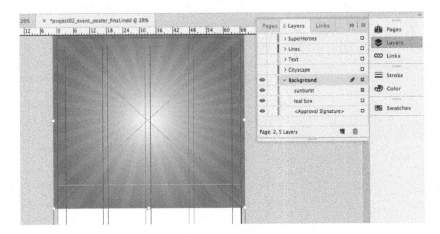

3   In the Layers panel, click to hide the eye icon for the first four layers: Super-heroes, Lines, Text, and Cityscape. You can also drag vertically across the four eye icons to hide them.

When a layer's eye icon is turned off, the objects on that layers are hidden. If the document were to be printed now, it would print as you see it here, with many objects missing.

4   Click the disclosure triangle to the left of the layer named Background.

The expanded layer listing reveals the names of objects on that layer. One of them is an object called Sunburst.

5   Click the selection dot to the right of the Sunburst object.

The Sunburst object is now selected. When an object is difficult to select on the layout because of other objects in front of it, selecting it in the Layers panel is a convenient alternative.

6   Choose Edit > Deselect All. Notice that no selection dots are highlighted now.

7   In the Layers panel, click to show the eye icon for the first four layers: Super-heroes, Lines, Text, and Cityscape. The objects on those layers appear again.

8 Click the disclosure triangle to the left of the layer named Background to collapse it.

The other great thing about the Layers panel is being able to control the stacking order of page elements by rearranging layers. Try it out:

9 In the Layers panel, drag the Superheroes layer down until the drag indicator line appears below the Cityscape layer, then release the mouse button (**Figure 2.9**).

All objects on the Superheroes layer now appear behind the Cityscape layer.

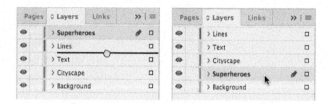

Figure 2.9 Change the layer stacking order by dragging layers up or down.

10 Choose Edit > Undo. The Superheroes layer is returned to the top of the layer stack, and the objects on it now appear in front of all other layers.

Building Layers for a New Document

Now let's create the layers needed in the new blank document you created.

1 Click the document tab for project02_event_poster, the poster you're building.

2 In the Layers panel, click Layer 1 to select it, wait a moment, and then click the Layer 1 text so that it becomes highlighted.

3 Type the name **Background** and then press Enter or Return (**Figure 2.10**).

You can also rename a layer in the Layer Options dialog, which you can open by double-clicking a layer. Opening Layer Options is useful when you want to change other layer attributes, such as whether it's printable. You don't have to rename layers, but having named layers provides useful clarity as a document becomes more complex.

Figure 2.10 Renaming a layer

One of the options in the Layer Options dialog is Color. The layer color doesn't change the printed appearance of any objects; it visually indicates the layer an object uses. You see the layer color on the selection dot at the right side of the Layers panel when a layer or object is selected, as well as on the bounding box and handles around an object selected on the layout.

4   At the bottom of the Layers panel, click the Create New Layer button, and change the name of the new layer to **Cityscape** (**Figure 2.11**).

A new layer is added at the top of the Layers panel if no layer is selected. If a layer is selected, the new layer appears above that layer. Let's create another new layer in a different way.

5   Click the Layers panel menu and choose New Layer (**Figure 2.12**). The New Layer dialog opens; it's basically the same as the Layer Options dialog but for an existing layer.

Figure 2.11 Adding a new layer named Cityscape

Figure 2.12 You can also add a new layer using the Layers panel menu.

6   In the Name field, type **Text**, and click OK (**Figure 2.13**).

Figure 2.13 The New Layer dialog contains additional options, but for now, you only need to name the layer.

7   Create two more layers using either of the methods you've learned so far; name them **Lines** and **Superheroes**.

SHORTCUT *When you want to select an object blocked by other objects, Ctrl-click (Windows) or Command-click (macOS) repeatedly to select each object in the stack in turn until the one you want becomes selected.*

8 Make sure the stacking order of the layers matches the order in the final document, project02_event_poster_final.indd, which should still be open in the other document tab. If the layer order doesn't match, drag to change the order until it matches (**Figure 2.14**).

9 Choose File > Save.

Figure 2.14 The Layers panel should contain layers with the names and stacking order shown here.

CHANGING STACKING ORDER WITHIN A LAYER

In the same way that you can drag in the Layers panel to change the stacking order of layers, you can also drag the objects on each layer. You can drag an object so that it appears in front of or behind a different object in the layout, or you can drag it to a completely different layer.

When you want to change the stacking order of objects within one layer, in addition to dragging them in the Layers panel you can use the commands on the Object > Arrange submenu for objects selected on the layout:

- **Bring To Front:** Moves the selected object to the top of its layer.
- **Bring Forward:** Moves the selected object above the next object up in its layer.
- **Send Backward:** Moves the selected object below the next object down in its layer.
- **Send To Back:** Moves the selected object to the bottom of its layer.

These commands move an object only within the stacking order in the layer containing the object. In other words, Bring Forward will not move an object to the next layer up.

Adding Guides and Changing Preferences

★ *ACA Objective 2.3*

**Video 2.4** *Adding Guides to a Document and Changing Preferences*

Creating a new document automatically adds to your page a number of nonprinting guides for margins, columns, bleed, and slugs. Along with these guides, you can also add ruler guides to help position the elements of the poster.

Using Ruler Guides

You can add a ruler guide by dragging it to any location on the layout, or you can have InDesign generate multiple ruler guides at regular intervals.

DISPLAYING RULERS

If you want to create a ruler guide manually, the onscreen rulers must be visible (**Figure 2.15**).

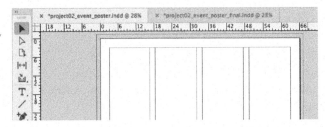

Figure 2.15 Make sure you can see the rulers along the left and top edges of the document window.

> **TIP**
>
> *One way that guides help you is by "snapping" objects to them when you drag an object near them. This helps ensure exact alignment to guides. Snapping is on by default, but if you don't want it to happen, choose View > Grids & Guides, and deselect Snap to Guides.*

To show or hide rulers, do one of the following:

- Choose View > Rulers.
- Press Ctrl+R (Windows) or Command+R (macOS).
- Select Rulers from the View Options menu in the application bar.

> **SHORTCUT** *You can also drag a guide that spans the entire pasteboard area by Ctrl-dragging (Windows) or Command-dragging (macOS) from the ruler. Pressing the Shift key when dragging a guide from the ruler snaps the guide to even ruler increments.*

ADDING AND MOVING RULER GUIDES

A guide can span a single page, or it can span all the pages in a spread (**Figure 2.16**).

- To add a ruler guide to a page, drag a guide from a ruler and drop it on the page.

> **TIP**
>
> *When a guide is selected, you can also position it by entering horizontal (Y) or vertical (X) values in the Control panel.*

- To add a ruler guide to a spread, drag a guide from a ruler and drop it on the pasteboard to the left or right of the spread. You can also drop it above or below the spread if you need a guide that never touches the pages.

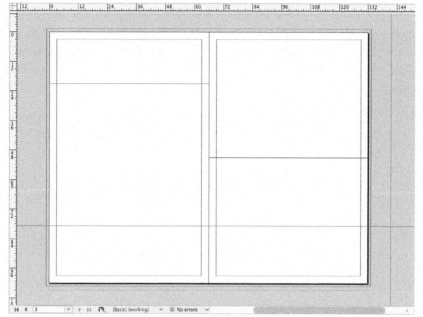

Figure 2.16 The upper ruler guide spans the left page, the center guide spans the right page, the lower guide spans the entire spread, and the guides on the right exist outside the page on the pasteboard. Guides are normally cyan, but these are shown darker for clarity.

To reposition an existing ruler guide, do one of the following:

- Using the Selection tool, click to select the guide, and drag it to a new position.
- To convert a page guide to a spread guide, hold Ctrl (Windows) or Command (macOS) as you drag the guide.

Ruler guides are cyan (kind of a light aqua color) by default.

Deleting Guides

You can remove one guide from the layout, or you can remove all guides at once.

To remove one guide:

1 With the Selection tool, click the guide to select it. The guide is highlighted in the layer color.

2 Press Delete.

To remove all guides on a spread:

Choose View > Grids & Guides > Delete All Guides on Spread.

NOTE

If you can't move a ruler guide, guides might be locked. Choose View > Grids & Guides, and if the Lock Guides command is selected, deselect it.

TIP

If you want to create evenly spaced ruler guides, choose Edit > Create Guides.

Changing the Unit of Measure

Although you've learned how to override the unit of measure, if you're always going to use the same unit of measure you should know how to set it as the active unit of measure. By doing this, you don't have to enter letters after the unit value; just enter the values alone. The active unit of measure is also what InDesign uses in various measurement displays, such as the onscreen rulers, the Control panel, the Info panel, and the transformation values that appear next to the pointer when you drag elements such as the ruler guides.

To change the unit of measure:

1   Open the Units and Increments panel of the Preferences dialog (**Figure 2.17**) using the method for your operating system:

In Windows, choose Edit > Preferences > Units & Increments.

On a Mac, choose InDesign CC > Preferences > Units & Increments.

Figure 2.17 The Units & Increments panel of the Preferences dialog

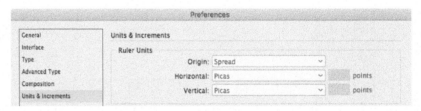

2   In the Ruler Units section, examine the Horizontal and Vertical units of measure, and set both to Inches for this lesson.

The reason there are separate Horizontal and Vertical units is that some traditional publication designs use one unit (such as picas) for widths and another unit (such as inches) for depth (such as when measuring "column inches"). Some of the units of measure are very specific to design or typography, such as the agate, and others are used in specific countries.

3   Click OK.

REVERTING TO DEFAULT PREFERENCES

If you ever want to return to InDesign's default preferences, you can delete the InDesign Preferences files:

1   Hold down Shift+Ctrl+Alt (Windows) or Shift+Ctrl+Option+Command (macOS) as you start up InDesign.

2   When the Startup Alert dialog appears, click Yes.

Adding Objects to a Document

★ ACA Objective 2.3

★ ACA Objective 4.1

▶ **Video 2.5** Adding Objects to a Document

With the new document created, layers created, and an understanding of guides, you've laid down a solid foundation for the structure of the design of the poster. Next, you'll add the actual guides you need and then add colored shapes, lines, images, and text.

Adding a Horizontal Guide for Poster Elements

You'll add one horizontal ruler guide to the page, as you did earlier, so that you can properly align a rectangle you'll draw soon:

1 Position the cursor over the horizontal ruler.

2 Drag a horizontal guide down out of the ruler, and when the Y transformation value next to the pointer indicates that the guide is 10 inches down (**Figure 2.18**), release the mouse button to drop the guide on the page.

TIP

If you have trouble dropping a new ruler guide at an exact dimension, such as 10 inches, hold down the Shift key while dragging to snap the guide to larger increments.

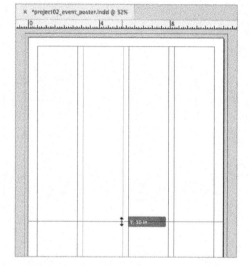

Figure 2.18 Add a horizontal guide at 10 inches from the top of the page.

Adding a Rectangle

You're about to add the teal-colored rectangle in the background of the poster. Because of the guide you just added, you'll know how large to draw the rectangle. In this way, guides are useful for communicating design intention for objects that haven't been created yet, especially if they're going to be created by someone else.

1 In the Layers panel, make sure the Background layer is selected, and expand it so you can see the list of objects on it.

    You selected the Background layer because you want the next object to be created on it.

2 Select the Rectangle tool (▢).

3 Position the cursor at the upper-left corner of the bleed area outside the page area (marked by red lines).

4 Drag the Rectangle tool down and to the right so that the lower-right corner of the rectangle meets the red bleed edge outside the right edge of the page and the horizontal guide you added earlier (**Figure 2.19**).

Figure 2.19 Drag the Rectangle tool diagonally to draw a rectangle.

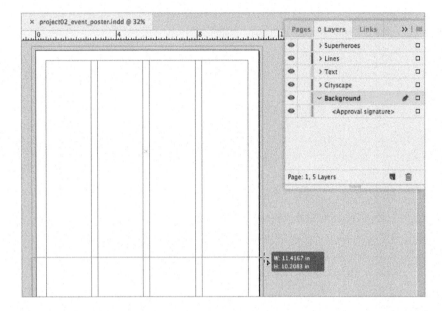

The new rectangle is in place. It needs to be filled with the correct color, so you'll do that next.

Applying Color to a Shape

There are several ways to add color to an object, but to start out you'll use the Swatches panel. You can store colors and gradients in the Swatches panel so that they're readily at hand to apply instantly to objects.

It's also possible to apply colors using the Colors panel, but the advantage of using the Swatches panel is that it saves a list of colors you defined. That way, if you need to apply a color to various objects during a project, you don't have to keep recreating the exact color specifications in the Colors panel.

Creating a Color Swatch

The teal color you need for the rectangle has not yet been defined in the Swatches panel, so you'll add it.

★ ACA Objective 4.5

1 Open the Swatches panel:

- If you can see the Swatches panel tab or button in the workspace, click it.

- If you can't see the Swatches panel tab in the workspace, choose Window > Color > Swatches.

The initial colors that you see in the Swatches panel are the default swatches. Because you started this document using a Print intent, the default swatches are CMYK colors.

The color needed for the poster background rectangle is not in the Swatches panel, so you'll define it and add it.

Figure 2.20 The New Color Swatch command on the Layers panel menu

2 Choose Edit > Deselect All to make sure nothing is selected. (You can also click the Selection tool in an empty area of the document.)

3 In the Swatches panel, click the panel menu and choose New Color Swatch (**Figure 2.20**).

4 In the New Color Swatch dialog, define the color as follows (**Figure 2.21**):

- For Cyan, enter **87**.

- For Magenta, enter **38**.

- For Yellow, enter **31**.

- For Black, enter **4**.

TIP

If you added a swatch to the Swatches panel and later want to change its settings, double-click the swatch.

NOTE

You can also create a new color swatch by clicking the New Swatch button at the bottom of the Swatches panel, but the New Swatch button may not be clickable unless an existing swatch is selected. Clicking New Swatch will duplicate that swatch, and then you can edit that one.

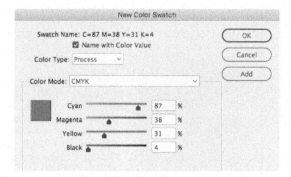

Figure 2.21 Defining a CMYK process color swatch

Figure 2.22 The Dark Teal color swatch you defined is added to the Swatches panel.

5 For Swatch Name, deselect Name With Color Value, and enter **Dark Teal**.

6 At the bottom of the New Color Swatch dialog, deselect Add to CC Library.

7 Click OK. The new swatch is added to the Swatches panel (**Figure 2.22**).

You might have noticed that there was an Add button in the New Color Swatch dialog. When you click Add, the new swatch is added to the Swatches panel, and the New Color Swatch dialog stays open in case you want to define more new swatches. Dark Teal is the only swatch we needed to add, so we clicked OK to close the dialog.

Applying a Color Swatch to an Object

Now that you have a rectangle object and a color swatch, you can apply the color swatch to the rectangle.

In InDesign, objects have two parts. A *stroke* is the outline of an object, and a *fill* is the area enclosed by the stroke. You'll see fill and stroke options almost anywhere you can apply a color in InDesign.

The rectangle in this poster currently has a black stroke and no fill. It needs to have a teal-colored fill and no stroke, so you'll color it accordingly.

TIP

You can also apply colors to a selected object using the Control panel, but instead of clicking the Fill or Stroke icons, click the arrow to the right of either icon and select None.

1 If the rectangle you drew earlier isn't still selected, use the Selection tool to select it.

2 In the Swatches panel, click the Fill icon and then select the Dark Teal swatch (**Figure 2.23**).

3 In the Swatches panel, click the Stroke icon and select None (the diagonal red line) (**Figure 2.24**).

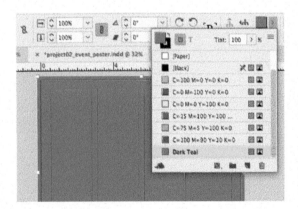

Figure 2.23 Applying the Dark Teal color swatch as the fill color for the rectangle

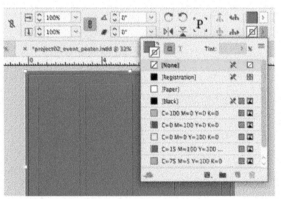

Figure 2.24 Removing the black outline from the rectangle (by applying the stroke color None)

You could have applied the colors using the Swatches panel, but the Control panel is a convenient alternative, especially when the Swatches panel isn't open.

4   Save the document.

Remember to always check both the fill and stroke when applying colors so that you don't accidentally leave a thin stroke around objects.

Applying a Gradient to an Object

Gradients are a popular design effect. A gradient transitions from one color to another. You can create two kinds of gradients in InDesign:

- Linear gradient. A linear gradient is straight, with a minimum of one color at either end.

- Radial gradient. A radial gradient is circular, with a minimum of one color at the center and another color at the edge.

▶ **Video 2.6** *Coloring an Object with a Gradient*

You apply gradients using the Gradient panel (**Figure 2.25**). A gradient can contain multiple colors. Each of the colors is represented by a square gradient stop below the gradient bar, which is at the bottom of the Gradient panel. The midpoint between two colors is represented by the diamond-shaped stops above the gradient bar. You can adjust the color transitions by dragging the stops along the bar.

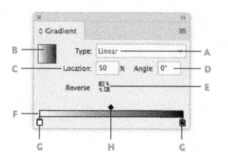

A   **Gradient type**
B   **Gradient icon**
C   **Location of selected gradient stop**
D   **Angle (for a linear gradient)**
E   **Reverse button**
F   **Gradient bar**
G   **Gradient stops for each color**
H   **Gradient midpoint stop (selected)**

Figure 2.25
The Gradient panel

You'll apply a radial gradient to the rectangle, with white at the center and teal at the edge.

To apply a radial gradient to the rectangle:

1   If the Gradient panel isn't visible, choose Window > Color > Gradient. Make sure you can see both the Gradient and Swatches panels.

2   Make sure the Fill icon is active (in front of the Stroke icon) in the Tools panel or Swatches panel; if it's behind the Stroke icon, click it.

COLOR THEORY BASICS

NOTE

If you're not sure whether to define color swatches as process colors or spot colors, ask your printing company. Until you know, use process colors, because that's how many color documents are printed. Adding spot colors may increase the cost of your print job, and it changes how the press is set up, so use spot colors only under the guidance of your commercial printer.

The options you have for creating color in InDesign are based on how your document will be delivered, because the color mode you use to define colors should be based on whether the document will be reproduced on a device display or a sheet of paper.

- **RGB color** stands for red, green, and blue. It's composed of the primary colors of light. Any device that captures or displays colors with light works with RGB color. When designing jobs exclusively for screens, such as digital publishing, eBooks, and websites, you would work with the Web or Mobile document intent and mix colors using RGB.

- **CMYK color** stands for cyan, magenta, yellow, and black (K). It's composed of the subtractive primary colors used in print, such as commercial presses and office printers. When designing jobs for print, you'll typically use CMYK color combinations to build up your colors.

- **Process colors** are made up of multiple color components. For instance, a CMYK process orange color might be 100% yellow and 50% magenta (**Figure 2.26**). An RGB process color for yellow might use 255 red and 255 green. In print terminology, process colors always refer to the mixing of CMYK colors.

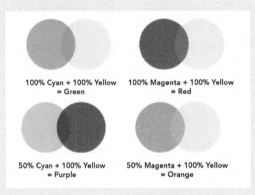

Figure 2.26 Examples of CMYK color mixing

100% Cyan + 100% Yellow = Green

100% Magenta + 100% Yellow = Red

50% Cyan + 100% Yellow = Purple

50% Magenta + 100% Yellow = Orange

- **Spot colors**, in contrast to process colors, are premixed inks created specifically for print. The Pantone Color Matching System (PMS), for example, is used to define spot colors. Spot colors are used for jobs that require:
  - Fewer than four colors
  - Accurate logo and branding colors
  - Colors that can't be achieved in process color-printing, such as a metallic or varnish

You'll learn more about spot versus process colors in Video Project 4 and later chapters.

3   In the Gradient panel, click the Gradient icon near the upper-left corner
    (**Figure 2.27**).

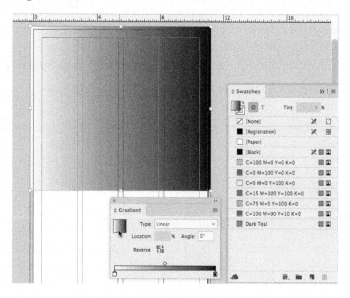

Figure 2.27 Clicking the Gradient icon applies the gradient to a selected object.

The default black and white gradient is applied to the rectangle; this is not
what you want, but you'll edit it.

4   With the rectangle still selected, drag the Dark Teal color swatch from the
    Swatches panel, and drop it in the Gradient panel on the gradient stop at the
    right side of the gradient bar (**Figure 2.28**).

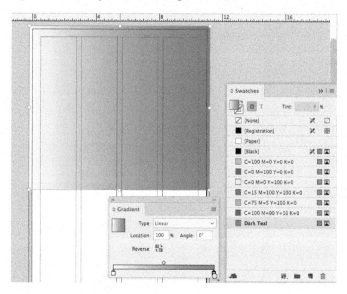

Figure 2.28 Customize a gradient stop by dropping a color swatch on it.

If a new, third gradient stop appears after you drop the swatch, choose Edit > Undo and try again. But this time, keep an eye out for a vertical line that may appear on the gradient bar. That line means that the swatch will create a new gradient stop. That isn't what you want here—you want to drop the swatch on an existing stop. So if you see the vertical line, move the mouse slightly so that the vertical line disappears but the pointer is still over the stop you want.

This is still a linear gradient, and we want it to be a radial gradient, so let's change that next.

5 With the rectangle still selected, in the Gradient panel click the Type menu and choose Radial (**Figure 2.29**).

Figure 2.29 You can change a linear gradient to a radial gradient in an instant.

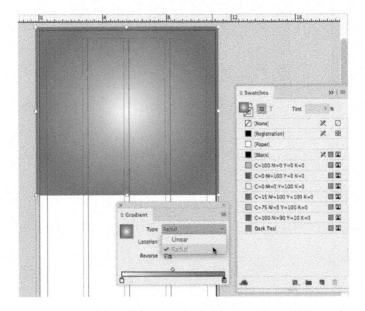

If you wanted to customize the gradient further, you could reposition the two stops or add more stops. But all we need for this project is a simple two-stop gradient with the stops at the ends of the gradient bar.

6 Close or collapse the Gradient and Swatches panels, and save your document.

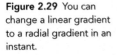

If you plan to use gradients frequently, consider changing your workspace to Advanced. This will add the Gradient panel to the docked panels onscreen.

Assigning Objects to Layers

★ ACA Objective 3.1

▶ Video 2.7
Assigning Objects
to Layers

It's time to take a closer look at organizing a document with layers. This poster design has just enough complexity that layers will help maintain easy access to any element in the layout.

Adding an Imported Graphic

First you need to add more elements to the page. The next one is an image. It's got a specific place on the layout, so you'll create a frame as a placeholder and then import the image into the frame.

1 In the Layers panel, make sure the Background layer is selected, and expand it so you can see the list of objects on it.

2 In the Tools panel, select the Rectangle Frame tool (⊠) (not the Rectangle tool).

3 Draw a rectangle frame at the same position and of the same size as the rectangle you created earlier (**Figure 2.30**).

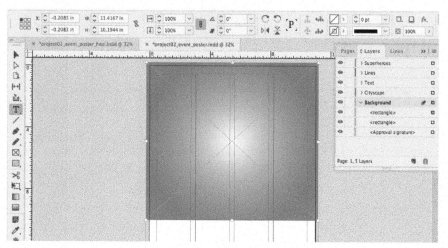

Figure 2.30 Drag the Rectangle Frame tool along the same margin and ruler guides you used for the previous rectangle.

Because the new object was created with the Background layer selected, the Layers panel shows the new object on the Background layer, and as long as the object is selected it displays a selection dot to the right of its name in the Layers panel.

The X inside the frame indicates that it's a graphics frame, which means it's a placeholder for a graphic to be added in the future.

To make objects and layers easier to identify in the Layers panel, you can rename them. Let's rename the objects you've created so far.

1 In the Layers panel, click the name of the rectangle frame you created (**Figure 2.31**) (it should be the topmost object on the Background layer), and when the text is highlighted after a couple of seconds, click the layer name again.

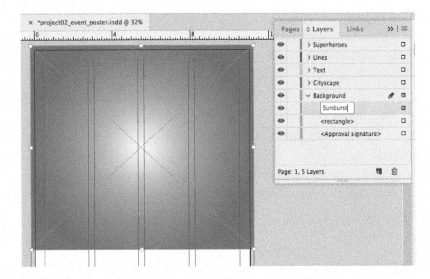

Figure 2.31 Click the name of a selected layer to highlight the name for editing.

You wait a couple of seconds between clicks because you don't want to double-click. The first click selects the layer, and the second click highlights the layer name.

2 Enter the text **Sunburst**, and press Enter or Return.

3 Select the other rectangle layer below **Sunburst**, name it **Teal rectangle**, and press Enter or Return.

4 In the Layers panel, click the selection dot to the right of the **Sunburst** object (**Figure 2.32**). The object is selected on the page if it isn't already, and the bounding box of the object as well as the selection dot are both highlighted with the layer color.

Figure 2.32 Selecting an object in the Layers panel is an alternative to selecting it on the layout.

Now we'll fill the placeholder graphics frame with the artwork intended for that space on the layout.

1   With the **Sunburst** object still selected, choose File > Place.

2   Navigate to the Project02-EventPoster folder, and then inside the Links folder, select the file proj2_poster_sunburst-lines.eps (**Figure 2.33**) and click Open.

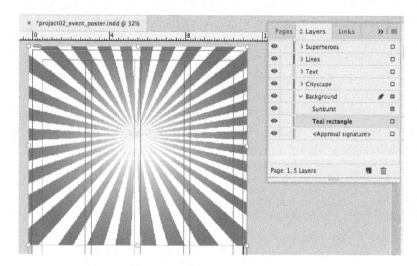

Figure 2.33 The sunburst lines graphic placed inside the rectangle frame

The graphic is placed inside the frame and fills it. The graphic is in EPS (Encapsulated PostScript) format, which is frequently used as an interchange format for vector-based artwork, such as for the clip art used in this lesson.

Normally, an object is added to the selected layer, which is the "Teal rectangle" layer at this point. But the sunburst graphic is on the Sunburst layer because it was placed inside a graphics frame that is on the Sunburst layer. It's a subtle but important distinction.

If you use Adobe Illustrator CC to create vector artwork, you don't have to save the artwork as EPS to place it into InDesign. Just leave the Illustrator artwork in its own native Adobe Illustrator (AI) format, and InDesign can place it directly. Not only is Illustrator format artwork easier to place, it is easier and more reliable to use because the AI format does not have some of the limitations of the EPS format.

TIP

The layer selected in the Layers panel can be different than the object selected in the Layer panel. The selected layer is highlighted in the Layers panel, while the object displays a highlighted selection dot.

Understanding Graphics Formats

Although you can complete a significant part of your design work in InDesign, images and graphics are generally created separately and supplied to you as individual files.

Pixel-based images, such as photos or photo compositions, are captured with a digital camera, scanned, or compiled in photo-editing programs, such as Adobe Photoshop. Vector-based graphics, such as a drawings, cartoons, logos, or technical drawings, are created in drawing programs, such as Adobe Illustrator. The shapes and lines that make up vector-based graphics are drawn mathematically, resulting in graphics that you can scale to different sizes without loss of quality. This means that vector-based graphics are resolution independent. In contrast, the quality of pixel-based images depends on their size and image resolution, measured in pixels per inch (ppi).

InDesign supports the import of native Photoshop and Illustrator files, as well as a range of other image and graphics file formats.

For pixel-based images (**Figure 2.34**), commonly supported file formats are:

- **Adobe Photoshop native files (PSD):** PSD files may contain transparency, layers, and layer comps (snapshots of layer visibility, appearance, and position). Top-level layers and layer comps can be enabled or disabled within InDesign.

Figure 2.34 When you magnify this photographic image, individual pixels become visible.

- **Tagged Image File Format (TIFF):** TIFF files can be compressed and may contain layers and transparency.

- **Joint Photographic Experts Group files (JPEG):** A compressed file format that significantly reduces file sizes, JPEG does not support transparency, layers, or spot color and should be used with caution, as high compression rates could result in significant loss of quality. JPEG format is more commonly used for web images.

For vector graphics (**Figure 2.35**) the more common formats are:

- **Adobe Illustrator native files (AI):** AI files retain transparency and layers. Top-level layers can be enabled or disabled within InDesign after import. During import, any available Illustrator artboard can be selected for import. Illustrator files appear as Adobe PDF Format in InDesign's Links panel.

Figure 2.35 When you magnify this illustration of a superhero, lines and shapes remain sharp, always at full device resolution.

- **Encapsulated PostScript (EPS):** An older file format that does not support transparency and is gradually being phased out. You will see this format used in the signage industry and with some older pagination systems newspapers use to place ads. Vector-based illustrations are fully opaque within the vector shape, but they can be see-through outside the area defined by the vector shapes.

- **Portable Document Format (PDF):** A document format that is platform independent and can be viewed with Adobe Acrobat Reader. PDF files embed images and graphics as well as fonts. The format is supported as an import format in InDesign. However, it is more commonly used to export finished art from InDesign for delivery to a printer or to provide a compatible version of the document for general viewing.

SHORTCUT *If you click the page with a loaded pointer instead of dragging, you place the image at that location at 100 percent size.*

These file formats work well for print publishing and can also be used for digital publishing. With the exception of JPEG, the file formats discussed here are not supported in web design. Common file formats used when designing for web are JPEG, PNG, and GIF.

TRANSPARENCY

Transparency is created when visual elements are no longer opaque. Changing the opacity level from 100 percent (opaque) to 50 percent, for example, creates transparency. Elements below transparent objects become visible. Additionally, effects applied to objects, such as drop shadows, create transparency. We'll cover transparency and effects in more detail in Chapter 3.

Resizing Objects and Adding Effects

▶ **Video 2.8** *Resizing Objects and Adding Effects*

When you place a graphic, it always exists inside a frame whether or not you drew one in advance. If you didn't draw one in advance, a placed graphic comes with a containing frame that matches the size of the graphic.

You'll resize the Sunburst graphic you just placed, and adjust its appearance by changing its effects settings.

RESIZING AN OBJECT TO FIT ITS FRAME

TIP

An alternative to using the Content Grabber is to select the Direct Selection tool in the toolbox. The Direct Selection tool bypasses the frame to give you direct access to its contents. When drawing paths and shapes, the Direct Selection tool bypasses the object level to give you direct access to points and paths.

Because a placed graphic always exists within a frame, use care when resizing because if you simply drag the corner handle of a selected graphic, you're actually resizing its frame; resizing the graphic itself requires a different method. Let's try some different methods for resizing a graphics frame and its contents:

1 If the Sunburst object isn't selected, select it by clicking anywhere on the frame except in the center of the frame.

2 Drag any corner handle outward (**Figure 2.36**).

   The frame around the graphic resized, revealing more of the graphic, but the graphic itself is unchanged. This isn't what we want, so we'll have to try again.

3 Choose Edit > Undo, and this time position the Selection tool over the center of the graphic, revealing the Content Grabber in the middle of the frame (**Figure 2.37**).

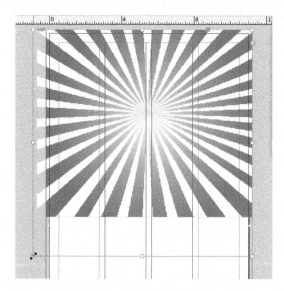

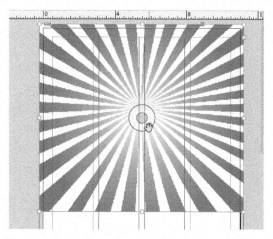

Figure 2.37 To select content inside a graphics frame, click only after you see the Content Grabber.

Figure 2.36 Resizing a graphics frame with the Selection tool

When the Content Grabber is visible, clicking it affects the contents of the frame (in this case, the Sunburst graphic) instead of the frame.

4   Click the Content Grabber. A different, larger bounding box appears (**Figure 2.38**). This is the graphic (the content), not the frame. If you grab one of the handles now, you resize the graphic, not the frame. (You can try this, but if you do, choose Edit > Undo afterward.)

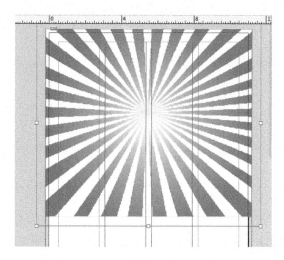

Figure 2.38 The content (the Sunburst graphic) inside the frame is bigger than the frame, so selecting the content reveals an image bounding box larger than the containing frame.

Is there a way to resize a frame and its contents together when you drag a bounding box handle? Yes: Hold down the Ctrl (Windows) or Command (macOS) key while dragging any of the frame's bounding box handles (also hold down Shift to resize proportionally).

Manual resizing is fine, but in this case we just want the graphic to fit its frame exactly, since the frame was drawn as a placeholder for that exact area of the page. Fortunately, InDesign has an automatic way to do this:

NOTE

For step 5, Video 2.8 demonstrates clicking the Fit Content to Frame icon in the Control panel. You can do that instead if you see those icons on the Control panel, but they may not appear on some smaller screen sizes.

5 With either the Sunburst graphic or frame selected, choose Object > Fitting > Fit Content to Frame (**Figure 2.39**).

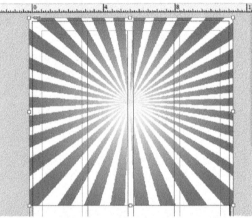

Figure 2.39 Applying the Fit Content to Frame command makes all four sides of the image content exactly match the four sides of the frame.

This makes the graphic exactly fit the height and width of the frame. Because the frame and the graphic are slightly different proportions, the resized graphic is slightly wider than its original proportions, so there is a small amount of distortion, but that's acceptable for this use. If you wanted to maintain the original proportions of the graphic without leaving any empty areas in the frame, you could choose Object > Fitting > Fill Frame Proportionally.

Applying an Effect

Visual effects are fun, but excessive or overdone effects can sometimes cause problems on a printing press. InDesign comes with a range of effects that are appropriate for print publishing and that can translate into web design or mobile device publishing.

One of the more useful and popular effects is opacity, where 100 percent opacity is completely opaque and 0 percent is completely transparent.

To apply an opacity effect to the Sunburst graphic:

1 Make sure the frame containing the Sunburst graphic is selected. If the contents are still selected, press the Esc key until you see the bounding box for the frame, which will appear in the layer color (**Figure 2.40**).

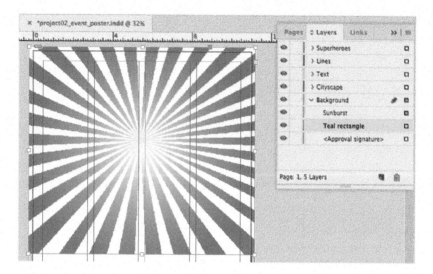

Figure 2.40 The frame containing the Sunburst graphic is selected.

2 Choose Object > Effects > Transparency.

The Effects dialog (**Figure 2.41**) opens, displaying the Transparency panel. Here you can see the other effects that are available, such as Drop Shadow, Outer Glow, and Bevel and Emboss, but for now we're concerned only with Transparency.

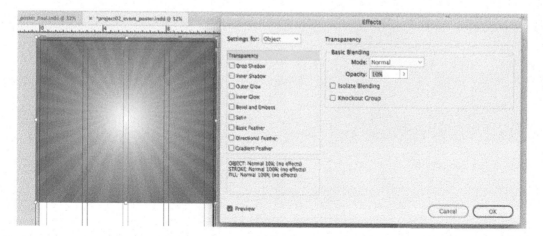

Figure 2.41 Transparency is one of the many graphic effects you can apply.

3   Make sure the Preview option is selected so that you can see the effects of your changes as you make them.

4   Change the Opacity setting to 10%, and click OK.

With the opacity lowered, the Sunburst looks fainter, and the teal background shows through it.

5   Save the document.

Creating a Shape with the Pathfinder Tools

★ ACA Objective 4.5

▶ **Video 2.9**
Introducing the Pathfinder Tools

▶ **Video 2.10** *Using the Pathfinder Tools to Create a Globe*

You can combine two or more shapes to create new shapes by using the Pathfinder panel and command in InDesign. This can often be easier and faster than drawing a complete shape by hand.

The poster design specifies that the superheroes stand on top of a globe. But the entire globe isn't shown, just the top section. To reduce clutter, the rest of the globe won't be used. Instead of having to perfectly draw an arc, it will be easier to draw an ellipse and a rectangle, and with the Pathfinder tools, use the rectangle to cut the desired section out of the ellipse.

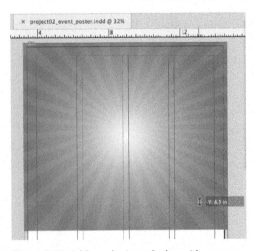

Figure 2.42 Adding a horizontal ruler guide

Let's create the partial globe for the poster by combining some of the basic shapes you can make with the InDesign drawing tools. First, create the shapes:

1   Drag a ruler guide down from the horizontal ruler, and when the Y transformation value next to the pointer says the guide is 8.5 inches down (**Figure 2.42**), release the mouse button.

2   In the Tools panel, select the Ellipse tool (⬭).

3   Drag an oval across the bottom of the page; the exact size isn't important yet.

4   With the oval still selected, in the Control panel click the arrow next to the Fill icon and apply the Black color swatch (**Figure 2.43**).

5   In the Control panel, click the arrow next to the Stroke icon and apply the None color swatch to remove the outline from the oval.

6   In the Control panel, set the width (W) of the selected oval to 17 inches and set the height (H) to 10 inches.

7   With the Selection tool, drag the black oval so that the top snaps to the guide you added in step 1 and so that the center of the ellipse is horizontally centered on the page (**Figure 2.44**).

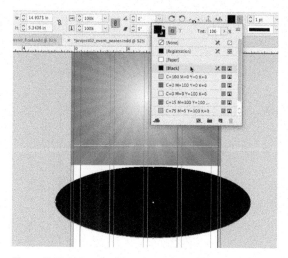

Figure 2.43 Using the Control panel to apply a black fill to the oval

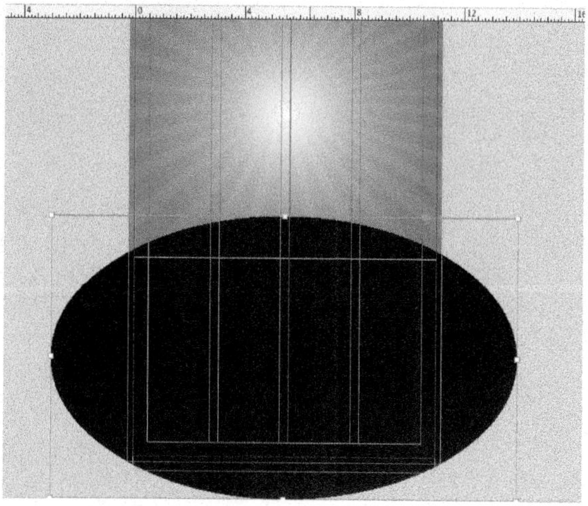

Figure 2.44 Positioning the oval

As you drag the oval near the horizontal center of the page, a vertical magenta guide should temporarily appear. This is a Smart Guide, which appears only when you drag an object close to alignment with another object or the page. Smart Guides help you align objects perfectly the first time so that you don't have to go back later and apply other alignment features. You can disable and enable Smart Guides by choosing View > Grids & Guides > Smart Guides.

Now you'll add a shape that will modify the oval feature when you apply a Pathfinder option.

8   In the Tools panel, select the Rectangle tool, and drag a rectangle in the pasteboard starting slightly beyond the left edge of the oval, until the right edge of the rectangle meets the left edge of the bleed area, and then release the mouse button (**Figure 2.45**).

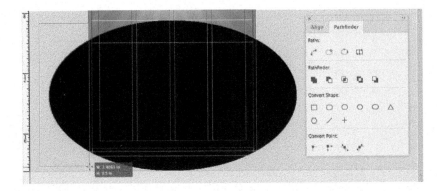

Figure 2.45 Drawing a rectangle that will be used to modify the oval

With two overlapping shapes drawn, you're ready to apply the Pathfinder tools to them.

1 If the Pathfinder panel isn't visible, choose Window > Object & Layout > Pathfinder.

2 If the rectangle is still selected, with the Selection tool Shift-click the oval so that both shapes are now selected.

3 In the Pathfinder panel, click the Subtract button (**Figure 2.46**). This subtracts the shape in front (the rectangle) from the shape in back (the oval).

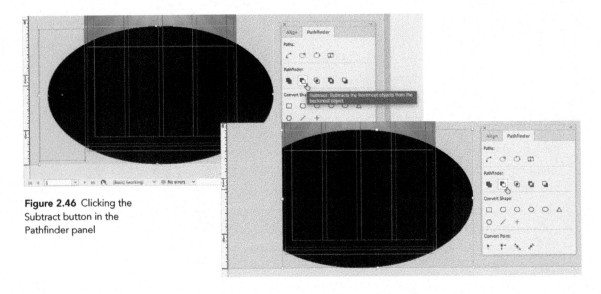

Figure 2.46 Clicking the Subtract button in the Pathfinder panel

4   In the same way, draw and subtract rectangles from the right and bottom sides of the oval (**Figure 2.47**).

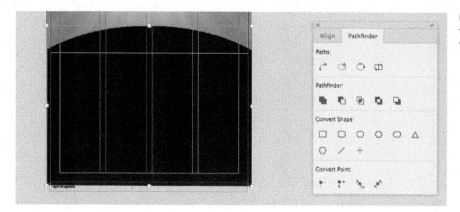

Figure 2.47 Subtracting the third rectangle from the oval

5   In the Layers panel, click the oval object, click the name to highlight it, rename it **Globe**, and then press Enter or Return.

6   Close the Pathfinder panel, and save your document.

That's it! You used the Pathfinder Subtract button with rectangle shapes to cut unwanted sections out of an oval, leaving you with the shape you really wanted.

Moving, Scaling, and Locking Objects

★ *ACA Objective 4.4*

▶ **Video 2.11**
Moving, Scaling, and Locking Objects

It's time to add more objects to the layout, but if we think about the big picture, you probably aren't going to drop a graphic on a page and move on. You'll fit the graphic into the page composition, moving it into the proper position and, if necessary, scaling it (changing its size).

Adding the Cityscape Graphics

Let's add the cityscape graphics that are needed to complete the poster. It isn't uncommon for even a one-page design to use several imported graphics.

1   In the Layers panel, if the Background layer isn't already expanded to show the list of objects on it, click the disclosure triangle to the left of the Background layer name.

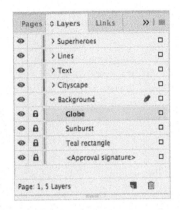

Figure 2.48 Setting up the Layers panel for the next task

You want to protect the existing objects on the Background layer from being accidentally altered. You could do this by enabling the lock icon for the Background layer, but that would also prevent you from unlocking individual objects on the Background layer. To preserve that option it's better to leave the Background layer unlocked but individually lock each object on the Background layer.

2 In the Layers panel, in the column to the left of the layer names, click to enable the lock icon for each object on the Background layer, but do not lock the Background layer itself (**Figure 2.48**).

Notice that in Normal screen mode, objects locked in the Layers panel display lock icons on their bounding boxes in the layout.

3 In the Layers panel, expand the Cityscape layer and select it.

4 In the Tools panel, select the Rectangle Frame tool.

5 Starting at the upper-left bleed edge, drag the Rectangle Frame tool down and to the right until the lower-right corner is slightly below where the arc ends at the right edge of the globe (**Figure 2.49**).

Figure 2.49 Drawing a placeholder graphics frame for the next image

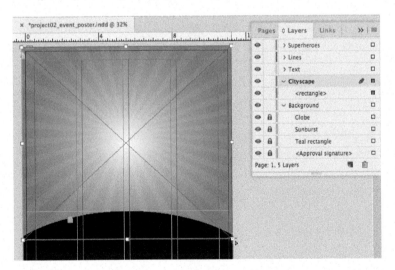

6 With the new rectangle frame still selected, choose File > Place.

7 In the Place dialog, navigate to the Links folder, select the file proj2_poster_city-back.eps, and click Open (**Figure 2.50**).

The file imports into the selected graphics frame, but it needs to be repositioned.

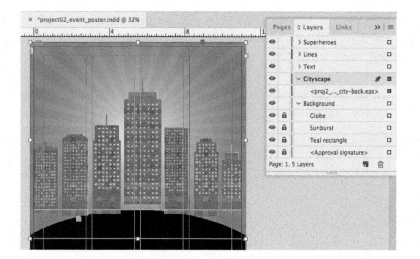

Figure 2.50 The first cityscape image placed inside the graphics frame

Now you'll adjust its size:

1. Make sure the image content, not the containing frame, is selected.

   Remember that you select graphics frame content by positioning the Selection tool over the center of the frame and clicking the Content Grabber after it appears. (Or by clicking inside the frame with the Direct Selection tool.)

2. Choose Object > Transform > Scale.

3. In the Scale dialog, do the following:

   - Make sure the Preview option is on so you can see your changes as you make them.

   - Make sure the link icon is closed; that will maintain the original proportions of the height and width as you change their values. (In other words, the height and width are linked.)

   - For Scale X, enter **94%**, and press the Tab key to apply the value (**Figure 2.51**).

   Because the link icon is closed, the Scale X and Scale Y values are linked, so applying 94 percent to Scale X also changes Scale Y to the same percentage, maintaining the graphic's proportions.

The link icon you saw in the Scale dialog is also next to the scale fields in the Control panel, and it has the same function there: to maintain the original proportions of a graphic as you change the H and W values.

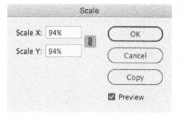

Figure 2.51 Using the Scale dialog to resize the first cityscape image

4   Click OK.

The graphic is scaled. With the size corrected, it's time to reposition the graphic.

5   With the Selection tool, position the pointer over the center of the cityscape graphic so that the Content Grabber circles appear, then drag the cityscape graphic until its bottom edge is roughly where the globe arc begins to rise (**Figure 2.52**). The graphic is repositioned within its frame.

> **TIP**
> *When you can't select an object on the layout, check the Layers panel to see if the object is locked or on a locked layer. Unlock the object to be able to select it.*

Figure 2.52 Repositioning the first cityscape image

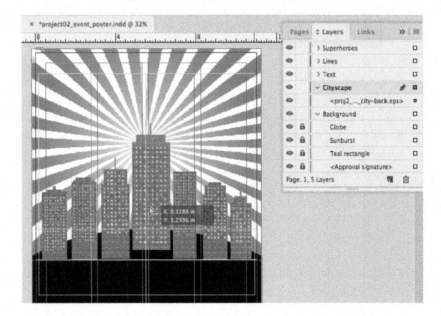

You can toggle the Preview screen mode to see how the design looks after trimming and without the InDesign guides and visual aids. The cityscape graphic would look better behind the globe.

1   In the Layers panel, click to hide the lock icon next to the Globe object so that it's unlocked.

2   In the Layers panel, drag the Globe object up until it's above the cityscape graphic in the list (**Figure 2.53**).

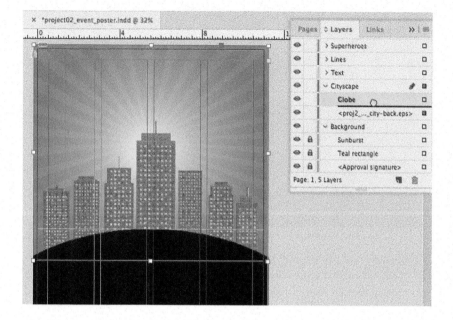

Figure 2.53 Correcting the object stacking order

There's another cityscape graphic specified for this poster, so let's add that:

1   Switch to Normal screen mode so that you can see the InDesign guides and visual aids.

2   In the Layers panel, make sure the Cityscape layer is selected.

3   With the Rectangle Frame tool, drag a rectangle frame in the same position and size as the one you drew earlier (with the upper-left corner at the upper-left bleed edge, and the lower-right corner slightly below where the arc ends at the right edge of the globe).

4   With the new rectangle frame still selected, choose File > Place.

5   In the Place dialog, navigate to the Links folder, select the file proj2_poster_city-front.eps, and click Open.

6   With the Selection tool, position the pointer over the center of the cityscape graphic so that the Content Grabber circles appear, then drag the cityscape graphic until its bottom edge merges with the black globe and the graphic is slightly offset from the other cityscape graphic to make the two graphics look more naturally layered (**Figure 2.54**).

Figure 2.54 Repositioning the second cityscape
graphic

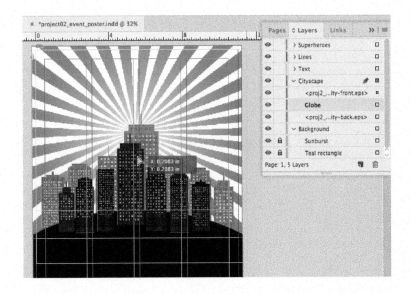

7 In the Layers panel, drag the Globe object above both cityscape graphics in the list for the same reason you did before—because the bottom of
   the cityscape graphic looks more natural if it's behind the arc of the globe
   (**Figure 2.55**).

Figure 2.55 Correcting
the object stacking order

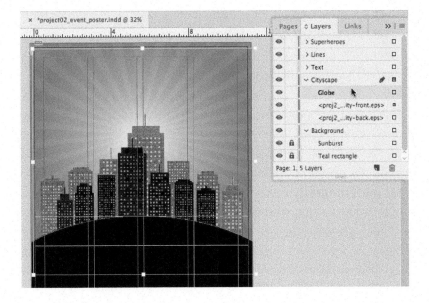

8 Choose Edit > Deselect All.

You've completed editing the Background and Cityscape layers, so to eliminate the chance that the objects on either layer might be accidentally altered, you'll lock both layers.

1   In the Layers panel, click in the lock column for the Background layer to enable its lock icon, and do the same for the Cityscape layer (**Figure 2.56**).

2   Save the document.

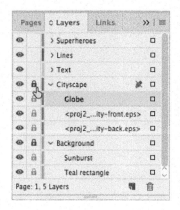

Figure 2.56 Locking the Background and Cityscape layers

TIP

When you want to deselect everything, you can also click in an empty area of the page or pasteboard as long as you're sure there isn't anything there. If you're not sure, it's safer to choose Edit > Deselect All or press Crl+Shift+A (Windows) or Cmd+Shift+A (macOS).

Adding the Superhero Figures to the Document

Placing graphics onto the page and adjusting them should be starting to feel routine now. Let's use the experience you've gained to add the superhero figures to the document.

1   Make sure Normal screen mode is active so that you can see the InDesign guides and visual aids.

2   In the Layers panel, make sure the Superheroes layer is selected.

3   With the Rectangle Frame tool, drag a rectangle frame from the upper-left corner of the page margin (not the bleed or page edge) to the lower horizontal guide where it meets the right margin of the second column (**Figure 2.57**). In other words, the rectangle should cover the first two columns without going into the page margins or middle column gutter.

▶ *Video 2.12* *Placing Graphics in a Document*

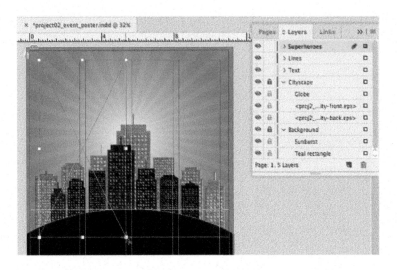

Figure 2.57 Drawing a placeholder frame for the female superhero

4   With the new rectangle frame still selected, choose File > Place.

5   In the Place dialog, navigate to the Links folder, select the file proj2_superhero-female_2020.eps, and click Open. The female superhero figure is placed inside the selected graphics frame (**Figure 2.58**).

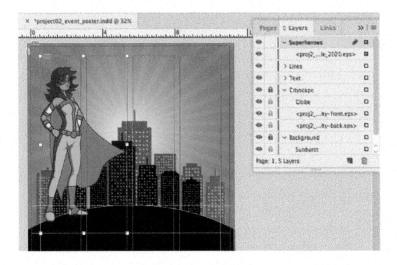

Figure 2.58 The female superhero figure in its designated graphics frame

6   With the Rectangle Frame tool, drag a rectangle frame that covers the second two columns down to the lower horizontal guide, without going into the page margins or middle column gutter. In other words, it should be the same as the previous graphics frame, but on the other side of the poster.

7 With the new rectangle frame still selected, choose File > Place.

8 In the Place dialog, navigate to the Links folder, select the file proj2_superhero-male-2020.eps, and click Open. The male superhero figure is placed inside the selected graphics frame (**Figure 2.59**).

Figure 2.59 The male superhero figure is placed in its graphics frame.

Now let's refine the size and positioning of the two figures. They both need to be slightly smaller and composed more effectively.

1 With the Selection tool, position the pointer over the center of the female figure so that the Content Grabber circles appear, then click it to select the image contents of the graphics frame (the female figure).

2 Drag the female figure until the feet rest on the lower horizontal guide (**Figure 2.60**).

Figure 2.60 Repositioning the female superhero

The female superhero figure needs to be resized, but this time you'll scale the graphic using the Control panel.

3 Click the middle point on the bottom of the Reference Point proxy (**Figure 2.61**). This will anchor the resizing operation at the bottom of the graphic so that the female superhero's feet stay where they are.

Figure 2.61 Resizing the female superhero

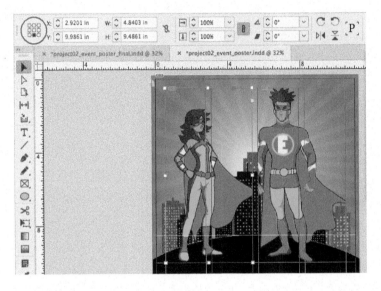

**NOTE**

After resizing in step 4, the Scale X Percentage and Scale Y Percentage fields may say 100% instead of 96%; if this happens it's because the graphics frame has become selected instead of its contents.

4 In the Control panel, make sure the link icon next to the Scale X Percentage and Scale Y Percentage fields is closed (to constrain proportions), type **96%** into the width field, and press Enter or Return.

Carefully examine the edges of the female figure. If repositioning the graphic now hides any sides of the female figure because they slid under the edge of the containing graphics frame (especially the right corner of her cape), perform step 5; otherwise, move on to step 6.

5 With the female superhero image still selected, press the Esc key to change the selection to its containing graphics frame, and drag any handle on the frame to make any hidden areas of the female figure visible again.

6 Repeat steps 1 through 4 for the male figure.

7 Choose Edit > Deselect All.

8 Save the document.

TIP

If step 5 is confusing, another way to select the containing frame of content is to deselect everything (Edit > Deselect All), and then with the Selection tool, click the frame of the graphic.

Adding Text

Similar to how graphics are always added to an InDesign document inside a graphics frame, text is always added to InDesign inside a text frame.

This poster design specifies that the text appear in multiple colors, so before adding the text, you'll set up some color swatches for the text color.

Setting Up Color Swatches

★ ACA Objective 4.2

▶ Video 2.13
Defining Swatches
and Coloring Text

Because this will be a printed poster, all the swatches for this document will use CMYK process colors. But how do you know what color values to enter to set up a particular color? The colors you see on your computer display do not always reliably represent how those colors will appear in print, so the best way to specify process colors accurately is to refer to printed swatch books. These books show printed samples of colors, along with the CMYK values that produced them. Similar swatch books exist for spot colors, but instead of specifying CMYK process colors, spot color swatch books show what the actual mixed ink color looks like when printed.

Let's add the color swatches you'll need for the text. You'll use more than one way to define a color swatch.

To create a color swatch using CMYK values:

1 In the Swatches panel (Window > Color > Swatches), choose New Color Swatch from the Swatches panel menu, and define a color using the following values:

    ■ For Cyan, enter **10**.

    ■ For Magenta, enter **91**.

    ■ For Yellow, enter **100**.

    ■ For Black, enter **18**.

2 Deselect Name with Color Value, and enter a name of **Dark Red** (**Figure 2.62**).

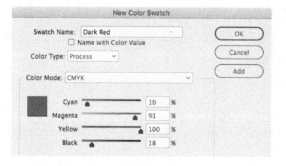

Figure 2.62 Adding the Dark Red color swatch

3 Deselect Add to CC Library, and click OK. The new color swatch appears in the Swatches panel.

Many color schemes are based on important colors in the images used in the design. You don't have to know the color values of those colors to use them; you can easily create a new color swatch by sampling any color in the document—even from imported graphics. Now you'll create color swatches based on colors found in the superhero costumes.

To define a color swatch by sampling a color in the image:

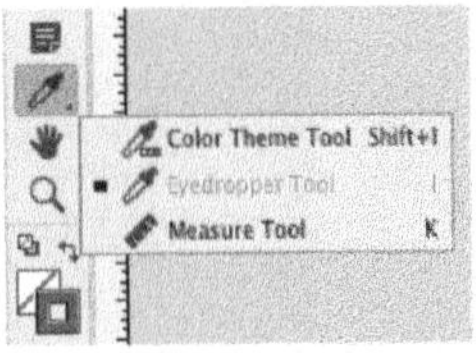

4 In the Tools panel, select the Eyedropper tool (![eyedropper]( )). If you can't find it right away, it's grouped with the Color Theme tool, so it may be a hidden tool in that group; press and hold down the mouse button on the Color Theme tool to reveal and select the Eyedropper tool (**Figure 2.63**).

Figure 2.63 Selecting the Eyedropper tool

5 Click the Eyedropper tool to sample the light teal color from the upper part of the male superhero's upper leg (**Figure 2.64**). If an alert message appears warning about a low-resolution RGB proxy, click OK.

6 In the Swatches panel, choose New Color Swatch from the Swatches panel menu. A new color swatch is created from the current color (**Figure 2.65**).

The swatch name in the Swatches panel indicates that it's defined using RGB color values. But this document uses CMYK values, so you need to convert the color values. Fortunately, that takes just a moment.

Figure 2.64 Sampling a color that exists in a graphic in the document

Figure 2.65 A new color swatch added after clicking the New Color Swatch button

7 Double-click the swatch you just created, and choose CMYK from the Color Mode pop-up menu.

8 Deselect the Name with Color Value option, and for Swatch Name, enter **Light Blue**. Click OK.

Now sample another color from the costume. Repeat steps 4 through 8, but this time, use the Eyedropper tool to sample the yellow color from the letter E on the male superhero's costume, and create a CMYK swatch from it named Light Yellow.

Adding Text Frames and Formatting Text

To add the text to the empty area below the superheroes, you'll draw text frames, fill them with text, add lines between the text frames, and then apply different fill colors to ranges of text characters.

To add the first text frame to the bottom of the poster:

1 Position the pointer over the horizontal ruler.

2 Drag a horizontal guide down out of the ruler, and when the Y transformation value next to the pointer indicates that the guide is 10.5 inches down, release the mouse button to drop the guide on the page (**Figure 2.66**).

Figure 2.66 Adding a horizontal guide for the text

3 With the Type tool, drag a text frame starting where the right edge of the first column meets the horizontal guide you just drew, and ending with the text frame about 3 inches tall at the left edge of the last column (**Figure 2.67**).

When you release the mouse button after drawing a text frame, a blinking insertion point is in the frame so that you can start typing. But first you'll set some options for the text you're about to type.

4 In the Control panel, set the following options (**Figure 2.68**):

■ From the font menu, choose Poplar Std (or another heavy display font).

■ Set the font size to **136pt**.

■ Click the arrow next to the Fill icon, and choose the Dark Red color swatch.

Figure 2.67 Creating the first text frame

Figure 2.68 Setting up type specifications in the Control panel

5 With the Type tool, click in the text frame, and type **EMPIRE** (**Figure 2.69**).

6 In the Control panel, click the Justify All Lines button (**Figure 2.70**).

Figure 2.70 Selecting Justify All Lines to distribute the text characters across the full width of the text frame

Figure 2.69 Typing text into the text frame

InDesign offers both alignment and justification of paragraph text. The alignment options align all lines in a paragraph to the left, center, or right side of the text frame. (The exact spacing from the edge can depend on other settings, such as paragraph indents.)

The justification options are different variations on automatically spacing the characters in lines of paragraph text so that both the left and right sides of a paragraph are aligned with the left and right edges of the text frame, respectively.

7 With the Type tool, click after the last character in the word EMPIRE, and apply a line break by pressing Shift+Enter (Windows) or Shift+Return (macOS). If you forget the shortcut, you can also choose Type > Insert Break Character > Forced Line Break.

8 In the Control panel, set the font size to **70pt**.

9 With the Type tool, type **COMICCON2020** (**Figure 2.71**).

Figure 2.71 Typing the second line of text

Figure 2.72 Setting a leading value to reduce the space between lines

There's a lot of space between the two lines of text, so you'll reduce the space by adjusting the leading value, which is the vertical space between lines. (If you wanted to adjust the space between entire paragraphs of text, you'd adjust paragraph spacing instead.) The leading value you currently see in the Control panel is in parentheses, indicating that it's automatic leading, which changes as you change the type size. You're about to set a manual leading value that will no longer change on its own.

10 Select the COMICCON2020 text, and in the Control panel, set the leading value to **66pt** (**Figure 2.72**).

Applying Colors to Text

Now it's time to apply the color swatches you created earlier to the text you just typed:

1 Select the COMICCON text.

2 In the Control panel, click the arrow next to the Fill icon, and apply the Light Yellow swatch from the menu that appears (**Figure 2.73**).

3 Select the 2020 text, and using the Fill icon menu in the Control panel, apply the Light Blue swatch (**Figure 2.74**).

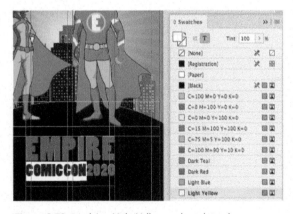

Figure 2.73 Applying Light Yellow to the selected text

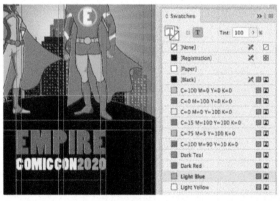

Figure 2.74 The ComicCon text filled with Light Yellow, and the 2020 text filled with Light Blue

USING TYPEKIT FONTS

Your computer's operating system comes with a set of fonts, and the Creative Cloud installer adds more fonts when you install InDesign. To make your designs unique so that they stand out, you'll often be on the lookout for new fonts. As part of your Creative Cloud membership, you have access to Adobe Typekit fonts that can be used across web and desktop designs, and many are available for both desktop and mobile use. (Adobe Typekit may not be available on computers in some schools and organizations.)

To use Typekit fonts in your designs, choose Type > Add Fonts From Type-kit. You can also choose Add Fonts From Typekit from the font menu in the Control panel or Character panel. You can try your own preview text, inspect different weights and styles, and if you want to use the font, click Sync or Sync All and the fonts will be synchronized to your computer, where you can use them in InDesign and other applications.

The Typekit web page opens in your default web browser (**Figure 2.75**).

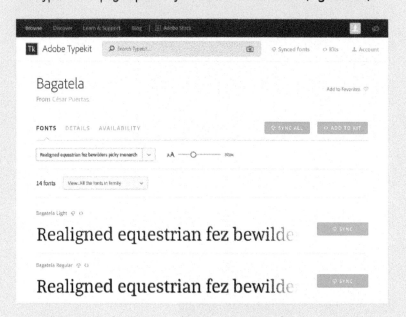

Figure 2.75 The Typekit web page, where you can evaluate fonts and sync them to your computer

4   Make sure there is not a third line in that text frame by clicking after the last character and pressing the Right Arrow key. If the blinking text insertion point moves to the next line, press the Backspace (Windows) or Delete (macOS) key until the text insertion point is after the last character in 2020 and still on the same line.

5   Choose Object > Fitting > Fit Frame to Content (**Figure 2.76**). This pulls up the bottom edge of the text frame until it meets the bottom of the last line of text and is an instant way to get rid of unneeded space at the end of a text frame.

Figure 2.76 Cleaning up extra space in a text frame

TIP

Although the colors you see on your computer display do not always reliably represent how those colors will appear in print, it is possible to produce a much closer match using advanced color-management methods such as display calibration and soft-proofing. Ask your commercial printer if they have advice on which methods work best with their InDesign workflow.

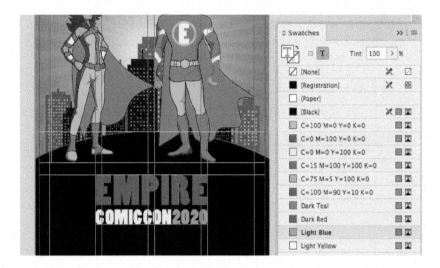

If there were one more empty line of text, Fit Frame to Content would have held open the text frame. That's why you checked for an unused last line in step 4.

6   With the Type tool, click between COMIC and CON and type a space. Also add a space between CON and 2020 (**Figure 2.77**).

Figure 2.77 Adding spaces to make the words more distinct

Moving and Sizing Text

★ *ACA Objective 4.2*

▶ **Video 2.14** *Moving and Sizing Text*

To complete the poster, there are a few more lines of text to add, along with some horizontal rules used as compositional elements.

1. If the document is in Preview mode, switch to Normal screen mode.

2. Magnify and scroll the document window to focus on the empty area below the existing text, using whatever methods you prefer (such as the Zoom tool, the magnification commands on the View menu, or the keyboard shortcuts for those commands).

3. In the Layers panel, expand the Text layer. Notice that the Text layer doesn't contain any objects.

    When you created the text frame, the Superheroes layer was selected, so the text frames were created on the Superheroes layer.

4. In the Layers panel, drag the text frame you created from the Superheroes layer to the Text layer (**Figure 2.78**).

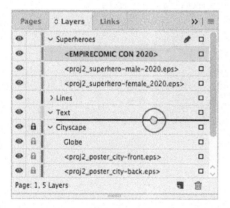 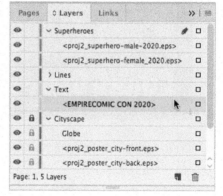

Figure 2.78 Correcting the object stacking order

Next you'll draw a line, which you'll want to create on the Lines layer.

1. In the Layers panel, select the Lines layer.

2. In the Tools panel, select the Line tool (✏).

3. In the Control panel, set the following options (**Figure 2.79**):

    - Click the arrow next to the Stroke icon, and choose Dark Red from the menu that appears.

    - Click the arrow next to the Fill icon, and choose None.

    - Set the stroke width to **2pt**.

Figure 2.79 Setting up object formatting in the Control panel

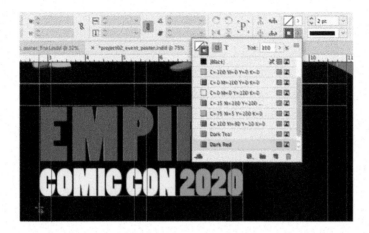

4　Position the Line tool slightly below the text frame, at the same column guide where the text frame starts, and Shift-drag to draw a line as wide as the text frame (**Figure 2.80**).

Figure 2.80 Drawing a line under the text

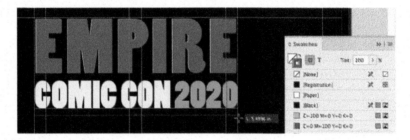

The next frame will contain some information about the convention.

1　Select the Text layer.

2　Select the Type tool, and draw a new text frame under the line, the same width as the line and text frame above it and about 0.65 inches tall (**Figure 2.81**).

Figure 2.81 Creating another text frame

3 In the Control panel, set the following options:

- From the font menu, choose Poplar Std Black (or another heavy display font).
- Set the font size to **33pt**.
- Click the arrow next to the Fill icon, and choose the Light Yellow color swatch.
- Make sure the Justify All Lines button is selected.

4 With the Type tool, click in the text frame and type **@PEACHPIT CONVENTION CENTER (Figure 2.82)**.

Figure 2.82 Typing the location of the convention

5 With the Selection tool, double-click the middle handle at the bottom of the text frame. This is a shortcut for fitting the frame to the text content, eliminating unused space at the bottom (**Figure 2.83**).

Figure 2.83 Unused space removed

The poster design calls for another line under this text frame, but instead of drawing another one from scratch, simply duplicate the one you already made:

1 Position the Selection tool over the line you drew that's between the two text frames.

2 Hold down the Alt key (Windows) or the Option key (macOS) as you drag the line down to just below the second text frame (**Figure 2.84**). Smart Guides will appear when the spacing equals the spacing of the line you drew farther up.

As in other graphics programs, Alt/Option-dragging an object copies it. This is faster than drawing the same object again.

Figure 2.84 Dragging a duplicate of the line

Now add another text frame:

1 Select the Text layer.

2 With the Type tool, draw a text frame the same width but about 1 inch tall.

3 In the Control panel, set the following options:

- From the font menu, choose Poplar Std Black (or another heavy display font).

- Set the font size to **42pt**.

- Click the arrow next to the Fill icon, and choose the Light Blue color swatch.

- Click the All Caps button to select it (**Figure 2.85**).

- Make sure the Justify All Lines button is selected.

Figure 2.85 The All Caps button ensures that all characters are capital letters, even if you didn't use the Shift or Caps Lock keys.

4 With the Type tool, click in the text frame and type **September 30-October 1**. Because you selected the All Caps button, this text appears in all capital letters, even if it was entered lowercase.

5 With the Selection tool, double-click the middle handle at the bottom of the text frame to collapse the empty space at the bottom. That finishes this text (**Figure 2.86**).

Figure 2.86 The completed text frame

There's only one more text frame to create before you're done creating the poster design:

1 Draw below the date a text frame that is the same width as the date text frame and about half an inch tall (**Figure 2.87**).

Figure 2.87 Adding the website address text frame

2 In the Control panel, set the following options:

- From the font menu, choose Poplar Std Black (or another heavy display font).
- Set the font size to **31pt**.
- Click the arrow next to the Fill icon, and choose the Light Yellow color swatch.
- Click the All Caps button to deselect it.
- Make sure the Justify All Lines button is selected.

3 Type **for more info go to empirecomiccon.com**.

4 With the Type tool, select the characters *empire* in the bottom text frame, and in the Swatches panel, make sure the Fill icon is active and click the Light Blue swatch.

5 With the Type tool, select the characters *con.com* in the bottom text frame, and in the Swatches panel, make sure the Fill icon is active and click the Light Blue swatch (**Figure 2.88**).

6 Save your document.

Figure 2.88 The text after applying the Light Blue color swatch to two ranges of selected text

TIP

If you want to close up the empty space at the bottom of any text frames or between graphics and their enclosing frames, select them and double-click the middle handle on the bottom edge. That's a shortcut for choosing Object > Fitting > Fit Frame to Content.

That's it, you finished the poster! You can check your work by switching to the Preview screen mode and zooming out to fit the page in the window.

Packaging Your Finished Project for Output

★ ACA Objective 5.2

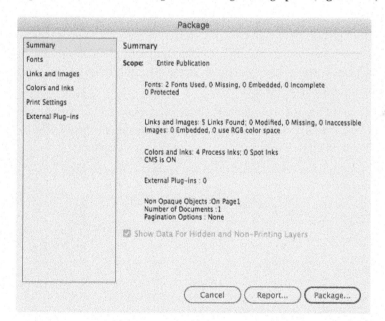

Video 2.15
Packaging Your
Finished Project
for Output

With the poster design completed, you're ready to send the job to your commercial printer. But you can't just send the InDesign document alone. You also have to send along all the components that the printer might not have, including all the fonts used in the document and all the graphics you imported. Graphics you import into InDesign are not actually copied inside the document file; instead, InDesign generates a small preview image for use in the layout and maintains a link to the original file that's outside the document.

Fortunately, you don't have to keep track of all of those files. InDesign can automatically collect and package everything to help ensure a successful print job.

To package a file for delivery to a commercial printer:

1   With the InDesign document open (in this case, the poster you've been working on), choose File > Package. The Package dialog opens (**Figure 2.89**).

Figure 2.89 The Package dialog

The Package dialog contains several panels that cover different critical aspects of a commercial print job. You can click each panel title to see what's in them:

- **Summary.** This panel provides an overview of the status of the packaging process. In particular, it will point out missing fonts, color inconsistencies, and other potential production issues.

- **Fonts.** This panel displays details of font usage, helping you identify potential problems. For example, if your commercial printer requires the use of OpenType fonts, the Type column in the Fonts panel will clearly identify any fonts that may be in an unapproved font format.

- **Links and Images.** This panel lists imported graphics and the status of the links to the original files. For example, if the Status column says a linked graphic is missing, that graphic will not print in high resolution and will have to be located before continuing to hand off the job.

- **Colors and Inks.** This panel lists the inks required to print the colors used in the document. This is important because the inks used must match the inks the printer is setting up on press; unexpected inks may cause costly rework.

- **Print Settings.** This panel lists the current settings of the Print dialog in InDesign. Reviewing this can provide a head start in understanding how the print settings need to be changed for the printer that will be used by the commercial printing service.

- **External Plug-ins.** This panel is useful when plug-in modules are used to create the InDesign document, because those plug-ins may need to be present when the commercial printer prints the document.

2 Click Package. The Printing Instructions dialog appears (**Figure 2.90**).

Figure 2.90 The Printing Instructions dialog

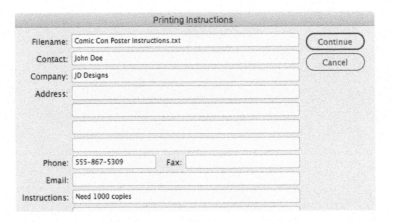

The Printing Instructions dialog is another tool that helps facilitate clear communication with your commercial printer. You should fill it out, especially with your contact information, and take the opportunity to think about any notes or other details that the printer should know about, although ideally you should discuss the important details with the commercial printer well in advance of the final handoff.

3 Click Continue. The Create Package Folder dialog appears (**Figure 2.91**).

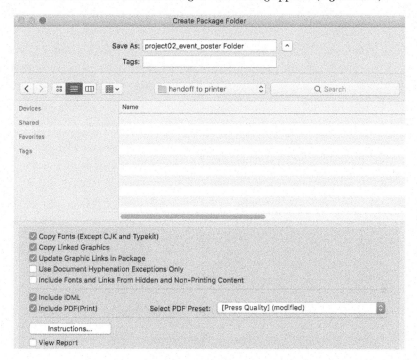

Figure 2.91 The Create Package Folder dialog

This is a standard Save dialog but with additional options; here are some of the highlights:

- **Copy Fonts** and **Copy Linked Graphics.** These options include those elements in the package. Typically, these two options are left on.

- **Update Graphic Links in Package.** This option changes the paths of linked graphics files so that they point to the folder specified in this dialog.

- **Include IDML.** This option includes a copy of the document in InDesign Markup Language. An IDML version can be useful for troubleshooting in case the original document has a problem, or if the commercial printer needs to open the document in a different version of InDesign than the one you're using.

- **Include PDF (Print).** This option includes a copy of the document in PDF format. Many commercial printers now create output from PDF files instead of from an InDesign file, because it's easier: Everything is in one optimized file—as long as the correct PDF preset was used. If a commercial printer prefers to output from the InDesign document, the PDF version is useful as a reference; the printer can compare what prints to what the PDF looks like.

- **Select PDF Preset.** PDF presets can be set up to exactly match the workflow of a particular commercial printer, helping ensure excellent output. If your commercial printer will print from the PDF, you must confirm which PDF preset to use. They will either tell you which preset to select or send you a preset that matches their production equipment and settings.

- **Instructions.** This is just a second chance to open the Printing Instructions dialog in case there's something you forgot to mention.

On a real job, before continuing you'd carefully review the settings in this dialog and make sure they match what your commercial printer recommended; they may require that specific options be selected.

4   Navigate to the folder in which you want InDesign to create a new folder containing the packaged files, and then click Package. InDesign collects all the components that were set to be included.

5   On your desktop, open the packaged folder that was created, and open the PDF file inside it (**Figure 2.92**).

Figure 2.92 The PDF file created by the Package dialog, shown in Adobe Acrobat DC

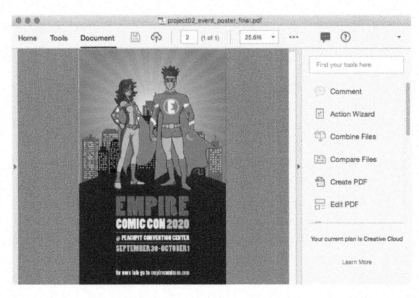

As demonstrated in Video 2.15, Jonathan's intention is to have the PDF include the bleed and slug values used in the document. This would be especially true if the commercial printer is going to print final output from the PDF version.

To replace the PDF version of the document:

1 Return to the InDesign poster document, which should still be open in InDesign.

2 Choose File > Export.

3 In the Export dialog, confirm the filename (change it slightly), make sure Adobe PDF (Print) is selected for Format, and click Save. The Export Adobe PDF dialog appears (**Figure 2.93**).

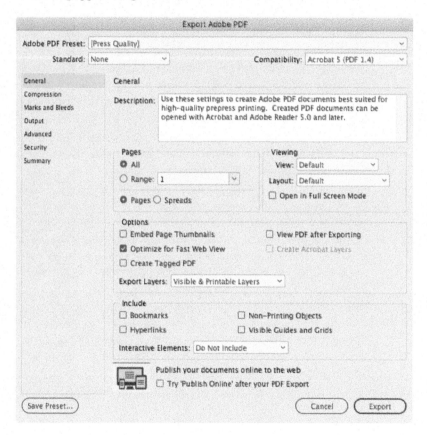

Figure 2.93 The Export Adobe PDF dialog

PDFs can be exported with different quality settings, and the PDF presets that ship with InDesign provide a great starting point. No matter which preset you choose, each will embed fonts and images and capture your design perfectly.

The following PDF export presets are available:

- **High Quality Print** retains transparency and leaves the document colors unchanged. Used for printing to desktop printers or proofing devices.

- **Press Quality** retains transparency, embeds all fonts, converts colors to CMYK (but retains spot colors), and retains high-resolution images. Used for submitting jobs to commercial printers.

- **Smallest File Size** retains transparency, converts all colors to sRGB (an RGB color space that captures the common RGB colors that can be displayed across a range of different devices, such as computer screens or scanners), and compresses and downsamples images to lower resolution. Used for web- or email-ready PDFs.

PDF/X is an International Standards Organization (ISO) standard for the exchange of documents within the graphics and printing industry. A number of PDF export presets meet ISO standard requirements:

- **PDF/X-1a:2001** flattens transparency, embeds all fonts, supports only CMYK and spot color, converts RGB color to CMYK, and retains high-resolution images. Used to submit designs to commercial printers.

- **PDF/X-3:2002** flattens transparency, embeds all fonts, retains color (CMYK, spot, and RGB), embeds color profiles, and retains high-resolution images. Used for combined CMYK/RGB print workflows (for example, when photos are placed in RGB and color swatches are defined as CMYK color).

- **PDF/X-4:2008** retains transparency, embeds all fonts, supports color models (CMYK, spot, and RGB), embeds color profiles, and retains high-resolution images. Used for combined CMYK/RGB print workflows that don't require transparency flattening.

To learn more about the various PDF/X standards, enter "PDF/X and print industry" in your favorite search engine. You will find great in-depth articles out there.

When submitting a press-ready PDF to your printer, always consult with the printer regarding the preferred export settings. In some cases, they may provide a PDF preset file for you to import.

4 Choose Press Quality from the Adobe PDF Preset pop-up menu. On a real job, you'd choose the PDF preset recommended by your commercial printer.

5 Click the Marks and Bleeds panel (**Figure 2.94**).

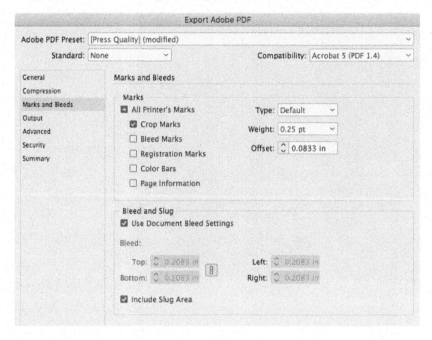

Figure 2.94 The Marks and Bleeds panel

6 In the Marks section, select Crop Marks. Crop marks are the marks that the commercial printer will use to trim the page, so crop marks represent the InDesign page size.

7 In the Bleed and Slug section, select Use Document Bleed Settings and Include Slug Area.

8 Click Export.

9 Open the Project02-EventPoster folder on your desktop, and open the PDF file that was created. It should now show the bleed and slug areas (**Figure 2.95**).

Figure 2.95 The updated PDF including bleed and slug areas

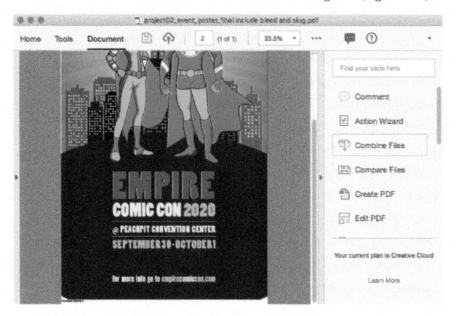

Challenge

Congratulations! You successfully created the Empire ComicCon 2020 poster from a blank document and prepared it for output at your commercial printer. You now have a sense of the complete end-to-end process of creating an InDesign document.

As a challenge, come up with your own design for a single-page InDesign document. It could be a poster promoting an event, a travel poster for a destination, or an advertisement for a product or service. As with the poster you created in this chapter, make the graphics the focus of your document, and design a strong, simple composition to maximize visual impact. Have fun with it!

CHAPTER OBJECTIVES

Chapter Learning Objectives

- Set up a new document.
- Select a workspace.
- Apply fill and stroke attributes to text and objects.
- Kern text.
- Apply effects to text and objects.
- Use paragraph styles.
- Draw a freeform frame with the Pen tool.
- Paste a graphic into a frame.
- Apply a text frame inset.
- Use groups.
- Use the Polygon tool.
- Preflight a document.

Chapter ACA Objectives

For full descriptions of the objectives, see the table on pages 270–276.

DOMAIN 1.0
WORKING IN THE DESIGN INDUSTRY
1.1

DOMAIN 2.0
PROJECT SETUP AND INTERFACE
2.1, 2.2, 2.3, 2.4, 2.5, 2.6

DOMAIN 3.0
ORGANIZATION OF DOCUMENTS
3.1

DOMAIN 4.0
CREATE AND MODIFY VISUAL ELEMENTS
4.1, 4.4, 4.5, 4.6,

DOMAIN 5.0
PUBLISHING DIGITAL MEDIA
5.1

CHAPTER 3

A Colorful Magazine Cover Design

The project for this chapter is a magazine cover design. You'll learn new techniques for applying and creating colors and gradients, and you'll work with creative effects. Plus, you will be introduced to new text-formatting options and amazing transparency effects that can make your designs pop (**Figure 3.1**).

Before submitting files to the printer, you always need to perform a pre-flight check that flags any errors in the InDesign document. This chapter will walk you through that process and teach you how to fix the most commonly encountered errors.

Figure 3.1 Finished cover design

Introducing the Magazine Cover Project

★ ACA Objective 1.1

▶ Video 3.1
Introducing the
Magazine Cover
Project

Take a look at the project that you'll work on. It's a magazine cover, and three versions are provided in the files for this lesson.

Open the three versions of the magazine cover and compare them (**Figure 3.2**):

1 In the project03_sample1_magazine_cover folder, open the file project03_magazine_cover-final.indd.

2 In the project03_sample2_magazine_cover folder, open the file project03_magazine_cover.indd.

3 In the project03_sample3_magazine_cover folder, open the file project03_magazine_cover.indd.

4 Click the Arrange Documents icon in the application bar, and choose 3-up.

The rest of this chapter focuses on using InDesign to create aspects of the image with the light purple background. But take a look at what all three covers have in common: layout elements such as the yellow bar across the top, the look of the masthead (the magazine title text), and the typography and layout of the teasers (the blurbs describing features in the magazine).

Figure 3.2 Three variations on the *COMIX* magazine cover

As you can see, while a magazine should have a consistent and recognizable look, there's nothing wrong with introducing creative variations on the overall theme from issue to issue.

When you're finished examining the three sample covers, close all the documents.

Starting a Magazine Cover Design

★ ACA Objective 1.1

★ ACA Objective 2.1

▶ **Video 3.2** Setting Up the Cover Design

A magazine cover has a different mission than do the pages inside the magazine. The cover must communicate what's inside the magazine, and just as importantly, it must be appealing enough to stand out among other publications that may be displayed around it. This magazine cover features a striking cover image, a bold and clear title, and "teaser" text written to draw the intended audience to the magazine.

Setting Up the New Document Dialog

As you've seen in previous projects, each design project starts with some questions that require answering. What questions would you ask and answer when designing a magazine cover? To begin, you might ask:

- Is this cover design going to be used for a print edition of the magazine? Or will it be used for a digital version?
- What unit of measure will be used?
- What is the trimmed size of the magazine?
- Does the design require a bleed?
- Will the design use a grid based on columns?

NOTE

This chapter supports the project created in Video Project 3. Go to the Project 3 page in the book's Web Edition to watch the entire lesson from beginning to end.

Answering these questions helps you set up the document in the New Document dialog. For this document, the answers to these questions are:

- This is for a printed edition of the magazine to be distributed to convention attendees.
- The unit of measure is inches.
- The trimmed size is Letter, 8.5 inches by 11 inches.
- The design requires a 0.25-inch bleed.
- The design is based on a 5-column grid.

With those questions answered, create the magazine cover document:

1 In the Start workspace, click the Create New button (or choose File > New Document).

2 Click the Print intent at the top of the New Document dialog (**Figure 3.3**).

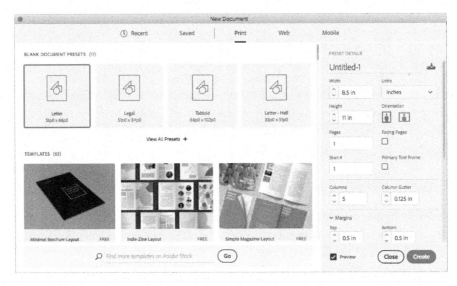

3 Click the Letter icon to set the page size, and make sure the Orientation icon is set to portrait (tall).

4 Choose Inches from the Units pop-up menu.

5 Deselect the Facing Pages check box, because this document will involve only the cover page of the magazine.

6 Leave both Pages and Start # set to 1.

7 Deselect Primary Text Frame.

8 For Columns, enter **5**.

9 For Column Gutter, enter **0.125** inches.

10 For Margins, set all values to **0.5** inches.

11 For Bleed, set all values to **0.25** inches. Leave the Slug section as it is.

12 If you want to see how the New Document settings affect the document that's about to be created, select Preview.

13 Click Create to close the New Document dialog. When it closes, InDesign creates the new document with the settings you applied (**Figure 3.4**).

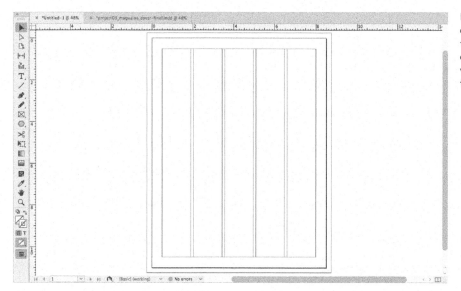

Figure 3.4 The new document with the settings for the cover. (The other tab is the finished version of the cover, open for reference.)

Setting Up Layers

The object stacking order of this cover design will be organized using layers.

Using the skills you learned in Chapter 2, set up the Layers panel with layers using the following names and stacking order (**Figure 3.5**):

- Top elements
- Coverlines
- Shapes
- Masthead
- Background

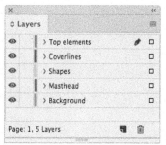

Figure 3.5 Layers panel set up for the magazine cover

The layer colors don't have to match the video and the project03_magazine_cover-final.indd sample file, but you may want to make the layer colors match to be consistent with them. The layer names will match the sample file if you name them from the bottom up. For example, the default Layer 1 has a light blue layer color, and you can name that Background. Create another new layer with the default layer color red, and you can name that Masthead, the name of the second layer from the bottom.

> **TIP**
>
> *To open the New Layer dialog as you create a new layer (so you can name it right away), Alt-click (Windows) or Option-click (macOS) the Create New Layer button in the Layers panel.*

Switching Workspaces

If you created the Learn workspace that was demonstrated in Video 1.7, and if it isn't already active, switch to it now.

If you did not create the Learn workspace, that's okay; you can do one of the following:

- Switch to the Typography workspace and simply open any other panels that you need to produce this project.
- Watch Video 1.7 again and follow the demonstration to build and save the Learn workspace.

Saving the Document

The document hasn't been saved yet, so this is a good time to save the work you've done so far.

1 Choose File > Save.

2 Navigate to the project03_sample1_magazine_cover folder.

3 Name the document **project03_sample1_magazine_cover**.

4 Click Save.

★ *ACA Objective 2.4*

★ *ACA Objective 2.5*

▶ **Video 3.3** *Placing an Image as the Background*

Placing the Featured Image on the Cover

To kick off the magazine cover, you'll create a graphics frame and then add the cover image to it. You'll also create a new color swatch based on a color in the cover image.

As you work through the projects from this point on, remember to zoom and scroll the document view as needed to clearly see the part of the document you're editing.

Adding the Cover Image

To add the cover image:

1 In the Layers panel, make sure the Background layer is selected.

Because you'll be adding the big image that goes behind everything else on the page, making the Background layer the active layer ensures that the next object you add will stay behind objects on all other layers.

2 Using the Rectangle Frame tool, draw a graphics frame that goes to the edge of the bleed area for all sides of the page.

The cover image is intended to be a full-bleed (borderless) image, so it has to extend past the page border into the bleed area. Therefore, the place-holder graphics frame you're creating for the image must also extend into the bleed area.

3 With the Selection tool, select the graphics frame.

4 Choose File > Place, navigate to the Lesson Files folder, open the Project03-Magazine Cover folder, open the project03_sample1_magazine_cover folder, open the Links (images) folder, select proj3_scifi-female.jpg, and click Open.

The image fills the selected graphics frame (**Figure 3.6**). It may be larger than needed, in that the top of the head may be cut off at the page edge.

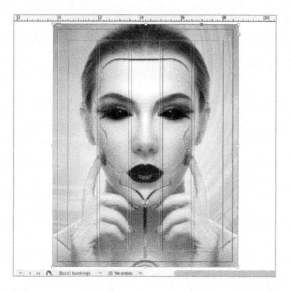

Figure 3.6 Cover image filling the graphics frame drawn for it

5 With the Direct Selection tool, click the image.

The image becomes selected instead of the graphics frame, and the image's bounding box may extend well beyond the graphics frame. That's why it's too big.

Also, note that clicking the image with the Direct Selection tool is one way to select the content inside a frame. Earlier, you selected the content of a frame by clicking a frame's Content Grabber (the concentric circle indicator) with the Selection tool; that's a shortcut you can use instead of having to switch to the Direct Selection tool.

6 In the Control panel, click the Fill Frame Proportionally icon (**Figure 3.7**). (If the icon is not visible in the Control panel, choose Object > Fitting > Fill Frame Proportionally. When the InDesign application frame or your display is not wide enough, some icons on the right side of the Control panel may not be shown.)

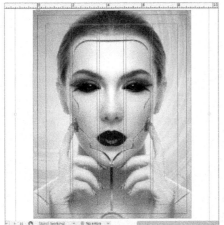 

The image should now be scaled so that it fills the graphics frame as much as it can without leaving any gaps and while maintaining the original proportions of the image. If you zoom out you will see that the image extends well beyond the top and bottom of the graphics frame, but that's unavoidable—if the image were scaled down any further, gaps would appear at the left and right sides of the graphics frame.

There's only one way that content can fit inside a graphics frame perfectly without gaps or areas outside the frame and without distorting the content: The content and the frame must have exactly the same dimensions.

7 Switch to Preview mode, using any of the techniques you have already learned.

Preview mode shows that the areas of the image cropped out by the graphics frame are not a problem here, because all the important content will be visible after the page is trimmed.

8 If you think the image needs to slide up or down a little, select the content inside the graphics frame and press the Up Arrow key or Down Arrow key to nudge it vertically. Leave room for the masthead (magazine title) that will be added later, and don't cut out too much of the medallion at the bottom.

Remember that you can use the finished cover document you opened earlier as a guide; you can refer to it in case you're not sure if you need to leave room on the cover for an element that's planned to be part of the design.

9   Choose Edit > Deselect All and save the document.

Creating a Swatch Based on a Color in the Image

To create color harmony in a design, a popular practice is to take a color from an image and use it in other elements on the page. You did this earlier in the poster project, when you sampled colors from a superhero graphic and applied it to text. This cover design will use a purple color from the image for some elements you'll add later.

1   Open the Swatches panel.

2   With the Eyedropper tool, click a dark purple area of the cover image.

Remember that the Eyedropper tool may not be immediately visible in the Tools panel because it's grouped with the Color Theme tool and Measure tool. And don't confuse the Eyedropper tool with the similar-looking Color Theme tool.

3   Choose New Color Swatch from the Swatches panel menu, make sure Color Type is set to Process, and make sure Color Mode is set to CMYK.

4   In the New Color Swatch dialog, deselect Name with Color Value.

5   For Swatch Name, enter **Purple**.

The sampled color can be a starting point for the color you'd actually like to use; in the New Color Swatch dialog, you can adjust the color values that define the swatch.

6   Enter the following color values (**Figure 3.8**):

- Cyan: **87%**
- Magenta: **87%**
- Yellow: **40%**
- Black: **17%**

7   Deselect Add to CC Library, and click OK.

With the cover image in place, and a new color swatch based on the image, you've laid a great foundation for the design work to come.

NOTE

If the Eyedropper tool doesn't pick up a color, make sure nothing is selected (choose Edit > Deselect All) and try again.

TIP

To clear the contents of the Eyedropper tool and pick up attributes from another object, Alt-click (Windows) or Option-click (macOS) the other object.

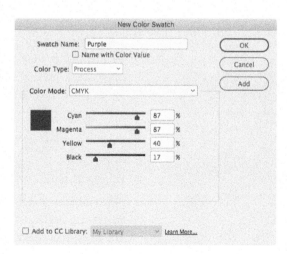

Figure 3.8 Editing the sampled color swatch

Adding Teaser Text

It's time to add a line of teaser text to the top of the cover (sometimes called a skyline), but first you'll add more color swatches that you'll need for the text.

Creating Color Swatches for the Text

Video 3.4 demonstrates two ways to create a 45% lighter version of the existing yellow swatch in the Swatches panel. You can create a light version of the existing yellow swatch by using the New Tint Swatch command or by duplicating the existing yellow swatch and editing it to be lighter.

It's important to understand that the consequences of each method depend on the Color Type setting:

- For a job that will be printed with only process colors, such as this magazine cover, you can use either method. Either way, four printing plates will be used (for cyan, magenta, yellow, and black).

- For a job that will be printed with spot colors, it's better to use the tint method because it creates the lighter version by screening the base color. For example, a 45% tint of yellow may be printed using a halftone screen on the yellow printing plate. Using the swatch duplication method is not a good idea for a job printed with spot colors, because every additional color swatch (that is not a tint) specifies one more ink to mix, which adds one more printing plate, and that may increase the cost of printing the job.

  It's important to note that for the light yellow example, the only reason it's just as easy to create the lighter version by duplicating the swatch is that you have to change only one color value: yellow. But if a swatch has multiple color values, making a lighter version without altering the hue is not as simple, so using the tint method can be more straightforward.

TIP

When a swatch uses multiple color values, you can quickly lighten or darken it by holding down Shift as you drag any of the color value sliders.

To create a lighter version of a swatch by tinting it:

1 Select the yellow swatch, and choose New Tint Swatch from the Swatches panel menu.

2 Edit the Tint value to 45% (**Figure 3.9**).

  The rest of the dialog is not editable because a true tint only screens back an existing swatch; it doesn't otherwise alter its color type, mode, or mix. The amount of the tint is added to the end of the swatch name in the Swatches panel.

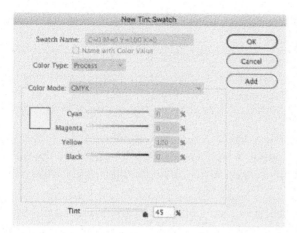

Figure 3.9 Creating a tint with the New Tint Swatch dialog

To create a lighter version of a swatch by duplicating it:

1 Select the yellow swatch and click the New Swatch button at the bottom of the Swatches panel (**Figure 3.10**).

   When a swatch is selected, the New Swatch button duplicates the selected swatch so that you can use it as a starting point.

2 Double-click the swatch to open the Swatch Options dialog, set the Yellow value to **45%**, and click OK.

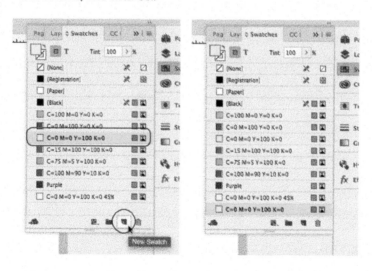

Figure 3.10 Creating a lighter color swatch by duplicating and editing an existing swatch

If you want to rename the new swatch, be aware of the naming differences between tint swatches and color swatches:

- You can't give a tint a custom name that's different from its parent swatch. The name of a tint swatch is always the name of its parent swatch with the tint percentage after it—for example,

  C=0 M=0 Y=0 K=0 45%

  Renaming a tint swatch also renames its parent swatch, because a true tint is always a derivative of a color swatch. Changing the color values of a tint will update the color values of its parent to match, so edit only the Tint slider in most cases.

  If you created the light yellow by tinting the existing yellow, use the swatch C=0 M=0 Y=0 K=0 45% when the cover design calls for light yellow.

- If you created a new light yellow swatch by duplicating, you can name it without affecting any other swatches. You can name it Light Yellow and use this swatch when the cover design calls for light yellow.

Adding the Teaser Text Across the Top

TIP

To set a fill or stroke to None using the keyboard, make sure the fill or stroke indicator is active, and press the slash key (/). If the wrong indicator is active, press the X key to swap which one is active and then press the / key.

If you refer to the finished sample version of this job, you'll see that although most of the teaser text sits over the cover image, the teaser line across the top is on a yellow rectangle.

To draw the yellow rectangle:

1 In the Layers panel, make sure the Background layer is selected.

2 Set the fill color to the Light Yellow swatch you created, using any of the methods you've learned so far, such as clicking the fill swatch in the Tools panel, the Control panel, or the Swatches panel. Set the stroke color to None.

3 With the Rectangle tool, draw a rectangle that extends across the top of the page, with the top, left, and right edges at the bleed edges, and the bottom edge at the top page margin.

   You can check your work by switching to Preview mode. The top, left, and right edges should be trimmed to the page edge, as they would be after printing. Remember to switch back to Normal mode for further editing.

4 In the Layers panel, select the Coverlines layer to make it the default layer for objects you create.

5 With the Type tool, drag to create a new text frame with the upper-left corner touching the top page edge and the left page margin, and the lower-right corner touching the top margin edge and the right page margin.

6   In the Character panel, set up the type specifications for the top teaser. Video 3.4 uses Myriad Pro Regular, 15 points.

7   Type to enter the text that goes into the top teaser, such as **Upcoming sequels coming out next summer: superheroes and robots top blockbuster list.**

8   The top teaser should be just one line. If the type wraps to a second line, make it fit on one line using any of the following methods, depending on which one you think looks the best:

- With the text selected, adjust the font size in the Character panel.
- With the text selected, adjust the tracking value in the Character panel.
- With the Selection tool, drag handles on the text frame bounding box to make it wider, but make sure the text is not too close to the top or sides of the page edge.

The teaser might look better if each word were capitalized. The Change Case submenu provides a quick way to change the capitalization of words in a sentence.

9   Select the text and choose Type > Change Case > Title Case.

10 With the text selected, apply Purple as the text fill color.

11 With the Selection tool, select the text frame and double-click the bottom middle handle so that the frame shrinks to fit the text, removing unused space in the text frame.

12 Center the text in the yellow rectangle (**Figure 3.11**). If the Selection tool is active, you can nudge the text frame by pressing the arrow keys.

Make sure you are centering the text between the top page edge (not the top bleed edge) and the top page margin. As always, the quick way to verify this is by switching into Preview mode.

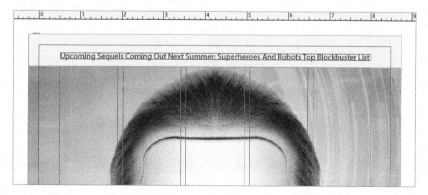

Figure 3.11 The completed teaser text in place

13 Check your work by switching into Preview mode and zooming out to fit the page in the document window. Make any adjustments that you think are needed.

14 Save the document.

★ *ACA Objective 4.2*

★ *ACA Objective 4.6*

▶ **Video 3.5**
Creating the Title Masthead

Creating the Title Masthead

The cover image and the masthead for the magazine title are the two most prominent features of the magazine cover. You've done the cover image, and now you'll add the masthead.

Adding the Masthead

Although the title masthead is a major element, it's really just another text frame, so you'll create it the same way that you've done before: by dragging to create a text frame with the Type tool.

To create the masthead:

1 Make sure you're in Normal mode so that you can see the margins.

2 In the Layers panel, make sure the Masthead layer is selected.

3 With the Type tool, drag to create a text frame near the top of the page from the left page margin to the right page margin, with the top edge just below the yellow rectangle and the bottom edge roughly where the hairline in the cover image ends at the forehead.

4 In the Character panel, set up the type specifications for the masthead. Video 3.5 uses Cooper Black, 143 points.

5 Type the magazine title, **Comix**.

6 Select the Comix text, and in the Control panel, click the All Caps icon (**Figure 3.12**).

Figure 3.12 Making the Comix text all capital letters with the All Caps button

Although you could have typed the text in all capital letters, the All Caps option lets you convert characters to all capital letters no matter how the text was entered, and you don't have to remember to use the Shift or Caps Lock keys.

7   With the text still selected, in the Paragraph panel, click the Align Center button.

8   With the Selection tool, select the COMIX text frame, and double-click the bottom middle handle of the frame to fit it to the text, removing the extra space.

Adjusting Masthead Kerning

When text is displayed at a large size, the spacing between letters can often appear less effective than at smaller sizes. You can tune the spacing between individual letter pairs; this is called kerning.

1   Click the Type tool between the O and the M in the COMIX text.

2   In the Character panel, lower the kerning value to tighten up the space between the O and the M (**Figure 3.13**).

Figure 3.13 Kerning manually between a pair of characters

The goal is not to eliminate all empty space, but to make the spaces between character pairs consistent in a way that will make the title appear more like a single graphic unit.

InDesign's default kerning technique is *metric kerning*, which kerns letter pairs based on information it draws from the specifications of the font in use. Extremely bad kerning can be improved by changing from metric to optical kerning. With *optical kerning*, InDesign does its very best to ensure that more even kerning is applied between letter pairs. However, even with optical kerning, you will often find yourself manually kerning letter pairs, especially when using larger font sizes. The capitalized text masthead set with the bold and bulky serif typeface Cooper Black is a good example of text that requires additional manual kerning.

To change the kerning from metric to optical (**Figure 3.14**):

1 Select the text.

2 From the Kerning menu in the Character panel, select Optical. (You can also find the Kerning menu in the Control panel.)

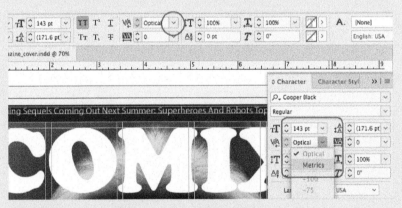

Figure 3.14 Applying optical kerning from the Character panel; the same control is in the Control panel when text is selected.

Adding a Line Under the Title

Many magazine titles have an additional short line of text that helps describe what the magazine is about. In this case, a line under the title indicates that the magazine is published by the convention organization.

To add the line under the title:

1 With the Type tool, drag to create a text frame about 0.3 inches high, starting at the left page margin under the COMIX title and ending halfway across the page.

To ensure that you have stopped halfway across the page, watch for a magenta Smart Guide to temporarily appear halfway across the page as you drag. Or you can first drag a vertical guide at that location, as demonstrated in Video 3.5.

2 In the Character panel, set up the type specifications for the text. Video 3.5 uses Myriad Pro Regular, 18 points.

3 Type the text **Empire Comic Con Magazine**.

4 Select the text you just typed, and in the Control panel, click the All Caps icon.

5 Switch to Preview mode and review where the masthead sits relative to the other parts of the cover. If the composition could be improved, continue to the next step; if it looks fine, skip the next step.

6 With the Selection tool, select the COMIX text frame, the text below the masthead, or both, and reposition them relative to the head and yellow rectangle until the composition appears balanced (**Figure 3.15**).

Figure 3.15 Adjusting the position of the masthead and the line below it

Applying Colors to the Masthead Text

The masthead is so large and bold that it does its basic job on a magazine cover, but it could do better. You'll apply separate colors to the fill and stroke of the masthead text to make it more visually appealing than just flat black text.

To apply colors and effects to the masthead:

1 With the Type tool, select the COMIX masthead text.

2 In the Swatches panel, apply Purple as the text fill color.

3 In the Swatches panel, apply Paper as the text stroke color.

4 With the Selection tool, select the COMIX masthead text and apply Purple as the text fill color.

If the text frame fill color changes instead, choose Edit > Undo and try again, but this time make sure that the Formatting Affects Text icon is selected. The Formatting Affects Text icon is automatically applied when you select text using the Type tool, but when you select a text frame with the Selection tool, as you did in step 4, Formatting Affects Text is not selected, so the fill and stroke colors affect the frame instead of the text inside. If you want to affect text but are not selecting with the Type tool, remember to make sure the Formatting Affects Text icon is selected.

5 Apply Paper as the stroke color, and apply a stroke width of 2 points (**Figure 3.16**).

Figure 3.16 Applying a stroke width to selected text with the Stroke panel

6 Select the line below the masthead and apply Purple as the text fill color.

7 Deselect the text.

Adding a Date Line to the Cover

A magazine cover typically includes a line of text called the date line that indicates the issue's date of publication. In this cover, the date line will be like the existing text under the title but on the right side. It will be formatted almost identically, so a quick way to create it is to simply duplicate the existing text frame.

To add a date line:

1 If the document window isn't already in Normal screen mode, switch to it.

2 With the Selection tool, Alt-drag (Windows) or Option-drag (macOS) the text under the title to the right until it snaps to the right page margin.

   Because you held down the Alt or Option key, dragging created a duplicate. It's the duplicate that you align with the right page margin.

   To make sure the copy stays aligned to the existing text as you drag, you can do any of the following:

   ▪ Keep the copy aligned to the Smart Guides that appear as you drag.

   ▪ Add the Shift key to the other key you hold down as you drag.

   ▪ Add a horizontal guide that lines up with the existing text, as demonstrated in Video 3.5, and keep the copy aligned to that guide as you drag.

3 With the Type tool, select the text in the copy and type **August 2020** to replace the original text.

4 Select the text or the text frame of the copy, and click the Align Right icon in the Paragraph panel or Control panel (**Figure 3.17**).

Figure 3.17 The completed date line

The text in the copy is now aligned to its right edge, so it should now mirror the original text on the other side of the page. But the purple text isn't standing out enough against the cover image, so you'll apply a glow effect.

5 With the Selection tool, select both of the text frames under the title (click one and Shift-click the other), and choose Object > Effects > Outer Glow.

   In the Effects dialog, notice that only Outer Glow is selected in the list of effects along the left side of the dialog.

6   Make sure Preview is selected so that you can see changes as you make them, and edit the following options (**Figure 3.18**):

  ■ For Mode, make sure that Normal is selected and that the color is Paper.

  ■ For Opacity, enter 84%.

  ■ Leave Technique set to Softer, Noise set to 0%, and Size set to 0.0972 in, but change Spread to **28%**.

7   Click OK.

Figure 3.18 Applying the Outer Glow effect to text

The Outer Glow effect helps increase the contrast of the type against the background by surrounding its edge with a very light background. You can experiment with other effects and settings in the Effects dialog to try other ways of improving type legibility on complex backgrounds; for example, later in this chapter you'll apply a drop shadow effect to text.

Adding to the Title Masthead

Many magazine covers create more visual interest by having the masthead interact with the cover image. For this cover, you'll make the woman's head appear in front of the masthead. The challenge is that the woman and the background are a single photo, so you have to find a way to put the masthead behind the woman's head. InDesign provides a way to do this.

Drawing a Freeform Frame with the Pen Tool

To make the masthead appear to be behind part of a cover photo, it's common to cut out part of the cover photo and bring that in front of the masthead. In

InDesign, you can use a drawing tool to create a frame that's an outline of the top of the woman's head, paste a copy of the cover photo into that frame, and then restack that frame in front of the masthead. This technique relies on the fact that a frame can be any shape.

To draw a frame for the top of the woman's head:

1 In the Layers panel hide the Masthead layer, and then select the Background layer because you'll want the next object to appear on it.

2 Select the Pen tool (✒).

The Pen tool works a little differently than a real pen because it's designed to create more precise corners and curves than most people can draw freehand. With the Pen tool, you click to create corners and you drag to create curves, resulting in a line called a path (see the sidebar "About Shapes"). For beginners, the way the Pen tool works is not immediately intuitive and takes time to master, but for this exercise you can keep it simple: Always click the Pen tool; don't drag it.

3 Position the Pen tool at the left side of the woman's head, at about the same level as the line that goes across her forehead, and click.

Clicking creates an anchor point. An anchor point defines the beginning and end of a path, and also defines each significant change in the direction of a path.

4 Look up along the woman's hair outline to where there's a significant change in direction, and click to create another anchor point there. Click more anchor points at each change in direction (**Figure 3.19**). Focus on the overall hairline; don't pay attention to individual hairs.

Figure 3.19 Clicking anchor points where the path changes direction

5 Continue along the hair outline as demonstrated in Video 3.6, doing any of the following as needed while the Pen tool is selected:

■ To reposition an anchor point without changing tools, hold down the Ctrl key (Windows) or the Command key (macOS) and drag the point.

■ As you draw with the Pen tool, the last point you clicked is selected (appears solid); to delete the selected anchor point, press the Delete key.

■ The next Pen tool click continues the existing path as long as the last point is still selected. If the path accidentally becomes deselected, click the last point with the Pen tool so that it becomes selected and now you can continue clicking new anchor points connected to the existing path.

6 When the path you draw reaches the opposite side of the head at the same vertical position, it's time to close the path. Position the Pen tool over the first anchor point you drew, and when you see a small circle appear below the Pen tool (**Figure 3.20**), click to close the path.

7 If you see any points you want to reposition, drag them with the Direct Selection tool.

Figure 3.20 When you position the Pen tool over a point and see a small loop next to the pen, clicking will complete the path.

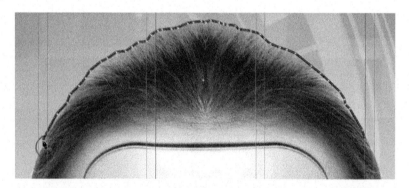

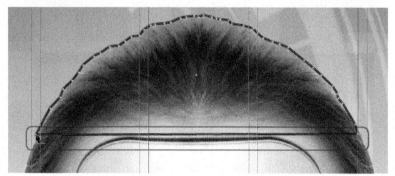

ABOUT SHAPES

In the Tools panel, you find tools for drawing shapes and frames, such as the Rectangle tool, the Rectangle Frame tool, and the Pen tool. Anything you can draw in InDesign is formed by an outline called a path. A path is a shape assembled from anchor points and path segments. Each path segment is joined by two anchor points. It's like how you would build a fence: A single corner post is placed first; a panel is then attached to the corner post and held in place with a second post at the opposite end, and so on. When the segments are curved, the anchor points contain a direction line that controls the curvature of the path as it extends from the point (**Figure 3.21**). To control the direction line, you drag the direction point at the end of the direction line.

You can edit frame outlines and shape outlines using the same tools and techniques. The only difference between shapes and frames is that a shape is intended to be a graphic on its own, and a frame either contains content or is a placeholder for content to come.

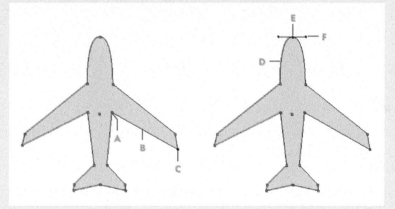

Figure 3.21 Parts of a path

A Anchor point	**D** Curved path segment
B Straight path segment	**E** Selected curve anchor point
C Selected corner anchor point	**F** Direction line and point

Pasting a Copy of the Cover Image into the Frame

Next you'll fill the frame you just drew with a copy of the cover image, completing the object that will interact with the masthead. The effect depends on the cover image being pasted into the frame at exactly the same position as the original cover image so that they appear to be a single image.

To paste a copy of the cover image into the frame:

1 Make sure the frame you just drew is still selected; if it isn't, select it with the Direct Selection tool.

2 Set the frame's fill color and stroke color to None (**Figure 3.22**).

Figure 3.22 The new path's fill and stroke set to None

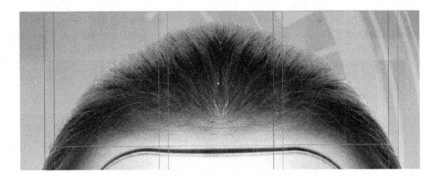

3 With the Direct Selection tool, select the cover image.

4 Choose Edit > Copy (or press its keyboard shortcut, Ctrl+C in Windows or Command+C in macOS).

5 In the Layers panel, expand the Background layer, and select the frame you drew by clicking the selection dot for the object named <polygon> (**Figure 3.23**).

Figure 3.23 Selecting the new path by clicking its selection dot in the Layers panel

You can also select the frame using the Selection tool or Direct Selection tool, but because its fill and stroke colors are both set to None, it is not visible, so you may not know where to click on the page. This is an example of when it can be easier to select an object in the Layers panel: If it's in the document, it's listed in the Layers panel, even if you can't see it on the page.

6 Choose Edit > Paste Into (or press its keyboard shortcut, Alt+Ctrl+V in Windows or Option+Command+V in macOS).

You may not see any difference after the Paste Into command, because the cover image was pasted into the selected frame without changing its position, so the copy inside the frame is perfectly aligned with the original.

Note that in the Layers panel, the name of the frame has changed to match the filename of its contents, <proj3_scifi-female.jpg>. The original cover image is also listed that way in the Layers panel, so remember that the upper instance in the Layers panel is the newer one.

7 To get a better view of what you've accomplished, hide the lower <proj3_scifi-female.jpg> object on the Background layer in the Layers panel (**Figure 3.24**).

NOTE

If you don't see a <polygon> object in the Layers panel but you do see a <path> object, that's the frame you drew, but it was not fully closed (there's a gap). This exercise still works with an open path, so you can simply continue, or you can go back and close the path before continuing.

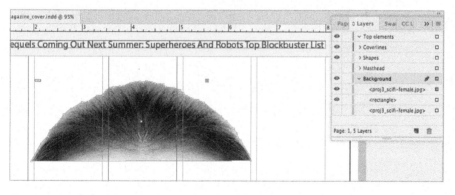

Figure 3.24 Temporarily hiding the original cover image lets you see more clearly the new path with the cover image pasted into it.

You'll see the frame you drew, filled with the copy of the cover image. Essentially, the frame is masking the copy of the cover image, because if you moved anchor points on the shape you drew, you'd reveal or hide different areas of the cover image. The only difference between this frame and other frames you've created is that this one is not a rectangle.

8 In the Layers panel, make the lower <proj3_scifi-female.jpg> object of the Background layer visible again.

Stacking the Masthead Behind
the Drawn Frame

The document is now set up for you to finish the effect that you've been working toward.

To stack the masthead behind the drawn frame:

1 In the Layers panel, click the eye icon for the Masthead layer to make it visible.

2 In the Layers panel, drag the upper object named <proj3_scifi-female.jpg> up and drop it in the Top Elements layer (**Figure 3.25**).

Figure 3.25 The top of the head stacked in front of the masthead

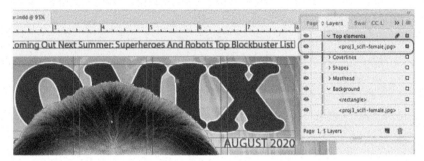

The masthead now appears behind the top of the woman's head. But the edge appears abrupt and harsh because the image is clipped by the path you drew. You can soften the transition by feathering, or slightly blurring, the edge.

3 With the <proj3_scifi-female.jpg> object selected on the Top Elements layer, choose Object > Effects > Basic Feather.

4 In the Effects dialog, specify a Feather Width of **0.05 in**, and leave the other settings as they are: Choke at 0%, Corners set to Diffused, and Noise at 0% (**Figure 3.26**).

5 Click OK.

With the masthead now behind the top of the head, the head appears to come forward, adding depth to the design.

Figure 3.26 Applying the Basic Feather effect to soften the hair edge

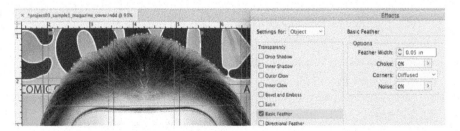

Grouping and Stacking the Text Below the Masthead

To enhance the 3D-like look of the cover, you can bring the text that's under the title forward of the woman's head. By now you should probably be able to guess that this will involve using the Layers panel.

To stack the text under the title in front of the head:

1   In the Layers panel, expand the Masthead layer so you can see the objects on that layer.

2   With the Selection tool, select both text frames under the title. If you find it easier to Shift-select the two items in the Layers panel, go ahead and do it that way instead.

    In the Layers panel, notice that the selection dots for those objects light up.

3   Choose Object > Group (or press its keyboard shortcut, Ctrl+G in Windows or Command+G in macOS).

    In the Layers panel, notice that the two objects have now been replaced by one object named <group>. You can expand the <group> object to show the objects that are part of that group.

    The Group command works much like the Group command in many graphics applications: It treats multiple objects as a unit so that you can move or edit them together. Grouped objects must be on the same layer.

4   In the Layers panel, drag the <group> object up and drop it at the top of the Top Elements layer (**Figure 3.27**).

    The text under the title now appears in front of the woman's head.

5   Save the document.

Figure 3.27 The two text frames below the masthead are now grouped and stacked in front of the woman's head.

★ *ACA Objective 4.1*

★ *ACA Objective 4.2*

▶ **Video 3.7**
*Finishing the
Title Masthead*

Finishing the Title Masthead

There are some final adjustments to be made before the masthead is finished. The masthead legibility is challenged by the top of the head that's now in front of it, and a superhero graphic needs to be added to the masthead.

Altering the Masthead for Better Legibility

Figure 3.28 The Baseline Shift option in the Character panel

When you play around with the stacking order of the masthead, one potential challenge is that the masthead may become less readable. At this point in this project, the head obscures the M in the masthead enough that it may not be read as an M by someone unfamiliar with the magazine. One potential solution is to alter the masthead to move the M away from the center so that it's more legible.

You can try your own solutions, but if you'd like to try the solution in Video 3.7, simply reduce the size of the masthead text, add a character after the masthead text, and use Baseline Shift (**Figure 3.28**) to adjust the vertical positioning of the character.

Adding the Superhero Graphic

There's a small graphic of a superhero that appears over the O in the COMIX masthead text; you can see this in the finished sample document of this magazine cover. This is a good time to add it.

To add the superhero graphic:

1 In the Layers panel, make sure the Top Elements layer is selected.

2 With the Rectangle Frame tool, drag a frame around the letter O in the COMIX text.

3 With the graphics frame selected, choose File > Place, navigate to the Lesson Files folder, open the Project03-Magazine Cover folder, open the project03_sample1_magazine_cover folder, open the Links (images) folder, and select proj3_superhero-2020.eps.

The graphic places much too large within the frame, but you've learned that you can automatically fit contents inside frames, so you'll do that next.

4   With the Direct Selection tool, select the graphic inside the frame.

5   In the Control panel, click the Fit Content Proportionally icon. (If the icon is not visible in the Control Panel because of the size of the InDesign application frame or your display, choose Object > Fitting > Fit Content Proportionally.)

6   As needed, adjust the size and positioning of the superhero graphic (**Figure 3.29**) using any of the methods you've learned so far, such as editing its dimensions in the Control panel.

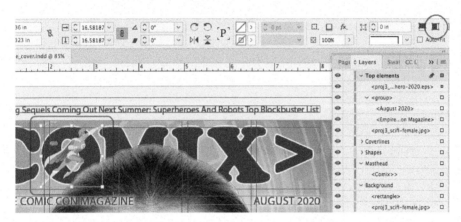

Figure 3.29 Fitting the superhero graphic into its frame while preserving its proportions

Adding a Coverline

★ ACA Objective 2.6

★ ACA Objective 4.6

▶ Video 3.8 Adding Teaser Text

Like many magazine covers, this design uses a number of coverline text items to attract potential readers and hopefully motivate them to pick up the magazine and read it.

To add the first teaser item:

1   Drag a guide out of the vertical ruler, and drop it 2.5 inches from the left side of the page edge.

2   In the Layers panel, make sure the Coverlines layer is selected.

3   With the Type tool, drag a text frame, starting about 6 inches down at the left margin and ending about 8 inches down at the guide you just drew.

4   In the Control panel, select the All Caps icon.

5 Type the text **Our Favorite Villain**; the All Caps setting should format it in all capital letters for you (**Figure 3.30**).

Figure 3.30 The left coverline added to the page

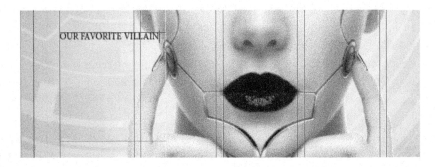

The text isn't completely formatted yet, but you'll do that next.

Creating and Applying a Paragraph Style

You'll apply a paragraph style to the text. A paragraph style can remember a set of specific type settings for you. It can include character settings such as font, size, leading, and color, as well as paragraph settings such as alignment, margins, and indents. Using a paragraph style saves you the trouble of having to remember to set all those options the same way across all paragraphs in a document. It's also quick and easy to update a style across all paragraphs in a document. For example, if you decide to reduce Space After for all headings in a document, if all headings use the same paragraph style, all you have to do is edit the style and all those paragraphs will update. The benefits and time savings of styles increase dramatically when you work with long documents.

It's common to define a paragraph style for each significant typographical format that's used in a document, such as body text (normal paragraphs), headings, number lists, bullet lists, and captions. For this magazine cover, you'll create a style for teaser text.

1 Select the text you just typed.

2 In the Character panel or Control panel, change the following character settings:

   ▪ Font: Arial Black Regular

   ▪ Font Size: 23

   ▪ Fill color: Purple

3   Choose New Paragraph Style from the Paragraph Styles panel menu
    (**Figure 3.31**).

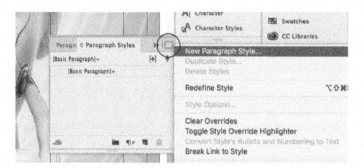

Figure 3.31 Choosing the New Paragraph Style command

When text is selected as you create a new paragraph style, the formatting of the selected text becomes part of the style definition. You can see this in the Style Settings section.

The New Paragraph Style dialog has a list of options along the left side. You can click each of these options to see what attributes can become part of a paragraph style. You can see that a paragraph style can contain a very wide range of attributes. You need to change only the settings you're interested in; settings you don't change are not altered by applying a paragraph style.

4   In the list on the left, click Hyphenation, and deselect the Hyphenate option.

    It's useful to have hyphenation disabled for this paragraph style, because teaser text doesn't look good if it's hyphenated. Now, any teaser text with this style applied will not be hyphenated.

5   In the list on the left, click General.

    The disabled hyphenation setting is now part of the style description in the Style Settings section (**Figure 3.32**).

6   For Style Name, enter **Purple Coverline**.

NOTE

A paragraph style formats an entire paragraph. If you want to create a style that affects just a range of selected text, that's a character style, which you manage in the Character Styles panel.

Figure 3.32 Setting up the new paragraph style

7   Make sure Add to CC Library is unselected, and then click OK.

8   With the text selected, click Purple Coverline in the Paragraph Styles panel. This is how you apply a paragraph style to text.

9   In the Character panel or Control panel, change the leading of the selected text to **24pt**.

Figure 3.33 The new paragraph style applied with an override

This leading change was made to text that has a paragraph style applied to it. Because the change was not applied by editing the style, it's in addition to the style. This is called a style override because although a paragraph style is applied, the 24pt leading setting is not part of the style and is not present in other paragraphs using this style. When the selected text has a style override, InDesign lets you know by adding a plus sign (+) to the end of the style name in the Paragraph Styles panel (**Figure 3.33**).

If a paragraph has style overrides and you want to make it conform to its applied paragraph style, you can select it and click the Clear Overrides in Selection button in the Paragraph Styles panel, but you don't have to do that here.

Creating a Paragraph Style Not Based on Selected Text

The coverlines are multiple lines of text with different formatting, so a different paragraph style will be needed for the next line of text, which you'll enter in a separate text frame. The previous paragraph style took its initial settings from the text that was selected when the style was created, but you'll define the next paragraph style from the ground up and then apply it.

To add another coverline:

1   With the Selection tool, double-click the middle bottom handle of the OUR FAVORITE VILLAIN coverline to fit the frame height to the content.

2   With the Type tool, drag to create another text frame below the previous one.

3   Enter the text **and why we love them**.

4   Choose New Paragraph Style from the Paragraph Styles panel menu.

5 In the New Paragraph Style dialog, click Basic Character Formats in the list on the left, and change the following settings:

- Font Family: Myriad Pro
- Font Style: Italic
- Font Size: 21

6 In the list on the left, click Hyphenation, and deselect the Hyphenate option.

7 In the list on the left, click Character Color (**Figure 3.34**), and set the fill color to Paper.

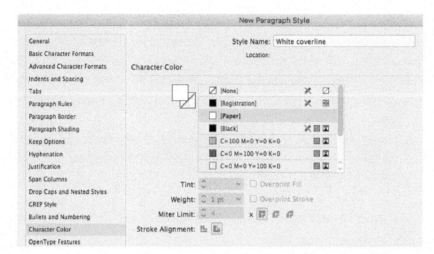

Figure 3.34 Defining another paragraph style

8 At the top of the New Paragraph Style dialog, for Style Name enter **White coverline**.

9 Click OK.

10 Select the text "and why we love them" and click White Coverline in the Paragraph Styles panel to apply the style to the text.

There are a couple of more formatting changes to apply that aren't part of the paragraph style.

Figure 3.35 The left coverline completed

11 With the text frame or the text selected, choose Type > Change Case > Title Case.

12 In the Character panel or Control panel, change the leading of the selected text to **21pt**.

13 With the Selection tool, double-click the middle bottom handle of the text frame to fit the frame height to the content (**Figure 3.35**).

The advantage of defining paragraph styles is not immediately apparent from creating one magazine cover. But if you were to do the magazine cover every month, having paragraph styles means that instead of entering numerous type specifications every time you create this coverline, you could apply all the formatting with one click of a paragraph style name. Paragraph styles also save a large amount of time on the pages inside the magazine, where a set of type specifications for a heading or a paragraph might need to be applied hundreds of times.

Adding a Drop Shadow to the Coverline

As with the text under the title, small or light-colored text can be difficult to see on a background that isn't solid. To improve contrast and readability, you can add a drop shadow to this text. A drop shadow is an effect built into InDesign, so this will be similar to when you applied the Outer Glow and Basic Feather effects earlier.

1 With the text frame or the text selected, choose Object > Effects > Drop Shadow.

2 In the Drop Shadow panel of the Effects dialog, change the settings so that the shadow is effective at setting off the white text (**Figure 3.36**). You can use the values specified in Video 3.8:

   ▪ For Distance, enter **0.0424** inches.

   ▪ For X Offset, Y Offset, and Size, enter **0.03** inches.

   ▪ For Spread, enter **12%**.

3 Leave the other settings as they are, and click OK.

4 Save your work.

Figure 3.36 Adding a drop shadow for the light-colored text

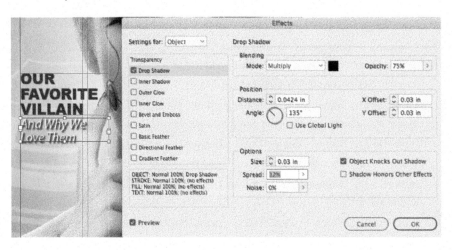

Adding the Main Coverline

★ ACA Objective 4.2

★ ACA Objective 4.6

▶ **Video 3.9** Adding the Main Coverline

The main coverline is near the lower-right corner of the page; you can see it in the sample finished cover page document. The process of creating this coverline is similar to that of the other coverline you created.

Creating the First Part of the Main Coverline

To create the main coverline:

1 In the Layers panel, make sure the Coverlines layer is selected.

2 With the Type tool, drag a text frame starting just below the woman's lips, at the center of the page, and ending about 10 inches down at the right page margin.

3 In the Control panel, set up the type specifications for the coverline: Myriad Pro Bold, 66 points, All Caps on.

4 Enter the text **VIOLET DREAMS**.

5 Select the text, and then use the Control panel or the Character panel along with your own judgment to improve the typographical appearance of the coverline by making adjustments such as the following suggested values:

- Tighten the spacing between lines: For leading, enter **53 pt**.
- Tighten the spacing between all characters: For tracking, enter **–20**.
- Make spacing across individual character pairs more consistent by clicking between characters and adjusting the kerning values.
- Apply a fill color of Light Yellow and a stroke color of Purple for additional edge contrast against the background.

6 In the Control panel or Paragraph panel, click the Align Right icon to align the paragraph along the right edge of the text frame (**Figure 3.37**).

7 With the Selection tool, double-click the middle bottom handle of the text frame to fit the frame height to the content.

Figure 3.37 The Align Right icon in the Paragraph panel applied to the main coverline text

Creating the Second Part of the Main Coverline

As with the first coverline you created, this one has additional text, formatted differently, that will be added in a separate text frame:

1   With the Type tool, drag a text frame starting just below the previous coverline at the right page margin and ending where the bottom page margin meets the center of the page.

2   In the Control panel, set up the type specifications for the coverline: Myriad Pro Semibold, 26 points tall on 25 points of leading, All Caps on, and tracking of –10.

3   Enter the text **KIERA RIPLEY SHINES IN NEW SCI-FI FLICK FROM ACA STUDIOS.**

If the end of the text disappears and a red plus sign appears near the lower-right corner of the text frame, the text is overset because it overflows the text frame at its current settings. You can make it fit by selecting the text frame (with the Selection tool) or all of the text (with the Type tool) and reducing character settings you've edited before, such as font size and leading.

4   Apply a fill color of Purple to the new coverline (**Figure 3.38**).

Figure 3.38 The second part of the main coverline formatted

To quickly adjust the height of an overset text frame, double-click the top-middle or bottom-middle handle of the text frame bounding box.

Adding Effects for Readability

As with the previous coverline, you can add effects to these two text frames to improve readability against the background:

1   Select the VIOLET DREAMS coverline and choose Object > Effects > Drop Shadow.

Because you're going to edit all the text uniformly, you can either select the text frame with the Selection tool or select all the text characters with the Type tool.

2   In the Drop Shadow panel of the Effects dialog, change the settings so that the shadow is effective at setting off the yellow text. You can use the values specified in Video 3.9:

   - Make sure the Mode is Multiply, the color is Purple, and the Opacity is 75%.

   - For Distance, enter **0.0628** inches.

   - For X Offset and Y Offset, enter **0.444** inches.

   - For Size, enter **0.0556**.

TIP

Typically, you don't need to enter inch values to more than two or three decimal places. When you see long decimal values in InDesign, the fractional results are often a result of converting between units of measure. For example, 2 points is 0.0278 inches.

3   Leave the other settings as they are, and click OK.

4   Select the KEIRA RIPLEY... coverline and choose Object > Effects > Outer Glow.

5   In the Outer Glow panel of the Effects dialog, change the settings so that the shadow is effective at setting off the purple text. You can use the values specified in Video 3.9:

   - Make sure the Mode is Screen, the color is Paper, and the Opacity is 75%.

   - For Size, enter **0.1875**.

   - For Spread, enter **27%**.

6   Leave the other settings as they are and click OK.

7   Check your work (**Figure 3.39**) by switching into Preview mode and zooming out to fit the page in the document window. Make any adjustments that you think are needed.

8   Save your work.

Figure 3.39 A drop shadow applied to the coverline text

You may have noticed that one effect used the Multiply blending mode and the other effect used the Screen blending mode. Blending modes affect how overlapping colors combine. They can lighten, darken, or alter the contrast between tones and colors. Multiply is a mode that darkens underlying colors, so it's useful for the purple drop shadow around the light text. Screen is a mode that lightens underlying colors, so it's useful for the white drop shadow around the dark text.

Applying an Inset to a Text Frame

You'll use some options you haven't used yet to create another coverline with additional formatting.

To create the third coverline:

1 Make sure the document window is displaying in Normal mode.

2 With the Type tool, drag a text frame that spans the last set of column guides, starting about 4 inches down at the left guide of the last column and ending about 7 inches down at the right page margin.

3 With the Selection tool, select the new text frame, and then apply a fill color of Purple.

   The Purple swatch is too dark, so you'll create a tint of it.

4 Choose New Tint Swatch from the Swatches panel menu, enter **30%** for Tint (**Figure 3.40**), and click OK.

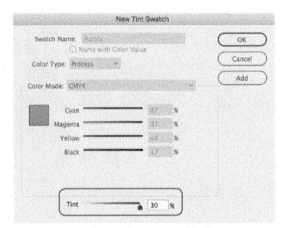

Figure 3.40 Creating a tint swatch

A new tint swatch named Purple 30% is added to the Swatches panel.

5 Apply a stroke color of Purple, and set the stroke weight to **1 pt**.

6 With the Type tool, click an insertion point in the text frame and type the following:

   Comic Book Psyche check out an interview with Dr. Otto Burken

   The text is right up against the edges of the text frame. This is not very readable, but there's an easy way to move away from all edges of the frame.

7 With the text frame still selected, choose Object > Text Frame Options.

8 For the Top option in the Inset Spacing section, enter **.125 in** (**Figure 3.41**) and click OK.

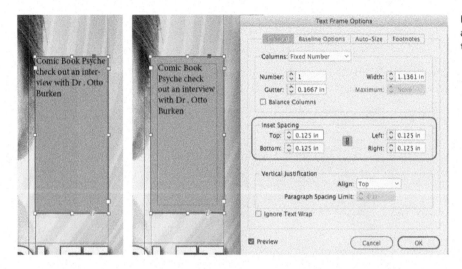

Figure 3.41 Before and after adding inset spacing to the text frame

As you saw earlier, if the link icon in that options group is enabled, when you change the value of any side, all four sides will change to the same value.

9 With the Type tool, select all the text inside the text frame and change its font to Myriad Pro Regular.

10 Select the text Comic Book Psyche. For font size enter **26 pt**, and for leading enter **25 pt**.

11 Select the text "check out an interview with." Change its font style to Italic. For font size enter **16 pt**, and for leading enter **17 pt**.

12 Select the text Dr. Otto Burken. Change its font style to Semibold. For font size enter **26 pt**, and for leading enter **23 pt**.

13 With the Type tool, click a text insertion point after the word "with" and press Shift+Enter (Windows) or Shift+Return (macOS) so that the Dr. Otto Burken text goes to the next line.

Shift+Enter/Shift+Return is the keyboard shortcut for the command Type > Insert Break Character > Forced Line Break.

Why not just press Enter or Return? When you press Enter or Return, you create a new paragraph, which could apply paragraph spacing and other attributes you don't want. A forced line break pushes text to the next line without starting a new paragraph.

14 If the text is overset at this point, select the text frame with the Selection tool and pull down the bottom-middle bounding box handle until all the text is revealed.

15 Apply a fill color of Paper to all the text in the frame.

16 Check your work (**Figure 3.42**) by switching into Preview mode and zooming out to fit the page in the document window. Make any adjustments that you think are needed.

17 Save your work.

Figure 3.42 The magazine cover so far

⭐ *ACA Objective 4.1*

▶ *Video 3.11*
Adding a Starburst

Adding a Starburst

The cover design calls for one coverline to be inside a starburst shape. There's more than one way to create a starburst shape in InDesign. You could create it by clicking with the Pen tool, but it's probably faster to create a shape that already contains multiple star points and modify that.

Creating a Starburst

The Polygon tool can create regular polygons, such as a hexagon, but it has settings you can use to create star points.

To create a starburst with the Polygon tool:

1 In the Layers panel, make sure the Shapes layer is selected.

2 Select the Polygon tool (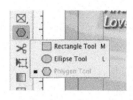), which is grouped with the Rectangle and Ellipse tools (**Figure 3.43**).

    You'll probably need to click and hold the Rectangle or Ellipse tool (whichever is visible in the Tools panel) to see and select the Polygon tool.

Figure 3.43 In the Tools panel, you'll find the Polygon tool grouped with the Rectangle and Ellipse tools.

3 Click the Polygon tool in the lower-left area of the cover page.

4 In the Polygon dialog that appears, do the following and then click OK (**Figure 3.44**):

    ▪ For Polygon Width, enter **3.6 in**.

    ▪ For Polygon Height, enter **2 in**.

    ▪ For Number of Sides, enter **20**.

    ▪ For Star Inset, enter **10%**.

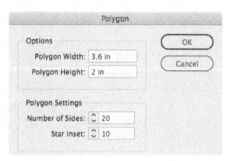

Figure 3.44 The Polygon dialog appears when you click the Polygon tool on the layout.

5 With the starburst shape selected, apply the following settings (**Figure 3.45**):

    ▪ Apply a fill color of Yellow.

    ▪ Apply a stroke color of Purple.

    ▪ For stroke weight, enter **3 pt**.

6 If you like, use the Direct Selection tool to customize the shape by dragging individual anchor points on the starburst.

    To be able to select individual anchor points, you may need to first deselect the starburst and then select it with the Direct Selection tool. An anchor point is selected when it appears solid.

7 Deselect the starburst.

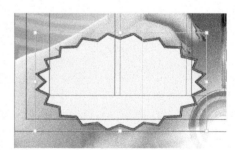

Figure 3.45 The starburst after applying graphics attributes

 TIP

To edit the settings for a polygon, double-click the polygon frame or the Polygon tool when a polygon frame is selected. You can even convert a nonpolygon or star-shaped frame into a polygon shape this way.

Adding a Coverline in Front of the Starburst

You can now add the coverline that's supposed to appear inside the starburst.

To add the text frame:

1   In the Layers panel, make sure the Coverlines layer is selected.

2   With the Type tool, drag to create a text frame within the starburst.

3   In the Character panel, change the following settings:

   - Font Family: Myriad Pro
   - Font Style: Bold
   - Font Size and Leading: 19

4   Enter the text **visit booth 300 for the new Thucydides graphic novel.**

5   With the Type tool, select the "visit booth 300" text and apply the All Caps button in the Control panel.

6   With the Type tool, click a text insertion point after the word "300" and press Shift+Enter (Windows) or Shift+Return (macOS) to add a forced line break.

7   Select the text after the forced line break and change its font style to Italic.

8   Select all the text in the frame, and click the Align Center button in the Control panel or Paragraph panel.

9   Select all the text and apply a fill color of Purple (**Figure 3.46**).

Figure 3.46 The formatted coverline over the starburst

10 Make any other adjustments you think are necessary to make the starburst and its coverline look like a graphic unit, such as repositioning the text over the starburst.

11 With the Selection tool, select both the starburst and its coverline (click one and Shift-click the other), and choose Object > Group.

12 Rotate the selected starburst coverline group about 18 degrees, using either of the following methods:

- In the Control panel, enter **13** into the Rotation Angle field, and press Enter or Return.

- Position the Selection tool pointer just outside any corner of the bounding box until the pointer becomes a rotation icon (**Figure 3.47**), and drag until the object reaches the rotation angle you want.

13 Check your work (**Figure 3.48**) by switching into Preview mode and zooming out to fit the page in the document window. Make any adjustments that you think are needed.

14 Save your work.

> **TIP**
>
> *The Direct Selection tool also allows you to select individual items within a group and edit them without ungrouping the group first.*

Figure 3.47 Rotating the starburst using the group bounding handle, with the Control panel Rotation value also highlighted

Figure 3.48 The completed magazine cover

Preflighting the Document

▶ *Video 3.12*
Preflighting the
Document

No one wants to see mistakes in a commercial printing job, because a big print job is expensive—think of a magazine that needs tens of thousands of copies printed. At worst, the job may need to be printed again at great expense. For this reason, InDesign provides ways to spot potential problems before they become costly printing mistakes. The process of reviewing a document for output issues is called preflighting, named after the preflight checklist that airplane pilots use to make sure the airplane is safe to fly.

Figure 3.49 The Preflight panel show-ing errors

To preflight a document:

1   Open the Preflight panel (Window > Output > Preflight) (**Figure 3.49**).

    ■ If everything is okay, the bottom of the Preflight panel will show a green light and say No Errors, and the Error list will be empty.

    ■ If there is a problem, the bottom of the Preflight panel will show a red light, and the Error list will show all the errors that were found.

2   If there aren't any errors, you're ready to package the document for output, as you did in Chapter 2.

    If there are errors, you can resolve them from the Error list. Click the page number on the error line to go to the object with the error so that you can resolve the problem.

The Preflight panel can alert you to many problems, including the following:

■ **Missing linked files.** Files you placed may no longer be in the folder from which they were originally placed, or the filename may have changed. You can resolve this by restoring missing files or changed filenames back to what was recorded in the document. You can also use options in the Links panel to point InDesign to the missing files' current locations and file-names; this has not yet been covered in this book.

■ **Missing fonts.** Fonts applied earlier may have become disabled or missing over time, or a document may have been moved to a different computer with different fonts available. You resolve this by making the necessary fonts available, by replacing the fonts with ones that are available, or by using Adobe Typekit to download matching fonts from the cloud.

■ **Overset text.** You have seen that overset text appears cut off and missing from the end of a text frame. You resolve this by editing the text or its type attributes so that it fits within the available space in a text frame.

If you have built the cover image correctly, it will probably pass the preflight check with no errors. If you get this result but you would like to see what an error would look like, do the following:

3   With the Selection tool, click the cover image.

4   Right-click (Windows) or Control-click (macOS) the cover image and choose Graphics > Reveal in Explorer (Windows) or Reveal in Finder (macOS).

The computer switches to the desktop, and the desktop folder containing the linked graphic opens, with the graphic selected.

5   Change the name of the graphic slightly (for example, add an **x** to the end) or move the graphic to a different folder.

6   Switch back to InDesign and look at the Preflight panel.

There should now be "missing link" errors, because the current name or location of the linked file does not match the name or location recorded in the InDesign document when you placed it.

7   Switch to the desktop, and reverse the change you made.

If you restored the file's name or location to its exact state before you changed it, there should no longer be errors in the Preflight panel in InDesign.

Challenge

Create your own magazine cover image based on one of your own favorite subjects, such as sports, school or neighborhood news, science, fashion, music, or entertainment. Come up with a title and find a strong image for the cover. Write some coverlines, and then integrate all those elements into a strong layout. Explore ways to keep text legible over a busy photograph, such as the effects that you applied to coverlines in this chapter.

As a bonus, come up with a cover layout grid, paragraph styles, and color swatches designed to work with a wide range of cover photos across a number of issues. Test your ideas with different cover photo images and coverlines. Produce a set of samples like the three sample COMIX covers you saw at the beginning of the chapter.

TIP

A quick way to preflight as you work is to look at the preflight area at the bottom of the document window. The green or red Preflight light appears there, and you can open the Preflight panel by clicking the arrow next to the status area and choosing the Preflight panel.

CHAPTER OBJECTIVES

Chapter Learning Objectives

- Create a multicolumn layout.
- Add master items to master pages.
- Apply master pages to document pages.
- Work with spot colors.
- Use dummy text to create a design proposal.
- Thread stories across multiple pages.
- Wrap text around images.
- Add form elements.
- Create an interactive PDF form.

Chapter ACA Objectives

For full descriptions of the objectives, see the table on pages 270–276.

DOMAIN 2.0
PROJECT SETUP AND INTERFACE
2.1, 2.5

DOMAIN 3.0
ORGANIZING DOCUMENTS
3.2, 3.8

DOMAIN 4.0
CREATING AND MODIFYING DOCUMENT ELEMENTS
4.1, 4.2, 4.4, 4.6, 4.7

DOMAIN 5.0
PUBLISHING DOCUMENTS
5.2

CHAPTER 4

Designing a Magazine Layout

In this design project, you will put together a basic layout to present to your customer. Specifically, you will provide design and text formatting ideas for the editor's note pages, a subscription form that will be included as a foldout in the print version of the magazine, and an interactive form that readers can fill out in the PDF version of the magazine. You'll be introduced to the concept of master pages, try additional paragraph formatting controls, and learn how to wrap text around images. Finally, you will gain an understanding of the various form elements used in PDF form designs (**Figure 4.1**).

▶ Video 4.1
*Introducing the
Magazine Interior
Layout Project*

Figure 4.1 Finished magazine design

As with the previous project, this project's primary output medium will be print. The magazine content is made up of photos, headlines, body copy, background tints, and line and form elements. The magazine example in this project is folded to a finished portrait letter size (8.5 inches by 11 inches). The magazine is designed with facing pages (left and right pages), and text appears in three columns. Additionally, its cover and some of its content design contain images and background color frames that extend to the edge of the page.

Setting Up the New Document Dialog

Start a new document for this project (**Figure 4.2**) using the following settings:

- **Intent:** Choose Print. This sets the document's default color mode to CMYK.
- **Name:** Type **project04_magazine_pages**.
- **Units:** Choose Inches.
- **Number of Pages:** Magazines are multipage documents. Start with four pages and add more pages as needed during production.
- **Page Size and Orientation:** In the Blank Document Presets section, click the Letter page size icon, and for Orientation click the portrait icon.
- **Facing Pages:** Select Facing Pages to create a document with spreads (left and right pages side by side). Notice that with Facing Pages enabled, the Left and Right margin fields change to Inside and Outside. The inside margin is the margin that appears on either side of the spine, where the magazine is bound. The outside margin is the margin that appears on the edge where there is no binding.
- **Columns:** Enter **3** for the number of columns. With Screen Mode set to Normal, the column guides assist with consistent and easy placement of design elements.
- **Margins:** Enter **0.5 inches** for all sides.
- **Bleed:** Enter **0.25 inches** on all sides.

The Slug option won't be used in this project.

After you click OK, remember to save the document.

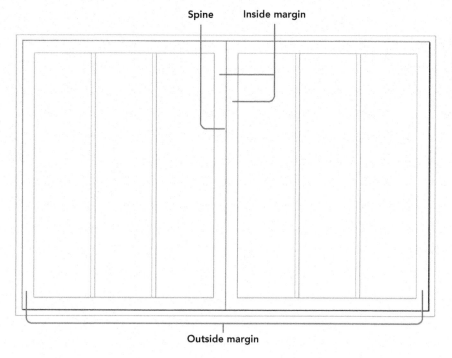

Spine   Inside margin

Outside margin

Figure 4.2 Viewing the second and third pages of a four-page facing-pages document, including three attributes when Facing Pages is enabled

Setting Up Master Pages

Master pages apply common design elements across the pages of your document. This saves you the time of adding those elements to each page individually, ensures consistency, and provides an easy method for making global changes across a document.

★ *ACA Objective 2.1*

If you have a magazine or other multipage publication nearby, flip through the pages. Can you spot common design elements or layout features? What design elements appear repeatedly across multiple pages in a report or book layout?

The magazine contains several examples of master items, which live on master pages. Page headers (the area above the top margin guide on a page) and footers (the area below the bottom margin guide) are areas on the page where you would position elements that repeat across different pages (**Figure 4.3**). Some examples of repeating header and footer elements are page numbers, company logos, and navigation controls.

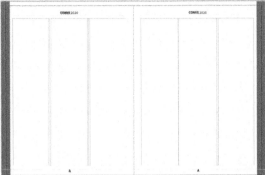

Figure 4.3 A two-page spread of a magazine layout and the master page that was applied to add the red bars, header, and footer

If you have an item you want to appear on many pages, add that item to a master page. Then, when you apply that master page to document pages, those master items appear on those document pages automatically.

★ *ACA Objective 4.1*

▶ **Video 4.3** *Adding Elements to Master Page A*

Creating and Editing Master Pages

When you create a new document, a blank document opens with the number of pages you specified. All the pages are automatically based on a default master page named A-Master. This default master page is applied to all empty pages and applies the original new document settings, such as the page size, orientation, margins, columns, and bleed settings.

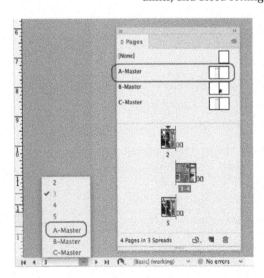

Before adding items to a master page, display the master page by doing one of the following:

- In the master pages area of the Pages panel, double-click the name of the master page (in this case, A-Master).
- In the Status bar, select the master page name (A-Master) from the Go to Page menu.
- Choose Layout > Go to Page, and then select the master page name (A-Master) from the Page menu (**Figure 4.4**).

Figure 4.4 ◀ A-Master selectable from the status bar at the bottom of the document window, and in the master page area of the Pages panel

The A-Master page or spread now appears in the document window. You can now start to add common master items.

When you use facing pages, a master page spread contains both a left and a right master page so that you can add items to just one page of each spread.

A special page number marker is often the first master item you add to a master page, especially for longer documents such as books, reports, or magazines. The marker automatically updates to display the current page number.

To add a current page number marker (**Figure 4.5**):

1 Using the Type tool, draw a text frame on the A-Master page, in the footer area, and click inside the frame.

2 Choose Type > Insert Special Character > Markers > Current Page Number.

   The special page number marker that is inserted appears as the letter A, matching the prefix of the master page. A page number on a B-Master would appear as the letter B. If you want to add more text to the footer text frame that contains the page number marker, such as the name of the magazine, go ahead.

3 When you return to a document page, you'll see the new master item on every page that uses that master.

   If you're using facing pages and you want to see a master item on every page, remember to add the master item to both the left and right pages of the master spread.

NOTE

Video 4.3 includes a layer group called Master Pages. This layer group was manually created to help organize the document; it isn't automatically created when you use master pages.

TIP

To customize how the Pages panel looks, such as making the page thumbnail icons larger, choose Panel Options from the Pages panel menu.

TIP

Include column guides and ruler guides on your master pages to help maintain layout consistency.

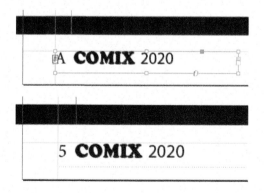

Figure 4.5 Current page number markers on the left side of A-Master (top), and how the marker looks on page 5

In the same way, you can add any other text or graphics to a master spread, such as a document title or issue date.

★ *ACA Objective 3.2*

Master pages aren't just for objects that appear on every page. They can also be useful for layouts that you want to reuse frequently. In Video 4.3, the Editor's Note page is being built on a master page because it's a specific page layout that will be needed for every issue. Instead of rebuilding the layout for every issue, having it ready as a master page lets you simply apply it to whichever page in the next issue will be used for the Editor's Note and fill it in with that issue's text.

Adding Master Pages

Documents are not limited to a single master page or master spread. For example, in a magazine layout, different sections might use different standard layouts.

To create a new master page, do any of the following:

- With a master page or spread selected, click the Create New Page button at the bottom of the Pages panel.

- Choose New Master from the Pages panel menu.

- Right-click the master page area in the Pages panel, and choose New Master.

If you choose the New Master command (or choose the Master Options command when a master is selected), you can change the settings for a master (**Figure 4.6**):

- **Prefix:** A short way of identifying a master when there isn't room to display the entire master name.

- **Name:** The name of the master.

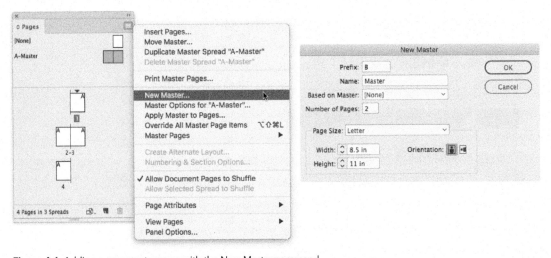

Figure 4.6 Adding a new master page with the New Master command

- **Based on Master:** Basing one master on another is a great way to handle variations. For example, if two sections of a catalog have identical rectangles in the header except for the rectangle fill color, you can base the second master on the first and just change the rectangle color. When you edit the first master, the changes also apply to the second (except for the fill color), so you edit just once to change both masters.

- **Number of Pages:** A master can have more than two pages; for example, you can design a master for a three-panel gatefold layout.

In addition to having different objects and guides, each master can also have its own page size, margin settings, and column settings.

Duplicating Master Pages

You can duplicate an existing master page to serve as the basis for a new master page. When you are creating multiple related masters, duplicating an existing master is faster than building a new master from a blank page.

To duplicate a master page or spread, do any of the following:

- With a master selected, choose Duplicate Master Spread from the Pages panel menu.

- Right-click a master and choose Duplicate Master.

- Drag a master onto the Create New Page button at the bottom of the Pages panel.

After you duplicate a spread, you can use the Master Options command to customize its name and attributes. Then you can add or remove items on the duplicate as needed.

▶ **Video 4.4** *Creating a Second Master Page*

TIP

To create a new master page that copies a document page design, select the document page in the Pages panel and then select Master Pages > Save As Master from the Master panel menu.

Putting Master Pages to Work

You can apply master pages to any document pages, and you can apply master pages to new pages as you add them.

★ *ACA Objective 3.2*

Applying Master Pages

When master pages are applied to document pages, the prefix letter (A for A-Master, for example) appears on the page thumbnail in the Pages panel. This makes it easy to see which master page is applied to a document page.

To apply a master page to a document page (**Figure 4.7**):

1 In the Pages panel, select the document pages for applying the master page.

2 Select Apply Master to Pages from the Pages panel menu.

3 In the Apply Master dialog, select a master to apply to the document page from the Apply Master menu.

4 Click OK.

Figure 4.7 Applying a master page to selected document pages in the Pages panel

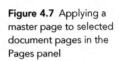

SHORTCUT *To select a continuous range of pages in the Pages panel, click the first page in the range and then Shift-click the last page in the range. To select non-contiguous pages, Ctrl-click (Windows) or Command-click (macOS) the page icons.*

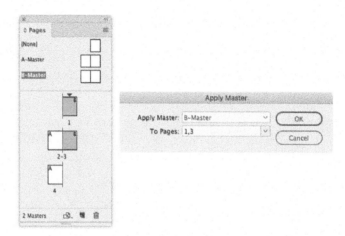

You can also apply a master in the Pages panel by dragging a master thumbnail and dropping it on page thumbnails in the Pages panel.

Adding Pages Based on Master Pages

When you add a new page, it uses the same master as the page that was selected at the time you added the new page.

TIP
You can also open the Insert Pages dialog by choosing Insert Pages from the Pages panel menu, or by Alt-clicking (Windows) or Option-clicking (macOS) the Create New Page button in the Layers panel.

If you want to choose which master is used for a new page, choose Layout > Pages > Insert Pages (**Figure 4.8**). In the Insert Pages dialog, you can choose where to add the new pages and which master they should use. You can also drag a master from the masters area of the Pages panel before or after any pages in the document pages area of the Pages panel.

Figure 4.8 Adding one or more pages and applying a master page

Deleting Masters

Deleting a master is nearly the same as creating one. In the Pages panel, you can simply drag a master page or spread to the Delete Selected Pages icon (🗑). When a master is selected, you can click the Delete Selected Pages icon or choose Delete Master from the Pages panel menu.

Editing Master Items on Document Pages

Master items are recognizable by a thin dotted border when Screen Mode is set to Normal. To protect master items from being altered accidentally, they are not normally editable on a document page.

There may be times when a master page is almost, but not quite, the layout you want. For example, if one page of the magazine is a special feature where background or header elements should be different, you can override, or release, master page items so that you can edit or delete them.

Keep in mind that overriding a master item may disconnect it from updates you make to the master page. For example, if you change the fill color of the overridden item on the page and later change the fill color of the master item, the color will not update on the document page with the override. If you want the master to change everywhere it's used, edit the master itself, not a document page.

To override a master item on a document page (**Figure 4.9**):

1 Using the Selection tool, Shift+Ctrl-click (Windows) or Shift+Command-click (macOS) the master item.

2 Make any design changes to the object, such as text or color changes. You can also delete the object if needed.

TIP

When pasting text, you may want to discard its formatting and have it take on the formatting of the text it's replacing. To do this, first select and copy the formatted text, excluding the paragraph return character (¶) at the end of the paragraph. Then choose Edit > Paste Without Formatting. To see the end-of-paragraph characters, choose Type > Show Hidden Characters, and set the Screen Mode to Normal.

SUBJECT

"Illaccatur? Per-est offic tempore perrume ipien-isto es et et eati berio elignimpor sit facil magnis"

Barry Garrick

SUBJECT

"Illaccatur? Per-est offic tempore perrume ipien-isto es et et eati berio elignimpor sit facil magnis"

Barry Garrick

Figure 4.9 Shift+Ctrl-click (Windows) or Shift+Command-click (macOS) the quote's text frame (a master item). The master item becomes a standard page object, so you can replace the placeholder text for the quote with real text.

Using Spot Colors in Print Designs

In Chapter 2, you were introduced to color theory and learned about RGB and CMYK color. In Videos 4.3 and 4.12 you see a document that is initially designed using spot colors and is later converted to process colors.

Adding Spot Colors from a Color Matching System

InDesign offers many built-in PANTONE color guides, along with TRUMATCH, TOYO, and HKS color matching systems. These color matching systems provide reference lists and printed sample books of precisely formulated colors. The sample books show exactly how a specific color will print, to overcome the limitations of trying to reproduce color consistently on computer displays. Even if designers, clients, and commercial printers are in different locations, as long as they refer to the same color swatch number, they will be looking at exactly the same color. One reason there are so many color systems is that some are optimized for certain types of materials, such as uncoated or matte paper, coated or glossy paper, or textiles; other color systems represent printing standards in different parts of the world.

To add a spot color to the Swatches panel (**Figure 4.10**):

1 Select New Color Swatch from the Swatches panel menu.

2 In the New Color Swatch dialog, select Spot from the Color Type menu.

Figure 4.10 Adding a
new PANTONE spot color
to the Swatches panel

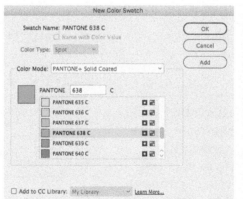

3   From the Color Mode menu, select one of the spot color guides, such as PANTONE+ Solid Coated.

Coated refers to the paper, or stock, that your publication is printed on. Coated papers work well for publications that are rich in color and detail. If you're not sure what color guide to pick, ask your commercial printer.

4   Select a color from the list, or enter a color reference number from the color guide.

5   Click OK.

TIP
You can create tints of spot colors the same way you did for process colors earlier by adjusting the Tint percentage in the Control panel or Swatches panel.

Working with Text Frames and Columns

⭐ *ACA Objective 4.1*

⭐ *ACA Objective 4.2*

▶ **Video 4.5** *Adding Text Frames*

▶ **Video 4.6** *Adding Body Copy to a Document*

When a design lays out a story using multiple columns, there's more than one way to implement the columns. You can specify multiple columns within the page margins of the entire page, or you can have a single text frame contain multiple columns (**Figure 4.11**). Many designs use both, where the columns at the page level define the overall design grid of the page, and columns at the text-frame level define how an individual story is laid out on the page.

You can create columns manually by drawing text frames and threading a single story through them (see "Threading Stories Through Text Frames" later in this chapter), but it's usually easier to draw one text frame and set it to contain multiple columns. Drawing text frames manually for each column may be better for highly creative layouts in which you want to vary column heights and positions.

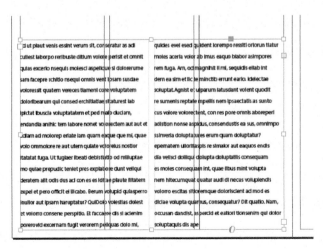

Figure 4.11 A page design using a three-column grid, and a text frame set up to contain text in two columns

Changing the Number of Columns in a Text Frame

To change the column settings for a text frame (**Figure 4.12**), select the text frame with the Selection tool and then do one of the following:

- In the Control panel, change the values in the Number of Columns field and the Gutter field.

- Choose Object > Text Frame Options, change the values in the Number of Columns field and the Gutter field, and click OK.

The gutter is the space between columns.

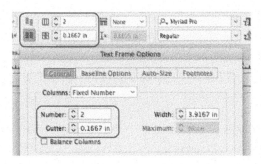

Figure 4.12 Number of Columns and Gutter options for a text frame, in the Control panel and in the Text Frame Options dialog

Changing How Far Text Sits Inside a Frame Edge

When you apply a background tint to a text frame to make a story stand out, the text can end up too close to the edges of the frame. To push the text in from the edges of the text frame, change the Inset Spacing values in the General tab of the Text Frame Options dialog.

★ ACA Objective 4.2

▶ **Video 4.6** Adding Body Copy to a Document

Creating a Drop Cap

Drop caps are often used to make the introductory paragraph for a story stand out. One or more characters are increased in size and extended several lines down into the paragraph. Although this effect might seem like a character format, it is actually a paragraph format that you can apply automatically through a paragraph style.

To start a paragraph with a drop cap (**Figure 4.13**):

1 Using the Type tool, click in the paragraph.

2 In the Control panel, click the Paragraph Formatting Controls button (¶), or show the Paragraph panel.

3 Enter a value in the Drop Cap Number of Lines field to specify how far the characters drop down.

4 To drop multiple characters—for example, when a paragraph starts with a quotation mark, you might want to drop the first two characters of the paragraph—increase the value in the Drop Cap One or More Characters field.

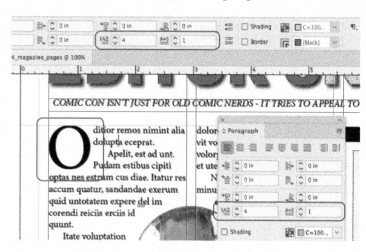

Figure 4.13 Starting a story with a drop cap, using the Control panel or the Paragraph panel

Now that you have started working with stories, there are more paragraph formatting controls that are handy to learn, such as working with spacing between paragraphs, indentation, and lists.

Adjusting Space Between Paragraphs

Spacing between paragraphs is an important part of typography and page layout. Correct spacing can help capture the relationship between different text elements and add harmony to the design.

★ ACA Objective 4.2

For example, the space between a heading and the rest of the text is important. If the space is too large, the bond between the heading and the following body paragraph could disappear. If the space is too small, it will be less eye-catching. Getting the spacing just right makes it clear to the reader that the heading and body paragraphs form a unit.

To add space before or after a paragraph (**Figure 4.14**):

1 Using the Type tool, click in a paragraph to select it, or select a range of paragraphs.

2 In the Control panel, select the Paragraph Formatting Controls.

3 Enter a value in the Space Before or Space After field, or click the arrows next to it.

Figure 4.14 Adding space between paragraphs, using the Control panel or the Paragraph panel

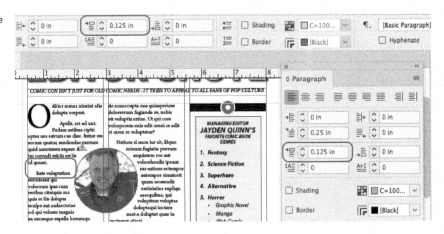

Setting Indents

Indents move paragraph text away from the left or right edge of a column. InDesign offers four indent controls, each of which determines how paragraph text moves away from the left or right edge of a column (**Figure 4.15**).

- **Left Indent:** Moves all lines in a paragraph away from the left side of the column.

- **Right Indent:** Moves all lines in a paragraph away from the right side of the column.

- **First Line Left Indent:** Affects only the first line of the paragraph, moving it away from the left side of the column.

- **Last Line Right Indent:** Moves the last line of the paragraph away from the right side of the column.

First Line
Left Indent   Left Indent   Right Indent   Last Line
Right Indent

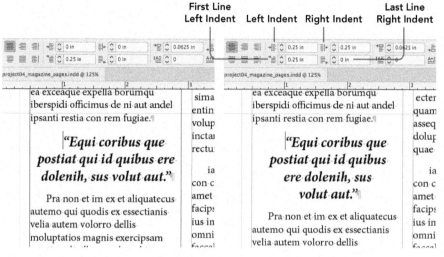

Figure 4.15 Adjusting paragraph indent settings in the Control panel helps set off the pull quote.

Setting Tabs

Unlike indents, which are intended for controlling whole paragraphs of text, tabs are intended to control lists or tables such as restaurant menus and schedules. This is done by setting tabs across a column so that each time you press the Tab key, the text insertion point moves to the next tab.

★ *ACA Objective 4.2*

An example of tabbed text is an evaluation form (**Figure 4.16**). It contains a table of questions and responses. Tabs align the columns of responses.

Left-justified tab

Center-justified tab

Right-justified tab

Align to Decimal (or Other Specified Character) tab

Tabs added to the tab ruler

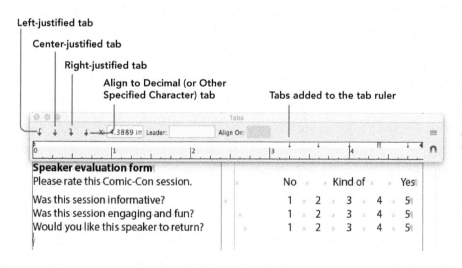

Figure 4.16 Text frame containing tabs, formatted using the Tabs panel

To add tabs:

1 If necessary, choose Type > Show Hidden Characters so you can see the tab characters in your text. (Make sure Screen Mode is Normal.)

2 Using the Type tool, click a text insertion point immediately before the word you want to align, and press Tab.

3 Choose Type > Tabs to display the Tabs panel.

4 Click one of the tab alignment icons on the tab ruler. The four tab types provide different ways to align text to a tab:

   ▪ Left-Justified tab aligns the left edge of the text immediately following the tab character to the tab stop.

   ▪ Center-Justified tab aligns the text equally on either side of the tab stop.

   ▪ Right-Justified tab aligns the right side of the text to the tab stop.

   ▪ Align to Decimal (or Other Specified Character) tab aligns the text on the decimal point or another character you specify.

5 Click just above the ruler in the white bar to insert a tab stop, then drag it to the right location. Or, with the tab stop selected, enter an exact position in the X field.

6 To adjust tabs for multiple lines, first use the Type tool to select the lines, and then adjust settings in the Tabs panel.

★ *ACA Objective 4.2*

Adjusting Hyphenation

▶ *Video 4.6 Adding Body Copy to a Document*

Hyphenation causes words that do not fit at the end of a line to split across two lines, with a hyphen appearing at the end of the first line. The use of hyphenation is a design and editorial choice. Enabling hyphenation assists in creating more even word spacing within a paragraph; for paragraph text that is justified, for example, enabling hyphenation could help reduce the word space variations.

To disable hyphenation for a paragraph (**Figure 4.17**):

1 Using the Type tool, click to select the paragraph.

2 In the Control panel or the Paragraph panel, deselect Hyphenate.

To customize hyphenation settings, choose Hyphenation from the Paragraph panel menu.

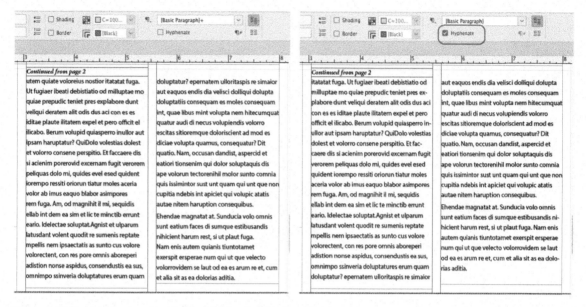

Figure 4.17 Text with hyphenation disabled (left) and enabled (right)

Wrapping Text Around Objects

★ *ACA Objective 4.2*

★ *ACA Objective 4.4*

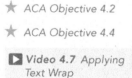
▶ *Video 4.7* Applying Text Wrap

The Text Wrap panel provides an easy way to wrap text around an object. Text is commonly wrapped around an imported graphic. But text wrap works with any type of frame; for example, you could wrap text around a text frame containing a pull quote (see "Adding a Pull Quote" later in this chapter). To handle various situations, the Text Wrap panel lets you flow the text around an object, an image's rectangular bounding box, or the contours of an imported image.

To wrap text around an object:

1 Select an object that overlaps (or is overlapped by) a text frame.

2 If the Text Wrap panel isn't visible, choose Window > Text Wrap.

3 Click a button at the top of the Text Wrap panel (**Figure 4.18**):

   ▪ **Wrap Around Bounding Box:** This wraps text around the rectangular bounding box of an object, regardless of the shape of the frame or the object inside it.

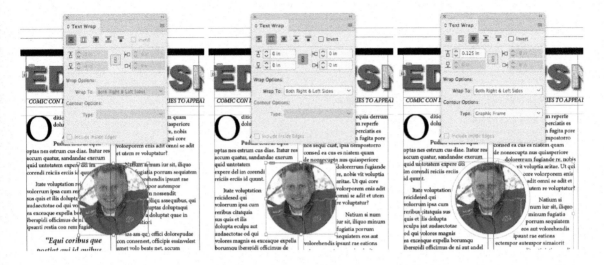

Figure 4.18 Applying Wrap options in the Text Wrap panel

- **Wrap Around Object Shape:** This wraps text around the shape of the frame instead of the shape of the bounding box. If the frame is a rectangle that contains a non-rectangular graphic, try choosing options from the Contour Options list depending on how the graphic indicates its shape. An alpha channel indicates shape using an extra image channel; a Photoshop path or clipping path indicates shape using vector paths saved with the image.

- **Jump Object:** Instead of wrapping text, this makes text jump over the object. That means text won't appear to the sides of the object. Jump to Next Column is similar, but instead of text resuming after the object, text resumes in the next column that the object doesn't overlap.

4 Enter Offset values as needed to push text away from the shape (**Figure 4.19**).

Figure 4.19 Applying Offset values in the Text Wrap panel

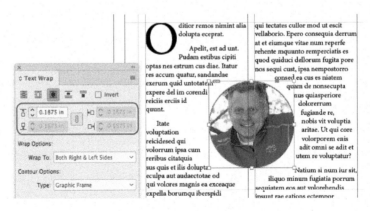

Creating Bulleted and Numbered Lists

★ ACA Objective 4.2

You can automatically add bullet characters or sequential numbers to paragraphs. Use numbered lists when the order or sequence of steps is specific. Use bulleted lists when the order isn't important. In a cookbook, for example, the ingredients might be in a bulleted list and the instructions might be in a numbered list.

▶ Video 4.8
Formatting Text

▶ Video 4.9
Designing a Sidebar with Lists and an Image

To create a bulleted or numbered list:

1 With the Type tool, select the paragraphs you want in the list.

2 Do one of the following (**Figure 4.20**):

   ▪ In the Control panel, click the Bulleted List or Numbered List icon.

   ▪ Choose Type > Bulleted & Numbered Lists, and choose Apply Bullets or Apply Numbers from the submenu.

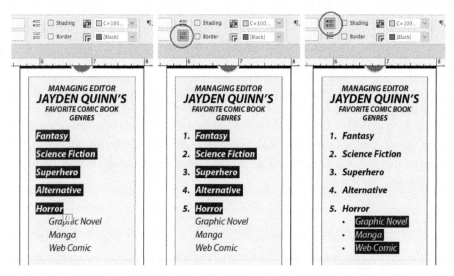

Figure 4.20 Creating a numbered list and then a bulleted list by clicking icons in the Control panel

To adjust the format of the list:

1 With the Type tool, select the paragraphs in the list.

2 Do one of the following:

   ▪ Alt-click (Windows) or Option-click (macOS) the Numbered List icon in the Control panel.

   ▪ Choose Bullets and Numbering from the Paragraph panel menu.

3 Adjust options as needed (**Figure 4.21**), and click OK. To learn more about the Bullets and Numbering options, see https://helpx.adobe.com/indesign/using/bullets-numbering.html.

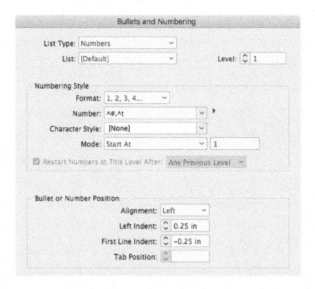

A bulleted or numbered list typically includes a hanging indent, where the first line of a paragraph is indented less than the rest of the paragraph (**Figure 4.22**) to make space for a bullet or number character. A hanging indent is the opposite of a first-line indent, where the first line is indented more than the rest of the lines. When you create your own list formatting, you can customize the hanging indent using Bullets and Numbering options.

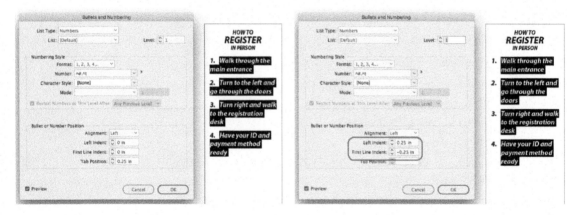

To create a hanging indent in the Bullets and Numbering dialog, set First Line Indent to be less than Left Indent. Typically, First Line Indent will be the same value as Left Indent but negative; for example, the default list formatting is a left indent of 0.25 inches and a first-line indent of –0.25 inches.

TIP

Because bulleted and numbered lists are at the paragraph level, you can save them as part of a paragraph style.

Threading Stories Through Text Frames

★ ACA Objective 4.2

▶ **Video 4.10** *Threading Text from One Page to the Next*

▶ **Video 4.11** *Adding Page Jumps to a Story*

In InDesign, the term story specifically means a single continuous article of text. A story can be a single text frame, such as a caption, but it can also flow among a series of threaded (linked) text frames. A story that's too long for the first text frame can be threaded through multiple linked text frames on the same page or spread (as in a story spanning multiple columns), and can also be threaded to text frames across multiple pages (as in a magazine). When you change the number of words in a threaded story, it affects the overall length of the story across all the threaded text frames.

Threading Text Frames

Text frames have an in port at the top left and an out port at the lower right (**Figure 4.23**). These ports connect text frames and allow text to flow across frames. You can draw text frames first and thread them later, or you can thread text frames interactively as you import text. Both ways involve using the in port and out port of a text frame.

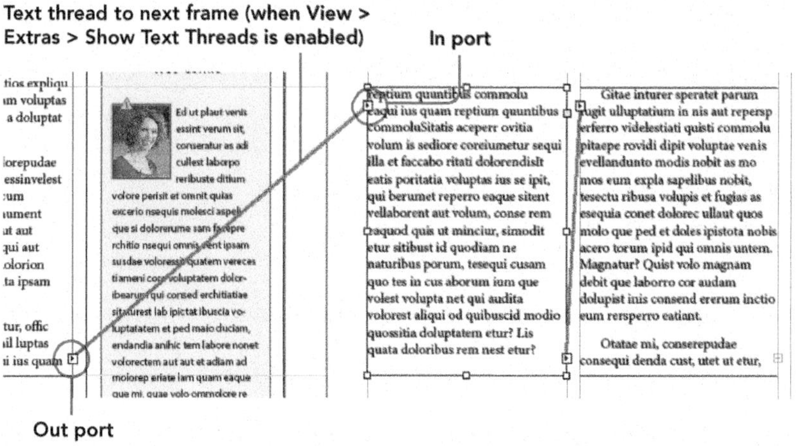

Text thread to next frame (when View > Extras > Show Text Threads is enabled)

In port

Out port

Figure 4.23 Text threading controls and indicators

If you want to see how text frames are threaded in Normal screen mode, choose View > Extras > Show Text Threads.

To thread text frames that already exist:

1   With the Selection tool, click the out port of the first text frame (**Figure 4.24**). The pointer changes into a loaded text icon with a link icon to indicate that the next text frame you click will be threaded to the previous one.

Figure 4.24 Threading text frames

2   Click the loaded text icon on an empty text frame. The two text frames are now threaded; overflow text from the first frame will appear in the second frame.

To thread text frames as you create them:

1   Choose File > Place, select a text file, and click Open. The pointer changes into a loaded text icon ( ).

2   Alt-drag (Windows) or Option-drag (macOS) to create a text frame. The loaded story flows into the frame, and the pointer is still loaded.

3   Repeat step 2 to create the next text frame. As long as you Alt/Option-drag the loaded text icon, the next text frame you drag will be linked to the previous one, even if there isn't any more text to flow. If you add text to the story, it will eventually flow through each threaded frame in the order you linked them.

To change the order in which text frames are threaded:

With the Selection tool, click the out port of a text frame that's already threaded, and then click a different text frame than the one it's currently linked to.

Creating Jump Lines

When a story continues on a different page, a jump line tells the reader where to find the remainder of the story, or where a story is continued from.

To add a "continued on" jump line (**Figure 4.25**):

1 With the Type tool, create a separate small text frame for the jump line.

2 Enter jump line text such as **Continued on page**.

3 With the text insertion point at the end of the line, choose Type > Insert Special Character > Markers > Next Page Number.

4 Using the Selection tool, position the text frame so that it touches or slightly overlaps the text area of the story that continues.

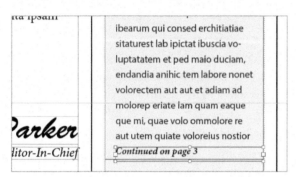
Continued on page 3

Figure 4.25 A jump line for a story that continues on another page

TIP

If the Next Page Number marker doesn't update to the jump page number until it seems too close to the story text, try extending the bottom of the story text frame. The jump page number updates only when it touches the actual story area of a text frame, not its frame edge or inset.

TIP

When creating a "continued from" jump line, choose Insert Special Character > Markers > Previous Page Number.

Resolving Overset Text

When there is more text than can fit in a frame, the out port displays a red plus sign. This is referred to as **overset text**, and it's marked in red (**Figure 4.26**). It means there's text that isn't currently displayed and so it won't appear on the final output.

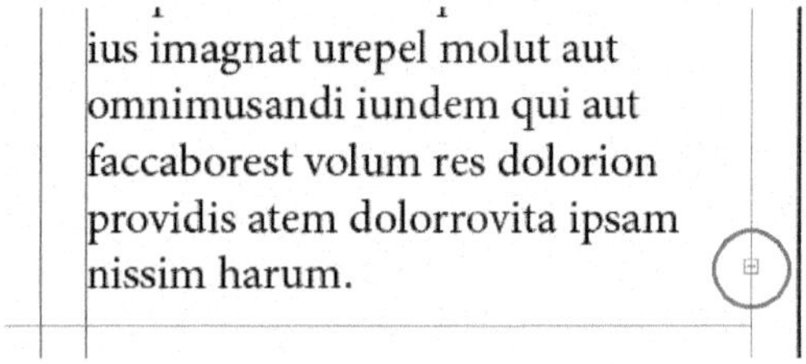

ius imagnat urepel molut aut omnimusandi iundem qui aut faccaborest volum res dolorion providis atem dolorrovita ipsam nissim harum.

Figure 4.26 Each text frame has an in port and out port. When the out port shows a red plus sign, the text is overset.

To resolve overset text, do one of the following:

- Shorten the text by editing it until all of the story fits in the frame.
- Make the text frame taller until all of the story fits in the frame.
- Thread the story to an empty text frame so that it can continue there.

 TIP

Stories threaded through multiple frames can be a challenge to edit when you can't see the entire story at once. Choose Edit > Edit in Story Editor to see and edit the story in a single window. Changes you make in Story Editor are reflected in the layout, and vice versa.

★ *ACA Objective 4.4*

 **Video 4.12**
Replacing Spot Colors with Process Colors

TIP

To un-anchor the text-shaped frame, select the frame, choose Edit > Cut, click anywhere on the page, and then choose Edit > Paste.

Converting Text into a Graphic

It isn't always possible to achieve the text effect you want using the type controls alone. For example, you might want some headline type to apply a kind of fill that is not possible in InDesign, even though it's possible in applications such as Adobe Photoshop and Adobe Illustrator. In these situations you can convert text to outlines.

When you convert text to outlines, the individual text characters become graphics frames. At that point you can do anything with them that you can do with a graphics frame, such as edit their paths (for customized letterforms) or fill them with images. But there's one downside: Once you convert the text to outlines, you can no longer edit the text using the Type tool. You may want to keep a copy of the original text on the pasteboard so that you have an easy fallback option if needed.

There are two ways to convert text to a graphic:

- **Convert all the text in the frame:** Using the Selection tool, select the text frame, and then choose Type > Create Outlines. This converts the text into a compound path, which is a series of paths that behave as a single frame or a group. Once it's selected, you can place a graphic inside the compound path (**Figure 4.27**).

Figure 4.27 Converting all the text in a frame to outlines

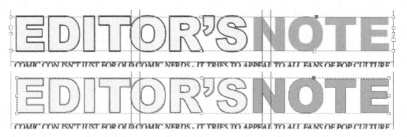

- **Convert selected text:** Using the Type tool, select the characters you want to convert, and then choose Type > Create Outlines. In this case, only the text you selected is converted. The new text-shaped frame is anchored within the rest of the text.

When you move the Direct Selection tool over the converted text, you can see all the anchor points and line segments (**Figure 4.28**).

Figure 4.28 Text converted to outlines results in a text-shaped frame.

How do you fill these outlines with an imported image? Because they're graphics frames, you do it the same way you have many times before when you were placing an image inside a rectangular graphics frame. The only difference is that these frames aren't rectangular. Just make sure the outlines are selected when you place an image, and the image will be placed inside the outlines (**Figure 4.29**).

TIP

Double-clicking a group with the Selection tool lets you select different elements within the group.

Figure 4.29 A blue pattern placed inside the converted text

You've previously edited inside graphics frames, and these work the same way: You can use the Direct Selection tool or the Content Grabber to adjust the image within the frame, and you can use the Direct Selection tool to edit the frame path.

Placing a Graphic Without a Placeholder

★ ACA Objective 4.1

▶ **Video 4.13** *Adding a Large Image with Caption*

So far, you've placed the majority of the graphics into the magazine by first drawing a graphics frame and then, while it's selected, placing an imported graphic into it. But that's not the only way to place a graphic.

You can freely place a graphic, even on a completely blank page, by dragging as you place it.

To place a graphic without a placeholder:

1   Choose File > Place, select a graphics file, and click Open. You can also import by dragging a graphics file from the desktop and dropping it in an InDesign document window.

2   Drag the loaded cursor to set the size of the graphic (**Figure 4.30**).

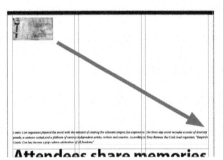

As you drag, a temporary rectangle appears to show you how big the graphic will be when you release the mouse button. The rectangle represents the proportions of the graphic you're placing, so you don't have to hold down Shift to place the graphic proportionally.

3   When the graphic is the size you want, release the mouse button.

The graphic is placed inside a graphics frame that InDesign created automatically.

Adding a Pull Quote

A **pull quote** is a text frame containing a short, provocative excerpt from a story, intended to draw reader interest to the story. It's often implemented as a separate text frame with the excerpt in large type.

All you need is a text frame with the pull quote text in it (**Figure 4.31**). The pull quote text frame should not be threaded to any other text frames. You've already learned the techniques you'll need to create a pull quote; you just have to put them all together:

1   Create a text frame and enter the pull quote text.

2   Format the text so that it's large and eye-catching.

3 If the pull quote will overlap columns of text, apply text wrap to the pull quote text frame, and set text wrap options so that the story flows around it.

Continued from page 2

Figure 4.31 A pull quote

Using Different Page Sizes in a Single Document

★ ACA Objective 3.2

▶ Video 4.15
Adding a Foldout
Subscription Form

As you add more pages to your magazine layout, each new page takes on the page size set for the master being used. You can change the size of any page independently of the rest so that your document uses multiple page sizes.

Preventing Pages from Shuffling

When working in a document with facing pages, odd-numbered pages are on the right and even-numbered pages are on the left. It's normally best to add two pages at a time so that the existing pages stay on their side of the spine. When you insert an odd number of new pages, each subsequent page will change from a right to a left page, and vice versa. In other words, InDesign automatically shuffles pages between sides of a spread. Shuffling can create unwanted changes—for example, a page specifically designed for the left side of a spread could end up on the right side.

If you want to keep left and right pages in their original page positions when adding new pages to a document, you can change that behavior. Simply ensure that the Allow Document Pages to Shuffle setting in the Pages panel menu is unselected. Pages will still be renumbered as you add more pages, but a left or right page will always remain a left or right page. Additionally, you can opt to keep entire page spreads together by selecting the spread in the Pages panel and selecting Allow Selected Spread to Shuffle from the Pages panel menu (**Figure 4.32**).

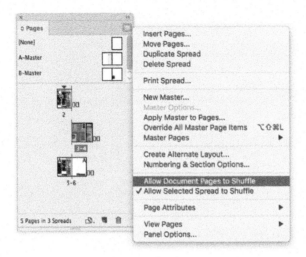

Figure 4.32 Deselecting the Allow Document Pages to Shuffle setting in the Pages panel prevents left pages from becoming right pages (and right pages from become left pages) when you insert or delete pages.

Adding a Foldout with a Different Page Size

When Allow Document Pages to Shuffle is disabled, as discussed in the previous section, you can add a foldout of a different size to a page spread without the other pages moving.

To adjust a page size for a page in the document (**Figure 4.33**):

1 Select the Page tool ( ).

2 In the Pages panel, click the page icon of the page you want to resize. You can also click the page itself in the document window.

3 In the Control panel, change the values in the Width and/or Height fields for the selected page. Or click the Edit Page Size button at the bottom of the Pages panel, choose Custom, enter the Width and Height settings in the Custom Page Size dialog, and click OK.

> **TIP**
>
> *You can save the foldout's page size as a reusable page size in the Custom Page Size dialog. Enter a name for the page size, and then click OK. Once you save a page size, you can select it from any Page Size menu, such as in the New Document dialog.*

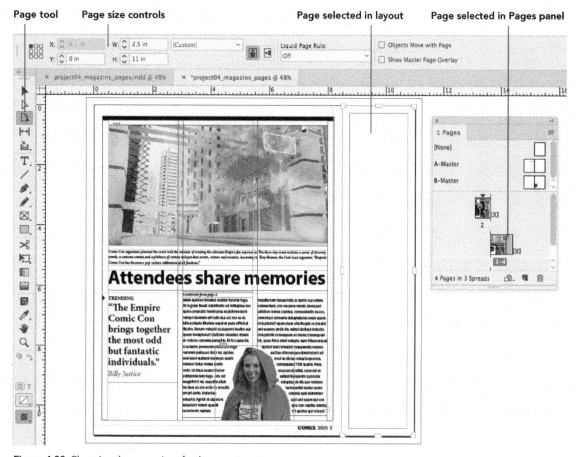

Page tool   Page size controls   Page selected in layout   Page selected in Pages panel

Figure 4.33 Changing the page size of a document page

Creating an Interactive Form

An interactive form is a PDF form that you can fill out electronically. For example, you can enter text in fields, select options from menus, and click radio buttons. Many tax forms, registration forms, and contracts arrive as interactive PDFs to be completed and returned via email.

★ *ACA Objective 4.7*

With the Buttons and Forms panel (Window > Interactive), you can add interactive form elements to an InDesign page and then export the document as an interactive PDF.

Understanding Form Elements

▶ *Video 4.16*
Adding Text Fields,
List Boxes, and
Radio Buttons to
a Form

InDesign supports a number of different form elements. Review the list of form elements and their typical uses before designing your form. You've probably used many of these elements on websites.

- **Text field:** A rectangular box for entering one or more lines of text. This might be a first name and last name (single line) or written feedback (multiple lines).

- **List box:** A scrollable list with options from which one or more items are selected. This might be a list of event dates to choose from.

- **Combo box:** A menu or list of options from which only one option is chosen—for example, a list of all the states or a list of age groups.

- **Check box:** A square box that's either selected (marked with a check or X) or not.

- **Radio buttons:** Round buttons that are part of a group of buttons. Only one button in a group can be selected at any time, making them mutually exclusive. An example of a radio button group is a series of buttons to select the length of a new subscription: one year, two years, or three years.

- **Signature field:** A rectangular box for inserting an e-signature or digital signature. Signature fields are used for PDF forms that are submitted electronically.

In addition to fields, PDF forms can contain buttons, for example:

- **Clear button:** To clear all the information entered in the form.

- **Print button:** To print the form once it's filled out.

- **Submit button:** To send the completed form via email to a recipient.

Designing and Creating Form Elements

▶ *Video 4.17*
Adding Check
Boxes and Control
Buttons to a Form

▶ *Video 4.18*
Making the Form
Interactive

You can create form elements with the frame tools or the Pen tool, so you can easily apply colors and styles to them. For example, you can create text fields and check boxes using the Rectangle tool. You can also use imported graphics. But don't let form elements become too ornate or decorative. A form should have a simple, clear design so that people of all ages and abilities can enter accurate information quickly.

After you add all the design elements for the form, you are ready to convert the elements to form fields.

To convert a rectangle to a text field (**Figure 4.34**):

1 Select a rectangle you drew for a text field.

2 Choose Object > Interactive > Convert to Text Field. Or choose Text Field from the Type menu in the Buttons and Forms panel.

3 In the Buttons and Forms panel, enter a unique name for the field. If multiple fields have identical names, text entered in those fields automatically appears in any other fields with the same field name.

4 Click the disclosure triangle to the left of PDF Options, and set the options for the text field you converted as follows:

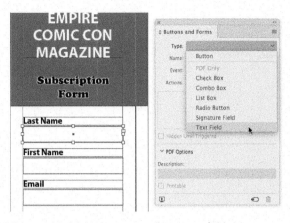

Figure 4.34 Converting a rectangle to a text field

- **Description:** Text you enter in the Description field appears as a tool tip in Acrobat Reader. In addition, it helps make the form more accessible to readers who rely on assistive technologies such as screen readers. As a best practice, always enter a description for each field.

- **Printable:** Select Printable to allow printing of a filled-out form field. In most cases, this should be enabled.

- **Required:** Select Required if someone must fill out this field before submitting the form electronically.

- **Password:** A Password field hides the text entered and replaces it with asterisks or bullets.

- **Read Only:** The user cannot select text in, or enter text into, a Read Only field.

- **Multiline:** Select Multiline for fields that require more text input, such as a feedback or more information field. Make sure to increase the depth of the field's rectangle to give enough room for multiple lines.

- **Scrollable:** Deselect Scrollable to limit the text entered in the field to the field size. For forms that are printed, deselect this option to avoid seeing only part of the entered text on the printout.

- **Font Size:** Select a font size for the text that is entered into the field.

If the document is exported to interactive PDF, the converted rectangle becomes a fillable text field.

You can use the same method to convert objects to any of the Type options in the Buttons and Forms panel.

Adding Buttons

▶ *Video 4.19*
Continue Making the Form Interactive & Animating Buttons

Buttons are interactive elements that can cause actions to take place. If you have ever placed an online order, you have clicked a Place Order button. When you clicked that button, your credit card details were checked and the order details were sent.

Making a button work involves two general steps:

1 Set the event: How does the user need to interact with the button for something to happen? Is it a tap on the button on a tablet device, or is it enough to roll your mouse pointer over the button?

2 Set the action: After the event, what should happen? Does a print dialog appear so that you can print a form? Does a movie start playing? Maybe you're taken to the web browser to look at a web page.

The most commonly used event is On Release Or Tap, which happens when you click and release the mouse button while the pointer is over the button, or tap the button on a tablet device or phone.

Various design elements can become a button:

- Use a graphic or image as a button.
- Use a simple text frame with a fill color and text.
- Group multiple objects (Object > Group), such as shapes, text in frames, and images.

Once you know how you want to set up your buttons, you can put it all together with steps such as the ones below, which were used to create the Print button for the magazine form:

To add a print button (**Figure 4.35**):

1 Using the Selection tool, select the object or group that will serve as the button.

2 Choose Object > Interactive > Convert to Button. Or, in the Buttons and Forms panel, select Button from the Type menu.

3 In the Buttons and Forms panel, enter a name for the button.

Figure 4.35 Converting a text frame to a Print button

4 Leave Event set to On Release Or Tap.

5 Select Print Form from the Action menu (+).

6 Click the disclosure triangle to the left of PDF Options.

7 To prevent the button from printing on the form, but have it remain visible when viewing the form onscreen, deselect Printable.

Setting Up Button Appearances

You've probably used buttons that change their appearance depending on whether you're hovering over the button or clicking the button. You can create InDesign buttons that respond in the same way: A button can have different appearances depending on its state (what's happening to it at the moment).

The Normal appearance is what you see when a PDF form is first opened in Adobe Acrobat Reader. The Rollover appearance happens when the mouse moves over the button itself. The Click appearance happens when you click the mouse button or tap the button on a tablet device.

To add a different appearance to a button (**Figure 4.36**):

1 Select the button.

2 In the Buttons and Forms panel, click the appearance you want to add, such as Rollover.

3 To be able to change the graphic formatting of the button for this appearance, such as changing the fill color, double-click the button.

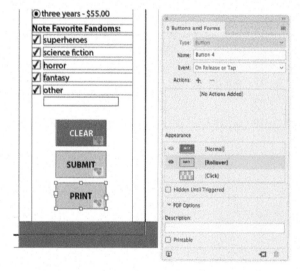

Figure 4.36 Adding an alternate appearance to a button

4 When you're finished editing the appearances of all buttons, set them all to the Normal appearance so that the form appearance in InDesign matches what you would first see in Acrobat Reader.

Numbering and Sections

An InDesign section consists of one or more ranges of pages. As you design different publications, such as magazines, books, and reports, you'll probably need to define different ranges of pages as multiple sections. For example:

- A printed magazine might have a cover that's printed on different paper from its inside pages. The cover itself might not require any page numbering; however, the first of the inside pages needs to start on page 1.

- The front matter in a book (the pages that precede the core text such as a preface or table of contents) might use Roman numerals (i, ii, iii, iv, and so on) instead of Arabic numbers (1, 2, 3, 4, and so on).

- You might want to add to a spread in a magazine a foldout page that doesn't affect the page numbering of the other pages.

The magazine foldout is one example of using a section. The magazine pages are numbered 1 through 4. With the foldout page added between pages 3 and 4, the page number of the last page increases to 5. Because you don't want the foldout to change the page numbering of the magazine, start by creating a new section for the foldout page. Then you can change the numbering style for this page (for example, to A, B, C) so that it does not clash with the Arabic numerals. Finally, you can start a new section after the foldout page to pick up where the sequential page numbering left off. Start the page numbering at page 4 and change the style back to Arabic numbers.

To start a new section and change the page numbering for that section (**Figure 4.37**):

1 In the Pages panel, double-click the page that marks the start of the section.

2 Choose Layout > Numbering & Section Options.

3 In the New Section dialog, select Start Section.

4 To adjust the page number on which that section starts, enter a number in the Start Page Numbering at field.

5 From the Style menu, select the preferred page numbering style, and click OK.

A section indicator icon (a small triangle) appears at the top of the page to indicate a section start.

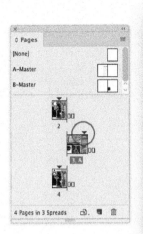

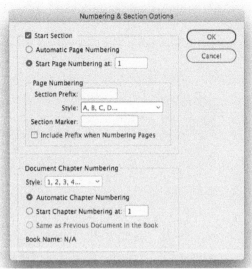

For the magazine design, you'll need to do this twice, first to set the foldout page as its own section with a non-Arabic numbering system (such as A, B, C, D), and again to set page 4 as another section that restarts Arabic page numbering at 4.

To edit the Numbering & Sections Options at any stage, do one of the following:

- Double-click the section indicator icon in the Pages panel.
- Select the page and select Numbering & Section Options from the Pages panel menu.
- Select the page and choose Layout > Numbering & Section Options.

TIP

To quickly create a section, right-click (Windows) or Control-click (macOS) a page icon in the Pages panel. Select Numbering & Section Options from the context menu.

Adding Page Transitions

Page transitions, such as a dissolve, take place when you navigate from page to page. You can apply different page transitions to each page spread in an InDesign document.

To add transitions to page spreads (**Figure 4.38**):

1 Select a spread in the Pages panel.

2 Choose Layout > Pages > Page Transitions > Choose to display the Page Transitions dialog.

3 To preview the transition, move the cursor over a thumbnail in the dialog.

★ *ACA Objective 4.7*

▶ *Video 4.20
Adding Transitions
& Exporting as
Animated PDF*

4 To apply the transition only to the selected spread(s), deselect Apply to All Spreads.

5 Select one of the transitions and click OK.

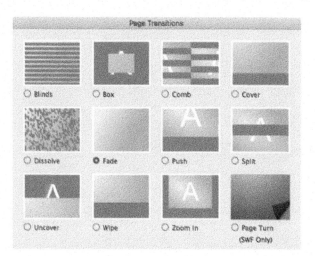

Figure 4.38 Applying a page transition to a selected spread

A small icon appears next to the spread in the Pages panel to indicate that the page has a transition applied to it. To change the transition, right-click (Windows) or Control-click (macOS) this icon and select Choose from the context menu.

To edit a transition, its duration, or the timing, do one of the following:

- Right-click (Windows) or Control-click (macOS) the transition icon in the Pages panel, and select Edit from the context menu.

- Select a page spread and choose Layout > Pages > Page Transitions > Edit.

Creating an Interactive PDF

To complete this project, there's only one more thing to do: Create a PDF so that you can test the transitions and the form elements.

To create an interactive PDF (**Figure 4.39**):

1 Choose File > Export.

2 From the Save As Type menu (Windows) or Format menu (macOS), select Adobe PDF (Interactive).

3 Enter the name for the PDF and navigate to the save location on your system.

4 Click Save. The Export to Interactive PDF dialog appears.

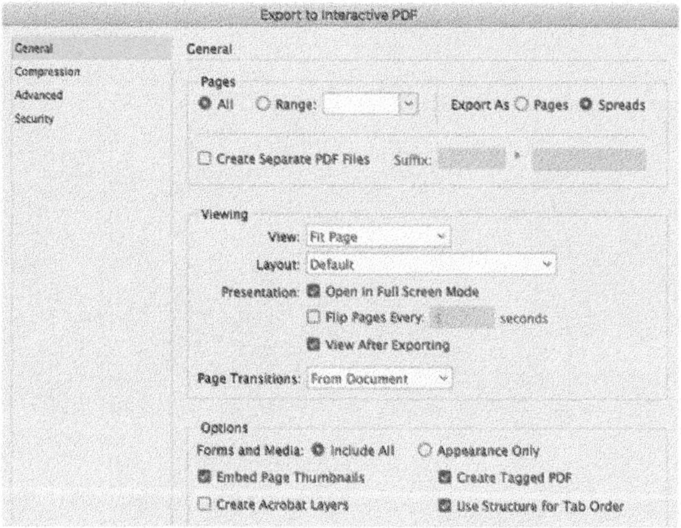

Figure 4.39 Exporting the interactive PDF

5 Ensure that the following settings are enabled:

- **View:** Select Fit Page so that the document opens to fit the size of the viewer's screen, not zoomed in or out.

- **View After Exporting:** This opens the PDF in Adobe Acrobat DC or Acrobat Reader DC so that you can test it.

- **Open In Full Screen Mode:** This enables you to view and test transitions.

- **Page Transitions:** Select From Document to retain each spread's different transition.

- **Include All:** Select Include All so that forms and media elements are working and interactive.

- **Create Tagged PDF** and **Use Structure for Tab Order:** To make the PDF more accessible for those relying on assistive technologies, enable Create Tagged PDF and Use Structure for Tab Order.

6 Click OK to save the PDF. You can now test it in Adobe Acrobat or Adobe Acrobat Reader.

To learn more about accessibility and accessible PDFs, see "Structuring PDFs" in InDesign Help (Help > InDesign Help).

Congratulations! You have just completed the magazine pages and interactive PDF project. In the next project you'll learn how to put a recipe book together, and how to speed up the production side of the design process using styles to format text, tables, and objects.

CHAPTER OBJECTIVES

Chapter Learning Objectives

- Style text with a gradient.
- Apply corner options to frames.
- Import text from other file formats.
- Format text with styles.
- Import text from other applications.
- Create and format tables.
- Create table and cell styles.
- Create a table of contents.

Chapter ACA Objectives

For full descriptions of the objectives, see the table on pages 270–276.

DOMAIN 2.0
PROJECT SETUP AND INTERFACE
2.1, 2.4, 2.5

DOMAIN 4.0
CREATING AND MODIFYING DOCUMENT ELEMENTS
4.2, 4.3, 4.4, 4.5, 4.6, 4.7, 4.8

CHAPTER 5

Styling a Recipe Book

You are becoming a seasoned InDesign user, so the project for this chapter focuses on learning to work smarter instead of harder. You will learn how to import text from other documents and quickly format it with paragraph and character styles. You'll format objects with object styles so you no longer need to write down all the settings, such as those for effects, in order to apply them to another object. Using tables, you'll format text in table format. Finally, you'll create a table of contents. All these new skills add up to make longer, more complex documents easier to build.

Setting Up the Recipe Book

InDesign allows you to create beautiful artwork, pages, and designs. By using master pages and styles, you can create beautiful designs faster and more efficiently. The theme for this chapter is to teach you skills that make the production side of design easier. You already learned a little about styles in the magazine cover project (Chapter 4), but in this chapter you'll really put them to work. With the help of styles, formatting text, tables, and objects becomes quick and easy, so you can spend more time on graphic design (**Figure 5.1**).

★ ACA Objective 2.1

▶ **Video 5.1** Introducing the Recipe Book Project

▶ **Video 5.2** Setting Up the Project File

> **NOTE**
> *This chapter supports the project created in Video Lesson 5. Go to the Project 5 page in the book's Web Edition to watch the entire lesson from beginning to end. Please refer to Appendix C, "Adjusting Master Pages," for detailed steps on the process demonstrated in Video 5.2.*

Create, set up, and save the new document the same way you have in earlier chapters, but this time use the New Document dialog settings described in Video 5.2, including setting up the master pages. Then customize the cover page as shown in Video 5.3.

Figure 5.1 Finished recipe book design

▶ **Video 5.3** Adding an Image & Creating Swatches

Deleting Unused Color Swatches

In Video 5.3, unused color swatches are removed from the document using the Delete Selected Swatch/Groups button in the Swatches panel (**Figure 5.2**).

When you delete color swatches that are applied to objects, InDesign doesn't leave those objects without any color applied. Instead, you can choose what color is applied to those objects (**Figure 5.3**):

- If you'd like objects to take on another existing swatch, select Defined Swatch and then choose a swatch from the Defined Swatch menu.

- If you'd like objects to keep their colors, choose Unnamed Swatch. This allows objects to keep the colors they're using, but without using named swatches.

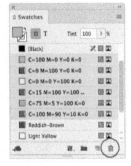

Figure 5.2 Delete Selected Swatch/Groups button

Figure 5.3 Delete Swatches dialog

The second option is better if you've selected multiple colors that are applied to objects and you don't want to apply the same color to all the objects.

Styling Text with Gradient Swatches

★ ACA Objective 2.5

▶ Video 5.4 Adding Title Text and Effects

In Chapter 2, you were introduced to gradients and working with the Gradient panel. Gradients are blends between two or more different colors or shades. For text set in larger font sizes, such as a book title, styling text with a gradient can help draw attention to it.

Earlier you applied a gradient to a frame, but you can also apply a gradient to all or some of the text in a text frame. To apply a gradient to text (**Figure 5.4**):

1 Do one of the following:

  ▪ To affect all text in the frame, use the Selection tool to click the text frame.

  ▪ To affect a range of characters, use the Type tool to select the text you want to edit.

2 Click the Fill box or the Stroke box in the Swatches panel or Control panel, and click the Formatting Affects Text icon.

3 Select the gradient swatch in the Swatches panel.

4 To adjust the gradient, open the Gradient panel and set the options as needed.

TIP

You can create a gradient from the Swatches panel menu by choosing New Gradient Swatch.

Figure 5.4 Applying a gradient fill to all the text in a text frame

When you want to apply or edit a gradient applied to text, keep the following in mind:

  ▪ Avoid applying a gradient to small body text, because that makes small text harder to read. It's best to apply gradients to large display text (headings and titles), especially those with thick character shapes.

- To edit a gradient applied to text, remember to select that text before changing gradient settings. If a gradient is applied to only some text in a frame, you'll need to select that text with the Type tool before editing the gradient settings.

- If you want to change only the angle of an applied gradient, you don't have to open the Gradient panel. Instead, drag the Gradient tool over the selected text at the angle you want. You will need to use the Gradient panel if you want to enter a specific value for the angle, such as 36 degrees.

- As with colors, when you edit a gradient applied to a selected text frame, remember to select the Formatting Affects Text icon to make sure your edit will affect the text and not the containing frame.

★ ACA Objective 4.2

Aligning Text Vertically in a Frame

▶ **Video 5.5**
*Finishing the
Front Cover*

You've already learned how to apply centered alignment to a paragraph. But how can you center text vertically in one step? You can do that using the Text Frame Options dialog.

To center text vertically in a frame (**Figure 5.5**):

1 Use the Selection tool to select a text frame.

2 Choose Object > Text Frame Options.

3 In the Vertical Justification section, select Center from the Align menu.

Figure 5.5 Vertically center text in a frame by choosing the Center option in the Text Frame Options dialog.

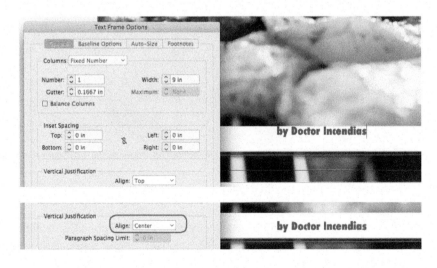

NOTE

Horizontal alignment is in the Paragraph panel because it's a paragraph attribute, whereas vertical alignment is in the Text Frame Options dialog because it's a text frame attribute.

Styling Corners

★ ACA Objective 4.4

▶ **Video 5.6** Adding Master Pages, Images, and Object Styles

Corner options enable you to change the appearance of design elements that contain sharp corners, such as rectangles, polygons, or starbursts. For instance, you can round those sharp corners, as demonstrated in the recipe book project.

Applying Corner Options

To apply corner options:

1 Select the design element with the Selection tool.

2 Choose Object > Corner Options.

3 If you want all corners to use the same settings, click the Make All Settings the Same icon (🔗) to select it. For this example from the cookbook, the icon is off because the upper-left and upper-right corners are set differently than the rest (**Figure 5.6**).

4 Enter the Corner Size amount, and select an option from the Shape menu. Select Preview to see the changes, and click OK when you're satisfied.

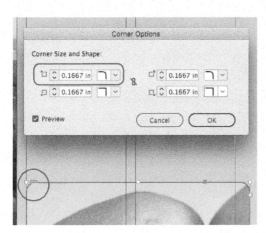

Figure 5.6 Applying rounded corners to the top corners

Working in Live Corner Mode

In the previous examples, you adjusted corner options by entering settings in the Corner Options dialog. Live Corner mode allows you to adjust the corner options with the mouse.

To edit corner options in Live Corner mode (**Figure 5.7**):

1 If necessary, choose View > Extras > Show Live Corner.

2 Using the Selection tool, select the frame. In Live Corner mode, a small yellow box appears in the upper-right corner of the frame's edge.

3 Click the yellow box, and drag the yellow diamonds inward to change the corner size.

 ▪ To change the corner radius, drag the diamond.

 ▪ To adjust an individual corner, Shift-drag the diamond.

 ▪ To change the shape of the corners, Alt-click (Windows) or Option-click (macOS) a diamond. Note that this changes all of the corners.

 ▪ To change the shape of an individual corner, Shift-Alt-click (Windows) or Shift-Option-click (macOS) a diamond.

4 Click outside the frame to exit Live Corner mode.

Figure 5.7 Editing corner shape and size in Live Corner mode

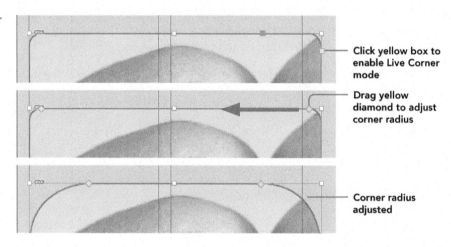

Click yellow box to enable Live Corner mode

Drag yellow diamond to adjust corner radius

Corner radius adjusted

★ ACA Objective 4.6

▶ **Video 5.7** Adding Text and Images to the Recipe Pages

▶ **Video 5.8** Using Character and Paragraph Styles to Refine the Layout

Formatting Faster with Styles

You've had some practice creating and applying paragraph and character styles, and in Video 5.6 you're introduced to object styles. By now you have hopefully noticed that in InDesign, a style is simply a way to let you apply a specific named combination of formatting settings in one click. But how do you manage and take full advantage of styles?

Deciding to Use Styles

You probably noticed that saving a combination of settings as a style takes longer than just applying those settings. That overhead of time and effort might make you ask: When is it worth using styles? The answer is that it's worth using styles when you would answer yes to at least one of the following questions:

▶ **Video 5.9**
Applying Character and Paragraph Styles

- Does a particular format involve a specific combination of many options to set? Applying a style in one click is obviously faster than locating and correctly applying several options that might be spread across multiple panels. And you don't have to remember the exact specifications for each format in your design, because a style remembers the settings completely and exactly.

- Will you apply the same formatting settings to many instances throughout the document? The longer the document, the more time styles save when you can apply one-click formatting. And when formatting needs to be updated, styles save time again, because instead of having to hunt down every instance of a specific combination of settings, you simply edit the style and every applied instance updates to match the new style definition. For example, if you created and applied a style to all the section headings in a 500-page book, it would take you just a few seconds to change the font size from 12 points to 14 points for every heading across all 500 pages, simply by editing the style you applied to the headings.

- Will the document be exported to a structured format such as CSS (such as a web or EPUB document) or XMP? Because a style tags (marks) an object or selected text, you can use styles to apply structure that can be translated to a structured document format.

If you answered yes to any of those questions, the time saved by using styles will far outweigh the time you spend setting up styles. Styles help you apply complex formatting faster, maintain design consistency and reduce formatting mistakes, and contribute to production speed and efficiency.

Understanding Style Types

This is a good time to review the different types of styles you've encountered so far, and their intended uses:

- **Paragraph styles** format text at the paragraph level, so a paragraph style always affects an entire paragraph even if you selected only one word or simply clicked an insertion point in a paragraph (**Figure 5.8**). A paragraph style applies up to the next return character or the end of a text story (whichever comes first), so a paragraph style will continue across line break characters that aren't paragraph return characters.

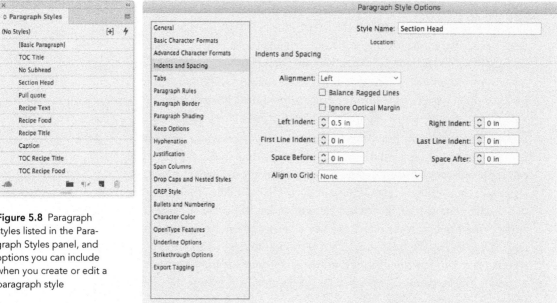

Figure 5.8 Paragraph styles listed in the Paragraph Styles panel, and options you can include when you create or edit a paragraph style

- **Character styles** format one or more characters of text (**Figure 5.9**). The main reason to use a character style is when you need to format text that's shorter than a paragraph, such as formatting important names with a blue fill color. Expect to use character styles much less often than paragraph styles, because paragraph styles can handle most general text formatting needs—such as your overall document type specifications, spacing between paragraphs, indents, and differentiating common text elements such as titles, headings, body text, page numbers, and lists.

- **Object styles** format the graphics attributes of any selected objects, such as corner options, fill and stroke options, and effects such as drop shadows. When applied to a frame, an object style can affect the frame and the content inside the frame (such as text) (**Figure 5.10**).

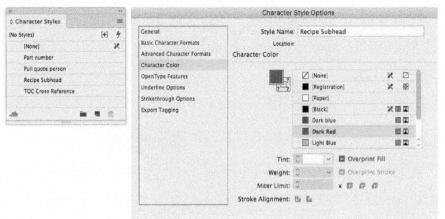

Figure 5.9 Character styles listed in the Character Styles panel, and options you can include when you create or edit a character style

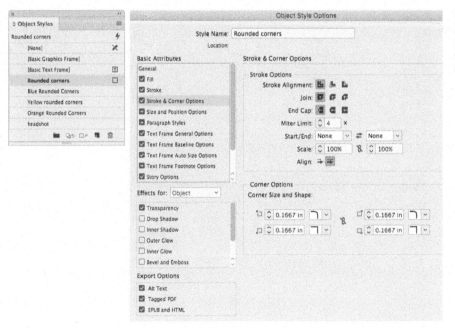

Figure 5.10 Object styles listed in the Object Styles panel, and options you can include when you create or edit an object style

- **Table styles** format the components of a table, such as the appearance of header, footer, and body rows; columns; and the border around a table (**Figure 5.11**). You will see table styles used later in this chapter.

- **Cell styles** format the graphics attributes of a selected table cell as well as the text attributes of text in the cell. You will see cell styles used later in this chapter.

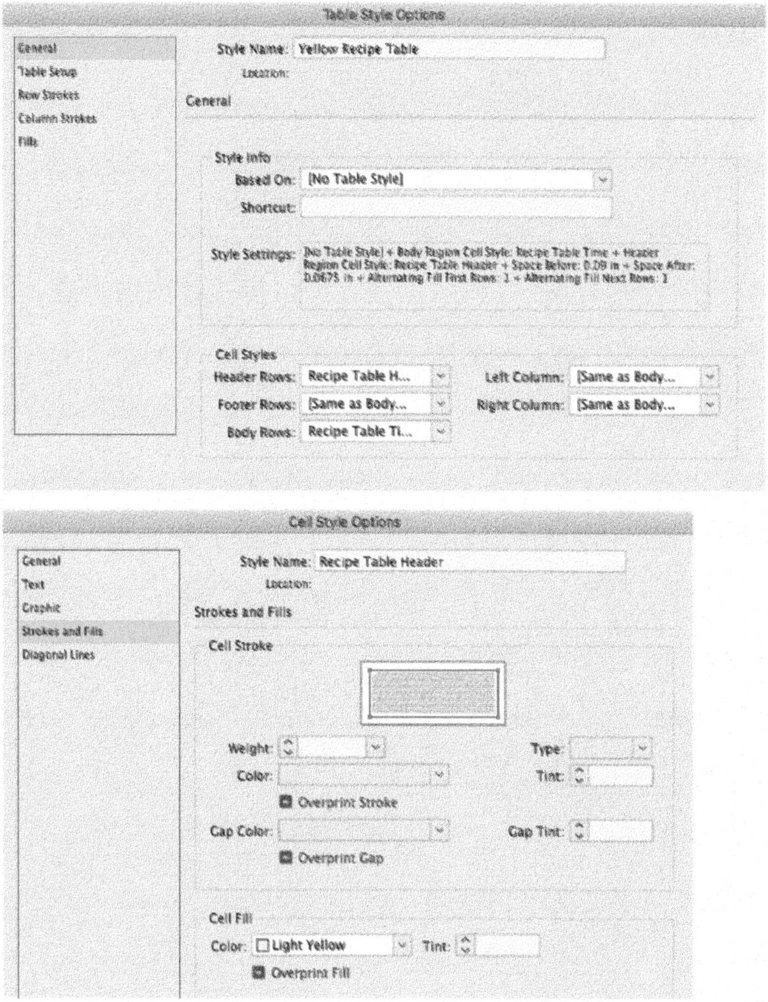

Figure 5.11 Options you can include in table styles and cell styles

Using Styles

Styles generally work the same way whether you are applying a paragraph style, a character style, an object style, or as you'll soon see, a table or cell style (**Figure 5.12**). The only differences you'll encounter are related to the natural differences among text, objects, and tables. For example, a paragraph style can include a font setting because paragraph styles are for text; an object style naturally doesn't have a font setting, but it can have a frame fitting option, because an object style can be applied to a frame.

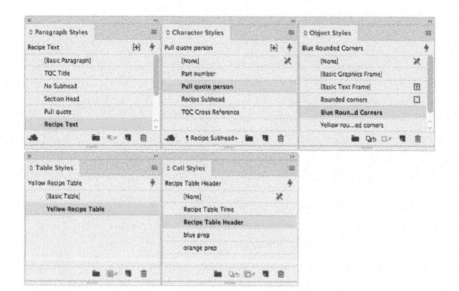

Figure 5.12 Once you learn the fundamentals of styles, you can apply that knowledge to all kinds of styles in InDesign.

TIP

If you have experience using Cascading Style Sheets (CSS) for web design, you already have a sense of how InDesign styles work. Many of the principles and concepts are similar.

CREATING A STYLE

You can create a style in two ways: Jump in and start setting options, or select something that is already formatted in the way you want and base the style on that. Because design is exploratory and iterative, chances are you'll usually create your styles the second way. After experimenting and trying out different design ideas, you'll produce a nice example that you can then use as the basis to define a style.

To create a new style based on a formatted object:

1 Select the object or text. For a paragraph, use the Type tool to click anywhere within the paragraph.

2 In the panel for the type of style you're creating, Alt-click (Windows) or Option-click (macOS) the Create New Style button at the bottom of the panel (**Figure 5.13**).

    The reason for adding the Alt or Option key is that it opens a dialog in which you can name the style and adjust its settings right away. If you don't add the Alt or Option key, a new style is added to the panel using a default name that requires an extra step to rename, and if you want to edit the style you have to then double-click its name in the panel.

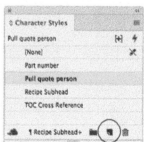

Figure 5.13 The Create New Style button in two different style panels

3 For Name, enter a descriptive name for the style.

4 Select Apply Style to Selection to ensure that the paragraph style you are creating is also applied to the object you selected in step 1. (Apply Style to Selection may not be available for all style types.)

5 Deselect Add to CC Library, and click OK.

APPLYING A STYLE

After you create a style, it's immediately available for you to start formatting design elements instantly.

To apply a style:

1 Select the object or text you want to format. For a paragraph, use the Type tool to click anywhere within the paragraph.

2 In the panel containing the style you want, click the style name in the list.

UPDATING A STYLE

Design is an iterative process, so it's natural to want to refine styles as you work on a document. It's easy to edit a style, and once you do, all of the applied instances of that style are updated right away.

To edit a style:

In the panel containing the style, double-click the style name, change the settings in the style options dialog, and click OK.

Sometimes you override a style (apply formatting that isn't part of the style definition) and you realize that the override looks better than the style. (See "Overriding a Style" later in this chapter.) Instead of having to remember what you did so that you can edit the style to match, in one step you can simply redefine the style to include the current overrides.

To redefine a style:

1 Select the text or object that contains a style override.

   In the panel for that style, the style should be selected, and the style panel should indicate the override for that style with a plus sign (+).

2 Choose Redefine Style from the panel menu (**Figure 5.14**) for that style type (such as the Paragraph Style panel menu or the Object Style panel menu).

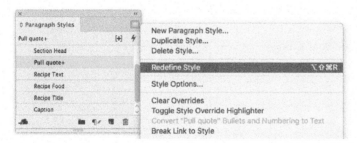

Figure 5.14
Updating a style
definition based
on an override

DELETING A STYLE

You can delete a style in the same way that you've deleted items in lists in other panels.

To delete a style:

1 In the panel containing the style, select the style and click the Delete Selected Style/Groups button, or drag the style to that button (**Figure 5.15**).

2 In the dialog that appears, select another style (or None) from the And Replace With menu. This determines how objects should be reformatted after you delete a style that was applied to them.

3 Click OK.

 TIP

To keep the current object settings when deleting an object style that is applied to design elements, choose [None] as the replacement style and select Preserve Formatting in the Delete Object Style dialog.

Figure 5.15 Delete Selected Style/Groups button

Common Style Options

Some useful style options are available to you in most or all of the style types available in InDesign.

BASING ONE STYLE ON ANOTHER

One style can be based on another to save time and reduce complexity. For example, the only difference between a body text paragraph style and a bullet list paragraph style might be the indents and the bullet character; they otherwise share all other attribute settings, such as font, size, and leading. You can define all of those attributes in the body text style, and then instead of starting from scratch to define the bullet list style, start by basing the bullet list style on the body text style using the Based On option (**Figure 5.16**). Then the only settings for you to change in the bullet list style would be the indents and the bullet character.

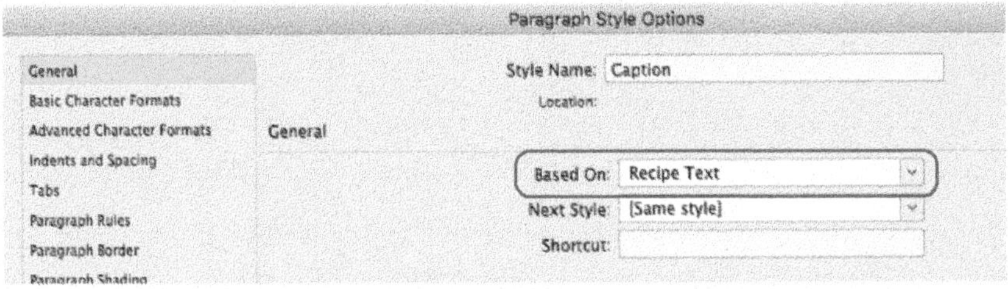

Figure 5.16 The Based On option in a Style Options dialog

Figure 5.16 The Based On option in a Style Options dialog

USING A STYLE AS PART OF ANOTHER STYLE

Some styles can be used as part of other styles. You've already seen how a character style can be used as part of a paragraph style, in the Drop Caps and Nested Styles panel in the Paragraph Styles dialog. Later in this chapter you'll work with table styles and table cell styles, and in those, a paragraph style can be used as part of a cell style definition, and a cell style can be used as part of a table style definition.

OVERRIDING A STYLE

You should be using a style for any group of formatting options that you'll use multiple times in a document. But when you want to apply a slight variation on a style and you'll use that variation only once in a document, there's usually no need to create a style for that. You can just apply the closest style and then manually apply the formatting that's different. The style panel will display a plus sign (+) next to the style name (**Figure 5.17**), showing that there's an override applied to the style.

Figure 5.17 A plus sign indicates overrides; you can remove them by selecting the Clear Overrides command or (if available) by clicking the Clear Overrides button.

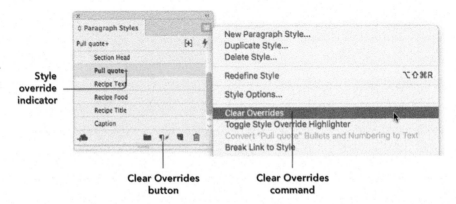

Style override indicator

Clear Overrides button

Clear Overrides command

You can remove overrides that are applied to a styled text or object to make them conform exactly to the applied style. Some style panels have a Clear Overrides button (¶✶); otherwise, there is a Clear Overrides command on the style panel menu.

GROUPING STYLES

In some list panels, such as the Swatches panel, you can organize items by grouping them. In those panels, groups appear as folder icons. You can group styles too.

To group styles:

1 In a style panel, click the Create New Style Group button (**Figure 5.18**), or choose Create New Style Group from the panel menu.

2 Drag any style names from the list and drop them into the new style group.

3 Double-click the style group name, edit the name, and then press Enter or Return.

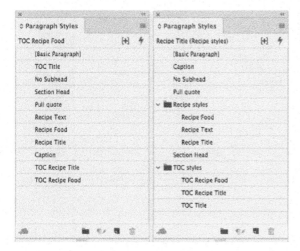

Figure 5.18 Before and after using groups to organize a long list of styles

TIP

Here's a shortcut for clearing overrides: With the object or text with the overrides selected, Alt-click (Windows) or Option-click (macOS) a style name. You'll see the plus sign disappear from the style name in its panel.

TIP

To name a style group when you create it, Alt-click (Windows) or Option-click (macOS) the Create New Style Group button.

Controlling How Object Styles Affect Existing Formatting

In the Object Style Options dialog, each option has next to it a check box (**Figure 5.19**) that controls whether that formatting attribute will alter the selected object when you apply the style:

- A check mark means the attribute will be applied to the object using the settings in the style. For example, if you apply an object style where the fill color is set to blue and it's checked, when you apply the style to objects their fill color will always be set to blue whether they have a fill or not.

- A dash means that the existing object settings for that attribute will be left unchanged. For example, if you apply the style example above to a rectangle that already has a fill, the style will not change the existing fill setting.

- An empty box means the attribute settings will be removed from the object (such as setting Drop Shadow to None).

To change how an attribute will apply, click the check box to cycle it through the check mark, dash, and empty box states.

Figure 5.19 Check boxes next to style attribute names control whether an object's existing attributes will be changed by the style.

TIP

To quickly toggle between ignoring all basic attributes except one and selecting all basic attributes except one, Alt-click (Windows) or Option-click (macOS) the selection box.

Nesting Text Styles

Sometimes a paragraph isn't just a simple block of text; it may have differently formatted parts. For example, the first sentence of each paragraph might need to be bold. It would be a lot of work to manually format the different parts of a paragraph, but fortunately you don't have to do that because InDesign provides **nested styles**. A nested style lets you apply different character styles to multiple parts of a paragraph; it's called a nested style because character styles are nested within the definition of a paragraph style.

For example, in the cookbook, each recipe starts with a heading in which the first part of the paragraph is formatted differently from the rest. How does InDesign know where to change the styles? You can tell InDesign which character should mark the end of the first character style. In the recipe heading, the style ends at the colon character (:). Of course, this works only if you use that character consistently in paragraphs in which that style is applied. The recipe headings do that, so their nested style works.

You can use a nested style to create the recipe heading on page 3 of the cookbook (**Figure 5.20**), which is shown in Video 5.8.

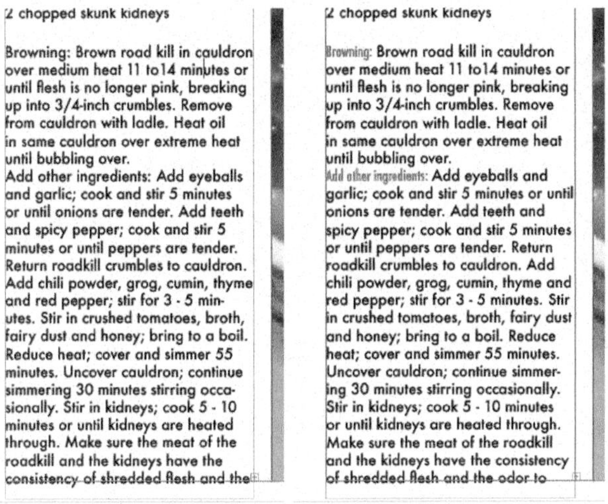

Figure 5.20 Before and after creating a nested style

To create a nested style for the recipe heading:

1   Double-click the Recipe Text style in the Paragraph Styles panel. The Paragraph Style Options dialog opens (**Figure 5.21**).

2   Select the Drop Caps and Nested Styles pane.

3   Select Preview to see the changes you make in your document.

4   Click New Nested Style under Nested Styles.

5   Select Recipe Subhead from the character style menu.

6   Select Through to ensure that the character style applies to the colon character as well.

Note that if you select Up To, the character style would stop just before the colon character.

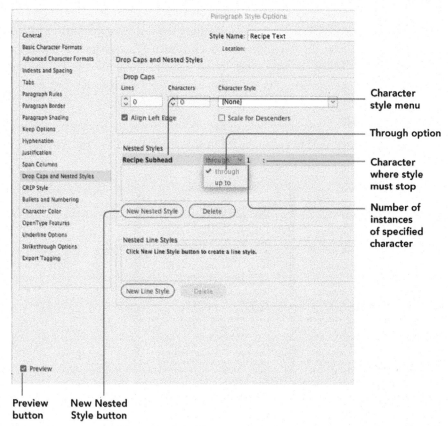

Figure 5.21 Creating a nested style that automatically applies the Recipe Subhead character style to the run-in head

Character style menu

Through option

Character where style must stop

Number of instances of specified character

Preview button

New Nested Style button

7   Leave the number of instances to encounter set to 1, as you want to apply the character style only through the first colon in the text.

The menu at the end defines the item that controls when to stop applying the character style. There is a long list of predefined items; however, the colon character isn't listed.

8   Instead of selecting from the menu, click where it says *Words*, and type a colon character.

9   Click OK to close the Paragraph Style Options dialog.

Congratulations! You have just created your first nested style. Figure 5.20 shows how the nested style would work in a paragraph that starts with a different number of words that end in a colon; feel free to experiment with different combinations of nested style settings and paragraph wording. You can see how flexible and powerful nested styles can be.

Adding Text from Other Applications ★ ACA Objective 2.4

▶ **Video 5.7** Adding Text and Images to the Recipe Pages

You've typed text into newly created text frames in InDesign, added placeholder text, and copied and pasted text. But the most common workflow for text is similar to how you've already worked with graphics: Receive the text for your design projects as documents in common text- and word-processing document formats, and then use the Place command to import them into your InDesign document. This workflow provides the most flexibility in production. Clients and writers can format text in a word processor, and InDesign can preserve the formatting, reducing the amount of formatting you have to do in InDesign. The Place command also provides advanced options that let you customize how formatted text imports into InDesign, especially when formats in the text document aren't consistent with the formats in the InDesign document.

Supported Text Formats

Text can be typed into InDesign or imported from a range of native text-editing applications, such as Microsoft Word. Additionally, text can be imported from TXT and RTF file formats.

The most commonly used file formats for text import are:

- **Microsoft Word (DOCX, DOC):** You can use the style formatting provided in the Word document, map it to InDesign styles, or remove any style formatting during import.

- **Rich Text Format (RTF):** An alternative export format supported by most text-editing programs, RTF retains style formatting, such as headings. When your client works with an unsupported text-editing application, you can ask them to export the text from their application as RTF.

- **Text Only or Plain Text (TXT):** This file format strips out all the styles applied to the text. As with RTF, this is an export format a client could use if they are unable to supply DOCX.

- **Microsoft Excel (XLSX, XLS):** Excel spreadsheets contain mostly numerical data. For example, the financials in an annual report might be supplied as an XLSX file. This text may be imported as tabbed text or in table format.

Importing Text and Tables

You might remember that when you were importing graphics, you could either create a frame first and place the graphic into it or choose the Place command first and then drag to define the size of the frame into which the graphic would be imported. It works the same way when importing text. You have already seen how to import text into an existing frame, so let's quickly review that for comparison.

To import text into an existing placeholder text frame:

1 Select the text frame.

2 Choose File > Place, and navigate to the location of the text file.

3 Select the file, and then click Open. The text flows into the selected frame.

To import text and create a text frame on the fly:

1 With no object selected, choose File > Place and navigate to the location of the text file.

2 Select the file, and then click Open.

3 With the loaded Place icon (▐), drag on the page to create the text frame and insert the text (**Figure 5.22**).

Figure 5.22 Creating a frame while placing a text file

TIP

To insert imported text into an existing text story, use the Type tool to click an insertion point in the story, and then choose the Place command.

Customizing Imported Word or RTF Files

Because RTF, DOCX, and DOC files can contain style information such as header styles, you might want to adjust how you import these files into your InDesign document. In some cases, you might opt to strip out any formatting your client has applied. In other cases, it might speed up the text formatting process to import text with formatting.

ENTERING TEXT FASTER WITH PRIMARY TEXT FRAMES

You've seen that text frames on master pages are useful because they save you from having to re-create a layout every time you add a page. But what's inconvenient is that, on a document page, you can't type in a master text frame until you first override (release) that text frame from the master page. If your document is long, constantly releasing master text frames can be tedious.

A primary text frame is like a master page text frame you don't have to release first. You simply click within the primary text frame on a document page and start typing, like you would in a word processing application. And if your text reaches the end of the frame and becomes overset, InDesign automatically adds another page and continues your text in a primary text frame on that page, threaded to the previous frame. You don't have to keep releasing frames or creating new pages; all you have to do is keep typing! In this way, a primary text frame can make it easier and faster to enter large amounts of text when the document has one main story, such as in a novel or an annual report.

You can have one primary text frame on each master. Remember the Primary Text Frame option in the New Document dialog? That automatically creates one primary text frame within the margins of each master. On a master page, you can also convert any text frame to a primary text frame by clicking the primary text frame indicator (**Figure 5.23**).

Primary text frames aren't used in the lesson files, because the sample documents have many different short stories in varied layouts. An appropriate use for primary text frames is formatting a novel, where the pages are dominated by one long text story across many pages that have a largely uniform layout.

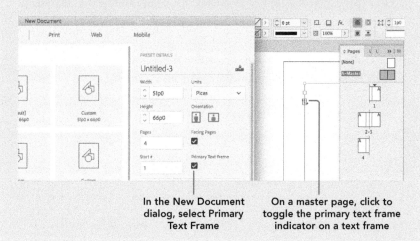

In the New Document dialog, select Primary Text Frame

On a master page, click to toggle the primary text frame indicator on a text frame

Figure 5.23 Two ways to make a primary text frame

To change the import options when placing text files:

1 Choose File > Place.

2 Select Show Import Options at the bottom of the Place dialog (**Figure 5.24**).

Figure 5.24 The Show
Import Options check box

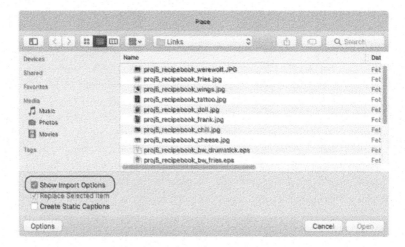

3 Navigate to the text file, select it, and click Open.

4 In the Import Options dialog (**Figure 5.25**), enter the settings to apply when importing the text. The Import Options dialogs for Rich Text and Microsoft Word files are similar.

- Select the Remove Styles and Formatting from Text and Tables option to clear any formatting applied in the text file before adding it to InDesign. This means you are in total control of the formatting once the text is added to your design.

- Select the Preserve Styles and Formatting from Text and Tables option to bring in all the formatting, including any inline graphics. This will add color swatches to the Swatches panel, as well as styles to the Paragraph Styles and Character Styles panels.

5 Click OK to add the text to the document.

TIP

You can place Microsoft Excel documents, which makes it easy to import tables and spreadsheets. When you select an Excel document in the Place dialog, make sure Show Import Options is selected so that you can control how the data imports. For example, InDesign can place an Excel spreadsheet as a table or as tab-delimited text.

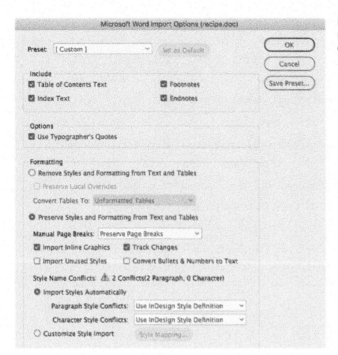

Figure 5.25 The Microsoft Word Import Options dialog

Using Tables

Tables provide an easy way to format content in a tabular or grid format, such as a restaurant menu, a bus schedule, and sports statistics. While many tables are text, you can also add graphics to table cells.

Some facts about tables:

- Tables consists of rows, columns, and cells (**Figure 5.26**).

- A table header row is the top row of the table, and it typically contains column titles; most tables use this.

- A table footer row is the bottom row of a table; not all tables use this.

★ *ACA Objective 4.8*

▶ **Video 5.10** *Adding and Styling a Table*

▶ **Video 5.11** *Guided Page Layout*

Recipe	Prep time	Ready in
Road Kill and Kidney Chili	15 Minutes	1 Hr 45 Min
Spicy Taco Cheeseballs	20 minutes	2 weeks
Twice Fried French Fries	15 Minutes	1 Hr 45 Min
Butter Beer Fudge Brownies	40 minutes	1 Hr 10 Min

Figure 5.26 A table with a header row, four body rows, and three columns

- Header and footer rows are generally formatted differently from the rest of the table (body rows). Additionally, they repeat themselves when a table is long and breaks across multiple text frames, columns, or pages.

- Tables are not standalone objects. Tables always appear inline with text, either as part of a story or in a standalone text frame.

- You edit tables using the Type tool.

You can add tables to your designs in various ways, which are covered in this section:

- Import Excel spreadsheets, or Word documents containing tables.

- Create a new table at a text insertion point in a story.

- Create a table in a new standalone text frame.

- Convert text to tables, based on a delimiter character for columns and rows, such as a tab character or an end of paragraph marker.

Creating Tables

★ ACA Objective 4.4

▶ **Video 5.8** *Using Character and Paragraph Styles to Refine the Layout*

Creating a table from scratch works best if you are going to enter (type) all the data in yourself. To create a new inline table:

1 Using the Type tool (**T**), click to set the insertion point for the table. You will usually want to click at the beginning of an empty paragraph.

2 Choose Table > Insert Table.

3 In the Insert Table dialog, enter the initial number of Body Rows and Columns you want in the table (**Figure 5.27**).

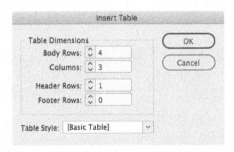

Figure 5.27 Setting up the Table Options dialog

4 If you want Header or Footer Rows, enter the number of rows as well. Click OK.

5 Click in any table cell with the Type tool to set the insertion point and enter the text for that cell. Repeat this process for each cell.

TIP

Instead of clicking in each cell with the Type tool to set the text insertion point, press the Tab key to move the insertion point to the next cell in the table. Press Shift-Tab to navigate to the previous cell.

TIP

To more easily see where you insert the table, ensure you view the document in Normal screen mode and choose Type > Show Hidden Characters.

To add a new table in a separate text frame:

1   Choose Edit > Deselect All to make sure nothing is selected on the page.

2   Choose Table > Create Table.

3   In the Create Table dialog, enter the initial number of Body Rows and Columns you want in the table.

4   If you want Header or Footer Rows, enter the number of rows as well. Click OK.

5   The table settings are loaded into the pointer (⌸). Drag to set the size of the text frame that will contain the table, as you would when creating a text frame on the fly (see "Importing Text and Tables" earlier in this chapter). When you release the mouse, the text frame fills with the number of rows and columns specified in step 3.

Adjusting Column Widths and Row Heights

You can change the width of the table columns.

To adjust the width of a column numerically:

1   Using the Type tool, click the top edge of a column to select the column.

2   To show the Table panel, choose Window > Type & Tables > Table.

3   In the Table panel, enter a value in the Column Width field (**Figure 5.28**). You can also set the column width in the Control panel.

TIP

To change the width of just the two columns on either side of a column divider, Shift-drag the divider.

Recipe	Prep time	Ready in
Road Kill and Kidney Chili	15 Minutes	1 Hr 45 Min
Spicy Taco Cheeseballs	20 minutes	2 weeks
Twice Fried French Fries	15 Minutes	1 Hr 45 Min
Butter Beer Fudge Brownies	40 minutes	1 Hr 10 Min

Figure 5.28 Selecting a column and changing the column width

TIP

You can also select a range of cells, such as a column, columns, or rows, by clicking in one cell with the Type tool and then dragging across the cell ranges you want to select.

To adjust the width of a column with the mouse:

Position the pointer over the right edge of a column. When a double arrow appears, drag left or right. The overall table width increases or decreases as you adjust the column width.

To make multiple contiguous columns the same width:

1 Using the Type tool, click the top edge of the first column to select the column.

2 Shift-click the top of the last column of the range of columns to select.

3 Choose Table > Distribute Columns Evenly (**Figure 5.29**). You can also right-click (Windows) or Control-click (macOS) the selected columns and select Distribute Columns Evenly from the context menu that appears.

> **TIP**
>
> *Another way to set the same column width for multiple columns is to select a range of columns and enter the column width amount. Each selected column will take on the width value entered.*

Figure 5.29 Distributing columns evenly

> **TIP**
>
> *To set the same row height for multiple rows, select a range of rows by clicking the left edge of the first row and then Shift-clicking the last row. In the Table panel or Control panel, enter a new Row Height value.*

> **TIP**
>
> *To see the hidden overset text in a cell, choose Edit > Edit in Story Editor.*

To change the height of a row, use the same techniques as those for changing the width of a column, but in the following ways:

- Select a row by clicking the left edge.

- In the Table panel or Control panel, enter a Row Height value.

- When adjusting row height with the Type tool, drag the top edge of a row.

Editing and Formatting a Table

★ *ACA Objective 4.8*

You can enhance the design of tables by applying settings such as fill and stroke color, borders, and various types of spacing and alignment to rows, columns, and individual table cells. When you first work with tables, the number of options can seem overwhelming, and they're in several panels and dialogs. Follow these guidelines to understand where to edit different aspects of a table:

- If the table options you want are not active, use the Type tool to click in the table or select the cells, rows, or columns you want to edit.

- Commands for selecting table elements are on the Table > Select submenu. These commands provide a quick and easy way to select a cell, a row, a column, or an entire table. If you like using keyboard shortcuts, it's useful to learn the shortcuts on the Table > Select submenu.

- Commands for editing tables are in the Table menu, in the panel menu of the Table panel, and in the context menu that appears when you use the Type tool to right-click (Windows) or Control-click (macOS) a table.

- The Table panel and the Control panel display table options when a table or table element is selected.

- If you can't find the way to format a specific part of the table, look in both the Table > Table Options submenu and the Table > Cell Options submenu.

- If you have text that you'd like to format as a table and it contains rows of items separated by a delimiter character (such as a comma or tab), you can easily convert it to a table. Select the text and choose Table > Convert Text to Table.

- You can create table styles and cell styles, which speed table production the way you have seen styles accelerate other work in InDesign. You'll find the Table Styles panel and the Cell Styles panel on the same Window > Styles submenu as the Paragraph Styles, Character Styles, and Objects Styles panels, because they work the same way (see "Formatting Faster with Styles" earlier in this chapter). Because tables generally contain mostly text, you can include paragraph styles in the style definitions for cell styles. For example, in the cookbook, the Recipe Table Header cell style uses the Recipe Text paragraph style to format cell text (**Figure 5.30**).

TIP

With the insertion point in a cell, press the Esc key to toggle between selecting that table cell and the text in the cell.

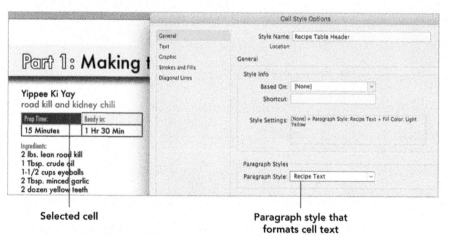

Selected cell

Paragraph style that formats cell text

Figure 5.30 How paragraph styles are used in a cell style

Using the Content Conveyor

★ *ACA Objective 4.4*

As a design-intensive document becomes longer, you might need to start reusing elements such as logos, standard graphics, and pre-styled blocks of text. The traditional way to reuse elements is by using the Edit > Copy and Edit > Paste commands in most applications, which moves a selection into and out of the Clipboard, respectively. However, copying and pasting can be tedious, and it's limited because you can transfer only one selection at a time.

The Content Conveyor is like a supercharged version of the Clipboard. You can move text and graphics items onto it, you can keep multiple items on it, and you can choose which items to drop into a different page or document.

Although the Clipboard is useful for a single transfer of content, the Content Conveyor really comes into its own when you have to move a lot of stuff to other pages or documents. For example, say you completed a catalog for a line of men's clothing and you now want to create the catalog for the same company's women's clothing, reusing a large number of the company's seasonal graphics that you used in the first document. You can use the Content Conveyor to select and load just the items you need from the first document, and then switch to the second document and drop off those items on their new pages.

To add page items to the Content Conveyor:

1 Select the Content Collector tool (📷). The Content Conveyor appears (**Figure 5.31**).

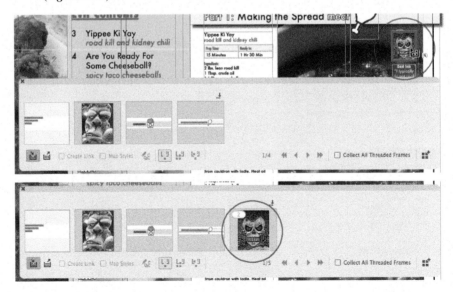

Figure 5.31 Clicking an object with the Content Collector tool adds it to the Content Conveyor.

2   With the Content Collector tool, click each object you want to add to the conveyor.

Note that if you want to add an object that's inside a group or frame, its containing group or frame will be added; you may want to remove the object from the group or frame.

To transfer items from the Content Conveyor to a page:

1   In the Content Conveyor, click the Content Placer button (![icon]) (**Figure 5.32**).

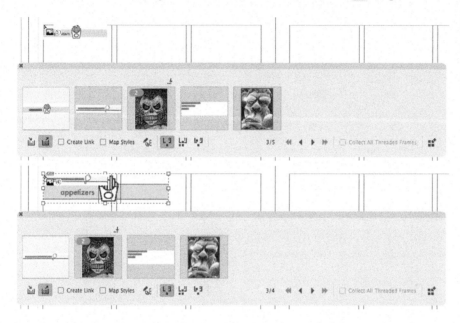

Different options are enabled in the Content Conveyor as it's switched to a mode for adding items to a layout. The pointer changes to a loaded Place icon containing the items on the Content Conveyor; it will work the same way as if you had selected multiple files on disk to place.

2   Go to a page that needs the items on the Content Conveyor; the page can be in a different document.

3   If the item loaded in the Place icon isn't the one you want to add to the layout, click the Previous or Next button in the Content Conveyor to switch to another item. You can also press the left arrow or right arrow key.

4   Position the pointer at the upper-left corner of the area on the layout where you would like to add the current item, and then click or drag to place the item on the layout.

When you use the Content Placer tool, the Content Conveyor provides three buttons (**Figure 5.33**) that change how the Content Placer works. For example, use the first button if you want to place each item only once (because it will remove items from the Conveyor as you place them), the second button if you want to place multiple instances of each item, and the third button if you want to be able to place any item at any time.

Figure 5.33 Content Placer options

NOTE

The Content Conveyor appears only when the Content Collector tool is selected, so the Content Conveyor isn't listed as a panel on the Window menu.

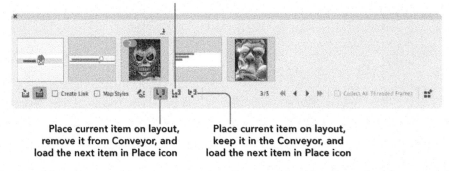

Place current item on layout, keep it in the Conveyor, and load the next item in Place icon

Place current item on layout, remove it from Conveyor, and load the next item in Place icon

Place current item on layout, keep it in the Conveyor, and load the next item in Place icon

The Content Collector has additional advanced features that aren't covered in this book, but you typically won't need them unless you maintain different versions of a document linked to the same content.

★ *ACA Objective 4.1*

▶ *Video 5.12*
Designing Page 5 on Your Own

Designing Page 5 On Your Own

Page 5 of the recipe book is a page you can design any way you want. Realistically, though, if you were given an assignment to create a page for a publication with an existing set of styles and design guidelines, like the recipe book, your job would actually be to create a new page design that's still visually consistent with the rest of the document. Draw your inspiration in part from the pages that are already designed, and put your own spin on it.

Video 5.12 mentions several features and tips you haven't seen yet, such as:

- **The Gap tool** helps you adjust the spaces between objects in your layout. Position the Gap tool over any empty areas—between objects, or between an object and the page edge. Drag to adjust the size of the gap (**Figure 5.34**). To reposition the two objects defining a gap, Alt-drag (Windows) or Option-drag (macOS) the Gap tool. To change the size of the gap, Control-drag (Windows) or Command-drag (macOS) the Gap tool.

- **Placing multiple images.** You can select multiple image files in the Place dialog. When you click Open, all selected images are loaded into the Place icon (**Figure 5.35**), and each time you click or drag you'll place one of those images on the layout, which is similar to how the Content Placer works. Press the left arrow or right arrow key to choose which image to place, or press Esc to unload an image without placing it. If you press Esc again until no more images are loaded in the Place icon, InDesign returns you to the tool you were using before you chose the Place command.

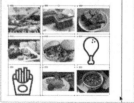

Figure 5.35 Nine graphics files were selected in the Place dialog, so they're loaded one by one into the Place icon to add to the layout.

- **Gridify.** You can interactively create a grid of rectangle frames by pressing the arrow keys as you drag the Rectangle Frame tool (**Figure 5.36**), the Rectangle tool, or a Place icon loaded with multiple graphics. The up arrow and down arrow keys control the number of rows in the grid, and the left arrow and right arrow keys control the number of columns in the grid.

TIP

If you drag multiple images from the desktop or another application and drop them in the InDesign document window, they'll be loaded into the Place icon as if you had used the Place command to select those images.

Figure 5.36 When multiple graphics files are loaded in the Place icon, press arrow keys to create a grid of them.

Creating a Table of Contents

A table of contents (TOC) is generally part of the front matter of a publication. Tables of contents most commonly list the different headings used throughout a publication—for example, the recipe titles and subtitles, or the chapter titles and the subheadings used within those chapters. As an exercise, find a book that has a table of contents in it, maybe even the one you are reading right now. Can you see a relationship between the table of contents text and the headings used throughout the book?

The key to building a table of contents is to use paragraph styles for any heading or other text you want to include in the TOC. For example, if you have styles called Heading 1 and Heading 2 and apply them to those heading levels in your document, you can tell InDesign to include those two styles in the TOC. The resulting table of contents will be a hierarchical list of paragraphs tagged with the Heading 1 and Heading 2 styles.

You'll also use paragraph styles to format the resulting TOC. Typically, you design a set of styles that control how the TOC text appears. These two uses of styles in a TOC can be a little confusing, so let's clarify: You'll select one set of paragraph styles that tells the Table of Contents feature which paragraphs to include, and you'll select another set of paragraph styles to format the text generated for the table of contents (**Figure 5.37**).

Figure 5.37 A table of contents automatically generated from document styles

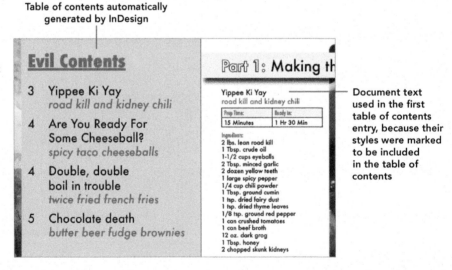

Table of contents automatically generated by InDesign

Document text used in the first table of contents entry, because their styles were marked to be included in the table of contents

Before you define a table of contents:

- Consistently apply paragraph styles to the text in your design project, especially titles and headings, because the table of contents relies on this formatting to create it.

- Create a dummy layout for the table of contents design.

- Create paragraph styles for the title of the table of contents as well as for the different levels.

- Determine which text from your document must be included in the table of contents, and check which paragraph styles are applied to that text. Jot down the style names, as well as the level of importance they have. For example, for a recipe book, you might consider the different types of recipes—such as appetizers, entrees, or desserts—as the top level (Level 1) in the table of contents, and under each of these you could list the names of the different recipes (Level 2).

- Record which paragraph styles are used to format text from your document that must appear in the TOC. These are the styles you will include in your TOC style.

Defining the Table of Contents Style

Once you've created the styles to format the table of contents text and determined which text needs to be added to it, you are ready to define the table of contents style. The table of contents style determines the included text, the hierarchy, and the formatting of the final table of contents.

To define a table of contents style:

1 Choose Layout > Table of Contents Styles.

2 Click New. The New Table of Contents Style dialog opens.

3 Click More Options to expand the dialog (**Figure 5.38**).

4 Enter a descriptive name for the table of contents style in the TOC Style field.

5 Type the title that will appear at the top of the table of contents (such as "Contents") in the Title field, and select a paragraph style from the Style menu to format the text. If the list doesn't already contain a style that will work for the TOC title, choose New Paragraph Style from the list to define a new paragraph style.

   You are now ready to add some of the styles used in your project to the Include Paragraph Styles list under Styles in Table of Contents.

Figure 5.38 New Table of
Contents Style dialog

Name of style for table of
contents title (appears in
Paragraph Styles panel)

Paragraph style used to
format the TOC title

Title of the table of
contents (appears
in generated TOC)

Styles of text to
include in the TOC
(select in right column,
then click Add)

Options for the paragraph
style selected in the left
column of the Styles in
Table of Contents section

Style that formats the text
of the selected paragraph
style, as it will appear in
the table of contents

Options for the
entire table of
contents

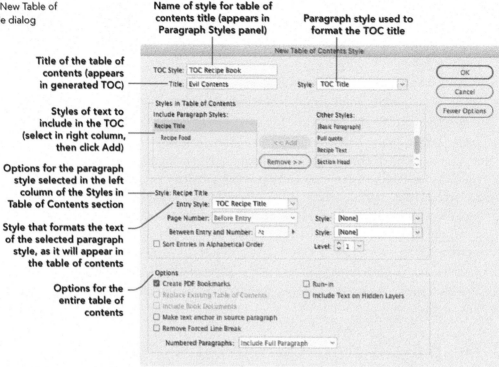

6 Under Other Styles, select a style you want to include in the TOC, and click Add. Repeat this step for each style that needs to be added. The styles will appear under Include Paragraph Styles.

With all the styles added, you can now set the formatting and levels for each of the included paragraph styles.

7 Select the style in the Include Paragraph Styles list, and select the hierarchy from the Level menu.

The level determines the order of the text in the table of contents. Level 1 is the top level, and Level 2 styles follow the Level 1 text.

8 From the Entry Style menu, select the paragraph style that formats the text in the table of contents.

9 From the Page Number menu, customize the page numbers to be used with each entry. Use the Between Entry and Number field and the Style menus to further customize the placement and look of the page numbers.

10 Repeat steps 7–9 for each style in the Include Paragraph Styles list.

11 Select Create PDF Bookmarks to automatically create navigation bookmarks that appear in Adobe Acrobat Reader's Bookmarks pane.

12 Click OK, and then click OK again.

Flowing the Table of Contents Text

With the table of contents style defined, you are now ready to add the table of contents text to the contents page in your project.

To add a table of contents to your document:

1 Choose Layout > Table of Contents.

2 Select your table of contents style from the TOC Style menu.

3 Click OK.

4 Click or drag with the loaded text icon to create a text frame filled with the table of contents text (**Figure 5.39**), or click an empty placeholder frame set aside earlier to contain the table of contents.

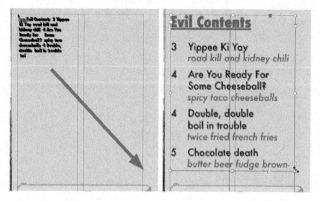

Figure 5.39 Adding the automatically generated table of contents text to the document

Updating a Table of Contents

As you make changes to your InDesign documents, remember that the table of contents you might have generated earlier does not update automatically. Headings that are included in the table of contents may have changed as part of client change requests, or they may appear on different pages after additional text inserts or cuts.

To update a table of contents:

1 Using the Type tool, click to place the text insertion point anywhere inside table of contents text.

2 Choose Layout > Update Table of Contents.

TIP

To ensure that the table of contents text is the latest and greatest, update the table of contents before you convert an InDesign file to PDF or package it for the printer.

CHAPTER OBJECTIVES

Chapter Learning Objectives

- Set up a new document for digital media.
- Use Creative Cloud libraries.
- Create object animations.
- Control the timing for animations.
- Animate along a motion path.
- Check spelling.
- Find and change content.
- Add video and audio.
- Build an image slide show.
- Set up control buttons to play interactive elements.
- Insert HTML to include an online map.
- Export a digital media project.

Chapter ACA Objectives

For full descriptions of the objectives, see the table on pages 270–276.

DOMAIN 2.0
UNDERSTANDING PRINT AND DIGITAL MEDIA PUBLICATIONS
2.1, 2.4

DOMAIN 3.0
ORGANIZING DOCUMENTS
3.1, 3.2

DOMAIN 4.0
CREATING AND MODIFYING DOCUMENT ELEMENTS
4.5, 4.7

DOMAIN 5.0
PUBLISHING DOCUMENTS
5.1, 5.2

CHAPTER 6

Creating an Interactive Digital Media Publication

In your final project, you'll learn to create an engaging and interactive digital media publication that you can publish in EPUB and other digital media formats (**Figure 6.1**). It represents an online application form for convention volunteers. You'll add animations that move along motion paths on your pages, create an interactive slide show of images, learn to embed audio and video into your documents, and even add an interactive Google Map. To conclude, you'll investigate exporting and publishing your publication to a number of interactive formats, such as a fixed-layout EPUB and an online document.

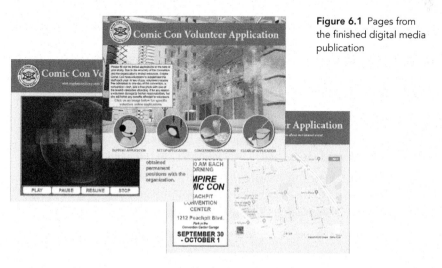

Figure 6.1 Pages from the finished digital media publication

Types of Digital Media

When you design a digital media document using Adobe InDesign CC, the final product can take many forms. Before you take on a digital media project, be clear about the final digital medium you're designing for. As with print, many critical decisions that affect the format and quality of the document depend on the exact specifications of the final medium.

Interactive PDF

Interactive PDF files support buttons, form elements, and page transitions, as well as media files such as video and audio. Hyperlinks, cross-references, table of contents entries, and index items all become clickable links when viewing the PDF in Adobe Acrobat or Adobe Acrobat Reader. Animations and multistate objects are not supported in PDF.

For quick access to all the interactive panels that work with interactive PDF, choose Window > Workspace > Interactive for PDF.

EPUBs

You can create two types of EPUBs from InDesign: reflowable EPUB and fixed-layout EPUB. EPUB files are designed for display on an e-reader, such as Kindle or Nook; in e-reader software that runs on your mobile devices, such as iBooks (macOS, iOS) or Google Play (Android); or with an extension for the Chrome web browser, such as Readium.

Reflowable EPUBs are well suited for text-heavy publications such as novels and nonfiction books. Reflowable means that the text and images flow to the width of the e-reader screen, a bit like web pages do when you make the browser window wider or narrower. When you increase the font size in the e-reader, the text automatically reflows as well. The layout from InDesign is not maintained, and the text and images from your InDesign project appear in a linear format.

Fixed-layout EPUBs retain the layout you create in InDesign, and they support animations, media files (audio and video), embedded HTML, and a number of button actions, such as play (for videos) and navigation (for slide shows). Fixed-layout EPUBs work well for illustrated publications that rely on engaging graphic design, such as comic books, children's books, cookbooks, or photography books.

Hyperlinks, cross-references, tables of contents, and indexes all become clickable links in fixed-layout and reflowable EPUBs.

Publish Online

By now, you'll have noticed the Publish Online button at the top of the application bar. This button allows you to publish your design projects to the web. Publish Online is a simple and immediate way to publish an interactive document. It's particularly useful when you don't have a distribution method set up for an EPUB or PDF file. The publication is hosted on an Adobe server. With Publish Online, your online designs will be available through a web address that is automatically generated, and you can even share your publications via social media—such as Facebook or Twitter—and email.

Your designs automatically convert to HTML5, the markup language used for web development; CSS3, which controls the styling and positioning of all the objects in your designs; and JavaScript, which provides some of the interactive control.

Publish Online supports many InDesign interactive features found in the Digital Publishing workspace, such as animations, audio, video, slide shows with navigation buttons, interactive tables of contents, hyperlinks, cross-references, indexes, and more.

Adobe Experience Manager

You can use InDesign to create interactive content for Adobe Experience Manager (AEM). AEM is a content management system that lets enterprises more easily and efficiently manage mobile apps and the content distributed through them. AEM integrates with Adobe services such as Adobe Marketing Cloud, which includes mobile marketing (such as in-app messages) and powerful mobile analytics to better understand user usage patterns.

You probably won't encounter AEM projects as a student or if you work with small business clients. You might work on them if you become employed by a company that has an AEM contract.

Setting Up for Digital Media

★ *ACA Objective 2.1*

 *Video 6.1*
Introducing the
Interactive Digital
Media Project

A document intended for digital media needs to be set up differently than a print document. You have used the New Document dialog to set up the print documents you've created so far, and with just a few different settings you can easily use the same dialog to set up a document for digital media.

▶ **Video 6.2** *Setting Up the EPUB Document*

To set up the online application form document:

1 Start a new document using any of the methods you have learned.

2 At the top of the New Document dialog, select the Mobile intent.

3 In the Blank Document Presets menu, click View All Presets to expand the list, and select the iPad preset.

4 Make sure the Orientation icon is set to landscape (wide), and click OK.

   The new document is created.

NOTE

This chapter supports the project created in Video Lesson 6. Go to the Project 6 page in the book's Web Edition to watch the entire lesson from beginning to end.

5 Choose the Digital Publishing workspace from the application bar, or choose Window > Workspace > Digital Publishing. This brings forward the panels that you'll need for designing interactive digital media.

Because you selected the Mobile intent, some settings will differ in your document when compared to the Print intent:

- The default color mode for the document is RGB. The default swatch colors are defined using RGB values, and the transparency blend space is also set to RGB.

- The unit of measure is set to pixels.

- The blank document presets provided represent the screen sizes of mobile devices.

★ *ACA Objective 2.4*

Working with Libraries

▶ **Video 6.3** *Creating a Logo*

As you work on design projects, you'll find that you reuse design elements such as caption boxes, speech bubbles, images, text, colors, and styles. This occurs not just within the same project, but across projects. Libraries can make those frequently needed elements available to you at any time.

InDesign offers two types of libraries:

- **Creative Cloud libraries.** Creative Cloud (CC) libraries store their content on Adobe servers. CC libraries can contain more than page objects; for example, they can also contain colors and paragraph styles. CC libraries synchronize over the Internet, so the same libraries and assets appear across Adobe applications (such as Photoshop and Illustrator) and Adobe mobile apps (such as Adobe Capture CC). If you share a library with other designers, the library contents are available to them. For these reasons, CC libraries are a reliable way to transfer content from other Adobe applications to and from InDesign.

- **Object libraries.** These libraries are separate files that you create by choosing File > New > Library; they are stored on your local computer. They can contain only objects, such as frames and groups of objects. Although you can share your library files with other designers, you can't provide live updates to the objects in them. Object libraries are older and less useful than Creative Cloud libraries, and they are not covered in this book.

CREATING A CREATIVE CLOUD LIBRARY

Working with Creative Cloud libraries is similar to working with content in other panels that you've already used. CC library content appears as a list that you can edit by using panel buttons, by using the CC Libraries panel menu, or by dragging and dropping.

To create a new library:

1   Choose Window > CC Libraries to show the CC Libraries panel.

2   Click the libraries menu at the top of the panel, and select Create New Library (**Figure 6.2**).

3   Enter the name for the library and click Create.

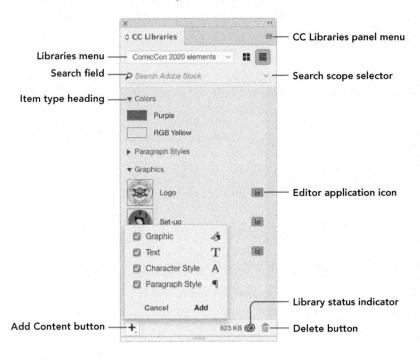

Figure 6.2 The CC Libraries panel

An empty library is created. You can start adding InDesign page elements, colors, color themes, and more. You can even search Adobe Stock, an online resource that has millions of beautiful images, photos, and videos that you can use in your designs.

ADDING ITEMS TO A CC LIBRARY

The Libraries panel is slightly different than other panels you have used. This is partly because you can add many types of items to the library, from page objects to swatches and styles.

To add InDesign items to a library:

1 Select the destination library from the library menu in the CC Libraries panel.

2 Drag the artwork from an InDesign page into the CC Libraries panel, or click the Add Content button at the bottom of the panel.

Depending on what you have selected on the InDesign page, you can also add character styles, paragraph styles, fill color, or stroke color. For example, if you have a shape selected with a red fill, clicking the Add Fill Color button at the bottom of the CC Libraries panel adds the color below the Colors heading in the CC Libraries panel. If you have text selected, clicking Add Paragraph Style adds its formatting to the panel.

The library item is added to the library under the Graphics heading, and automatically named. When items are displayed in the list view, an icon on the right indicates the application from which the item was added. For example, artwork added from Adobe Illustrator will display an Ai icon.

RENAMING A LIBRARY ITEM

To rename library items:

1 Right-click (Windows) or Control-click (macOS) the added artwork, and select Rename.

2 Type the new name, and press Enter (Windows) or Return (macOS).

USING CC LIBRARY ITEMS IN DOCUMENTS

With colors, color themes, styles, and graphics loaded in CC libraries, you can now use them for your design projects.

TIP

Some panels, such as the Swatches panel, may include within the New Swatch dialog an Add to Library button, which you can use to add items from that panel to the active CC library.

NOTE

When you are not connected to the Internet, you can still add items to and update items in CC libraries. Synchronizing will happen once you're back online.

TIP

You can also rename a selected library item by choosing Rename from the CC Libraries panel menu.

To add a graphic to the page:

1   From the library menu at the top of the CC Libraries panel, select a library. If needed, expand an item type heading to reveal the item you want to add.

2   Drag the graphic from the library to the page.

You can also right-click (Windows) or Control-click (macOS) a graphic and select Place Copy or Place Linked. Place Copy detaches the placed graphic from the item in the library. Place Linked maintains a link to the parent object in the library. When a linked item, such as a sound effect graphic created in Illustrator, is placed, a modified or missing link warning might appear in the Links panel (this happens when the item has been edited or removed from the library). You update these links just like any other link in InDesign: Select the object and select Update Link from the Links panel menu.

To work with other library items, such as styles, select text on the page and click the style name in the library in the CC Libraries panel. Styles are automatically added to the Paragraph Styles or Character Styles panel for the document you are working on. The same applies when using colors from a CC library. The colors are added to the Swatches panel.

Library items that are graphics can be edited in their native applications—for example, to edit an item with an Id icon.

To edit an InDesign graphic in the library:

1   Double-click the item in the library. It will open in InDesign as a randomly named file.

2   Make the changes; for example, you could change the fill color.

3   Choose File > Save, and then choose File > Close.

The item in the library is updated, and any designers you've shared the library with will see the updated item in their libraries once Creative Cloud has synchronized the files.

If a library item displays the icon of another Adobe application, double-clicking it opens the item in the application that created it.

Releasing Master Page Items

★ *ACA Objective 3.1*

★ *ACA Objective 3.2*

Earlier you learned that items on master pages are not accessible from document pages unless you release them (by Ctrl-Shift-clicking a master page item in Windows, or Command-Shift-clicking a master page item in macOS).

If you have master page items that overlap each other and you want to release more than one of them, pay attention to the order in which you release them.

On the same layer, items on document pages are higher than items on master pages. When you release overlapping master page items, release the top object first and then work your way down. If you release them in any other order, the resulting layer order on the document page may not be as expected.

★ *ACA Objective 4.7*

Laying Out Buttons Precisely

Video 6.5
Designing Buttons

The volunteer application project calls for four interactive buttons along the bottom of the page. A common task is to evenly space buttons on a layout. You have at least three tools available to help you quickly arrange buttons evenly on a page:

- **Columns.** The volunteer application document is an example of using four columns to organize not columns of text, but the layout of objects. If you've already created the page, you can specify these by choosing Layout > Margins and Columns.

- **Smart Guides.** If the layout uses columns with the spacing you want, you can center a button within one column as you drag it. As the center of the button you drag approaches the center of a column, a Smart Guide appears, and you can snap the center of the button to it. You can also use Smart Guides to align a button to other buttons or objects.

- **Align and Distribute options.** Use the Align options to ensure that selected buttons are aligned by their centers or edges. Use the Distribute options to ensure a uniform amount of space between buttons. You'll find Align and Distribute options in the Align panel (Window > Object & Layout > Align), or on the Control panel.

★ *ACA Objective 4.7*

Working with Animations and Timing

Video 6.6
Animating the Buttons

Animations cause objects to move or transform on the page. With the help of the Animation panel and the Timing panel (Window > Interactive), you can control the type of movement that occurs; for example, you could control the motion path that the object follows as it moves, or the length of time over which that movement occurs.

Creating Simple Animations

The Animation panel comes with a number of motion presets; these are predefined animations with their own motion path and timing and transform settings applied. The motion presets make it easy to get started with animations.

APPLYING PRESETS

Before you apply an animation, have a general idea of how you want the animation to perform.

To apply a motion preset:

1 Choose View > Screen Mode > Normal so that you can see the motion paths added to page elements.

2 Choose Window > Interactive > Animation to show the Animation panel (**Figure 6.3**).

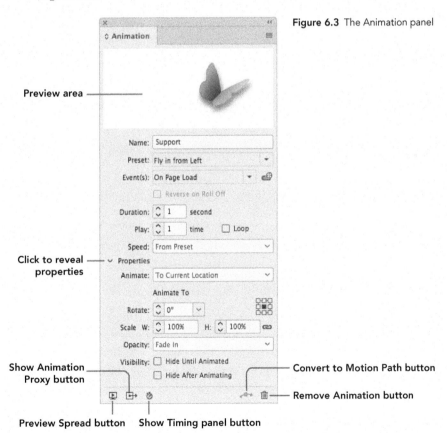

Figure 6.3 The Animation panel

Preview area

Click to reveal properties

Show Animation Proxy button

Convert to Motion Path button

Remove Animation button

Preview Spread button   Show Timing panel button

3 Select a page element to animate.

4 Select a motion preset from the Preset menu.

5 In the Name field, enter a descriptive name for the animation, such as **Support** for the Support Application button. Easily identifiable names are important if you want to animate several objects on a page, because you'll be selecting those names later for tasks such as controlling the timing of each object.

6 Enter a value in the Duration field to control the length of time it will take for the animation to complete.

7 In the Play field, enter the number of times the animation plays. To play the animation continuously, select Loop.

8 From the Speed menu, select a speed option to control whether the animation runs at a constant speed, accelerates, or slows down.

- **From Preset:** The selected motion preset settings are used.
- **None:** The animation runs at a constant speed for the length of the animation.
- **Ease In:** The animation accelerates slowly at the beginning.
- **Ease Out:** The animation slows down toward the end.
- **Ease In And Out:** The animation starts slowly and finishes by slowing down.

The motion preset applies its default settings to the object. Repeat the process for each animation on the page.

PREVIEWING INTERACTIVITY

To see the animation on the page, you can do either of the following:

- Click the Preview Spread button at the bottom of the Animation panel.
- Choose Window > Interactive > EPUB Interactivity Preview.

The EPUB Interactivity Preview panel appears (**Figure 6.4**), and the animation on the active page automatically plays.

The EPUB Interactivity Preview panel lets you preview a complete interactive InDesign document, test animations, test button controls, play movies, navigate slide shows, and more. You can drag the corners or sides of the EPUB Interactivity Preview panel to make the panel larger if needed.

To preview all the pages in a document, click the Set Preview Document Mode button (🗋) at the bottom of the EPUB Interactivity Preview panel, then click the Play Preview icon. Click the Go to Next Page and Go to Previous Page buttons to navigate to different pages.

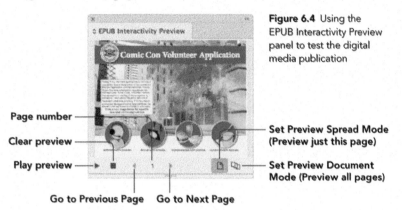

Figure 6.4 Using the EPUB Interactivity Preview panel to test the digital media publication

Page number

Clear preview

Play preview

Go to Previous Page   Go to Next Page

Set Preview Spread Mode (Preview just this page)

Set Preview Document Mode (Preview all pages)

CREATING A HYPERLINK BUTTON

When working with interactive documents, you can convert any design element to a button, as you did when you created the online form. You can set up the button to link to an address on the web.

▶ *Video 6.7* Adding Interactivity to the Buttons

To create a hyperlink button:

1   Using the Selection tool, select the object or group that will serve as the button.

2   Choose Object > Interactive > Convert To Button. Or in the Buttons and Forms panel, select Button from the Type menu (**Figure 6.5**).

The bounding box changes to a dashed line to indicate that it's now a button.

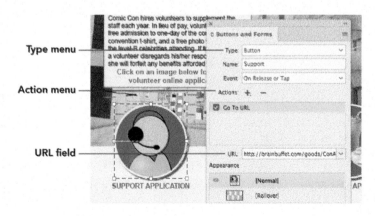

Type menu

Action menu

URL field

Figure 6.5 Creating a hyperlink button in the Buttons and Forms panel

3 In the Name field, enter a name for the button.

4 Leave Event set to On Release or Tap.

5 Select Go to URL from the action menu (+).

6 Enter or paste the web address in the URL field.

Controlling Animation Timing

By default, animations play in sequential order, one after the other. The first animation you created on a page plays first, followed by the second, and so on. There might be times when you want to change the order in which animations play, or you might want multiple animations to start playing at the same time.

You can use the Timing panel (Window > Interactive > Timing) to change the order in which animations play, set multiple animations to play at the same time, and add a delay to an animation.

One reason for delaying an animation could be that you want to ensure that the full page is loaded and visible before any animations start playing. In that case, set a delay timing on the first animation in the Timing panel.

To change the timing for animations:

1 Choose Window > Interactive > Timing to show the Timing panel (**Figure 6.6**).

   If the list of animations is empty, choose Edit > Deselect All to make sure nothing is selected.

2 To change the order in which animations play, drag an animation up or down in the Timing panel list.

3 Enter a Delay amount for a selected animation to prevent that animation from playing immediately.

Figure 6.6 The Timing panel

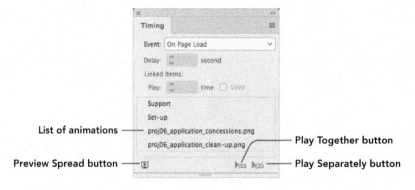

List of animations

Preview Spread button

Play Together button

Play Separately button

To play several animations at the same time:

1 In the Timing panel, Ctrl-click (Windows) or Command-click (macOS) the animations you want to group together.

2 Click the Play Together button at the bottom of the Timing panel.

Working with Motion Paths

Many of the motion presets automatically add a motion path to the animated object. This path is visible as a green line when Screen Mode is set to Normal and you select the animated object on the page. The motion path is the guide for the movement of the animation, and as such it provides some valuable information (**Figure 6.7**):

- The motion path is an arrow that indicates the direction of the animation.

- The dots along the path indicate the speed of the animation. Where dots are closer together, the speed is faster.

To see where an animation starts or finishes, click the Show Animation Proxy button at the bottom of the Animation panel. A gray preview shows you the start or end position.

TIP

To select a continuous range of animations in the Timing panel, Shift-click the first and last animation in the range.

NOTE

The animation proxy can appear at the start or end of an animation, depending on the direction of the animation.

Animation proxy

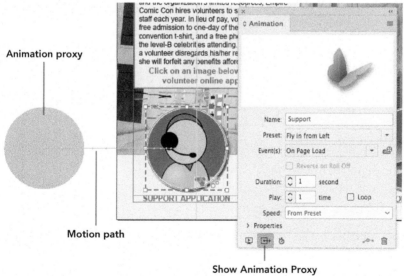

Motion path

Show Animation Proxy button in Animation panel

Figure 6.7 Parts of a motion path

EDITING THE MOTION PATH

TIP

If you're skilled with the Pen tool, you can use it to extend or customize a motion path.

You might not always be happy with the default start or end positions created by motion presets for your animations. For example, when using the Fly in from Top motion preset, you might want to extend the motion path so that the animation starts off the page and then flies in. Not to worry! You can edit a motion path the same way you edited paths earlier in this book. Can you remember which tools you used to edit paths?

You can use the Direct Selection tool to select the anchor points on a motion path and reposition them. To edit a motion path:

TIP

You can create your own motion path. Draw a path using tools such as the Pencil tool or Pen tool, select both the path and the object to animate, and click the Convert to Motion Path button at the bottom of the Animation panel.

1 Make sure Screen Mode is set to Normal.

2 With the Selection tool, select the object that has a motion path. When the selected object displays a dashed bounding box, the motion path is also visible.

3 With the Selection tool, select the motion path.

4 With the Direct Selection tool (▷), drag the anchor point at the end of the motion path to a new position (**Figure 6.8**).

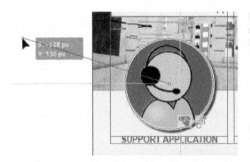

Figure 6.8 Editing the motion path with the Direct Selection tool

5 Preview the result in the EPUB Interactivity Preview panel, and make further adjustments as needed.

Animation Properties

TIP

A number of motion presets also change various properties in the Animation panel. You can adjust the properties set for those presets to customize the animation.

The Properties section of the Animation panel contains a number of fun animation properties. For example, you can make an object shrink to a smaller size (Scale) as part of the animation, or have it disappear by applying an Opacity setting of Fade Out.

To change any properties for an animation:

1 Select an animated page element.

2 Click the disclosure triangle to the left of Properties in the Animation panel to reveal additional options (**Figure 6.9**), and set the options as needed.

TIP

If you want the viewer of the document to initiate an animation, select an animated object, make sure no event is applied in the Animation panel, click the Create Button Trigger option in the Animation panel, and click the object. Now the reader can click the object to start its animation.

Checking Spelling

InDesign can detect incorrectly spelled words, capitalization errors (such as a lowercase letter at the start of a sentence), and repeated words. InDesign checks text against a dictionary for the language that is applied to the text.

TIP

To control what text in the document is checked, select an option from the Search menu in the Check Spelling dialog. You can check selected text (Selection), the text in a series of threaded text frames (Story), all text in the document (Document), or all open documents (All Documents).

Figure 6.9 Setting additional properties for animations

To check spelling for a document:

★ *ACA Objective 4.5*

1 Choose Edit > Spelling > Check Spelling.

The Check Spelling dialog opens (**Figure 6.10**), and the first suspect word in the text is highlighted.

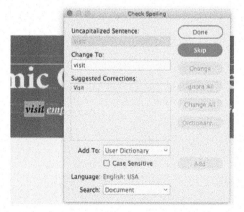

Figure 6.10 Checking the spelling for a document

2　Select the correctly spelled version of the highlighted word from the Suggested Corrections list, or enter the correct spelling in the Change To field.

3　Click Change to update just this occurrence of the error, or click Change All to fix all occurrences of this error.

The next suspect word is highlighted.

To ignore a spelling error, because it is a company name or a special term that does not appear in the dictionary, click Ignore or Ignore All. Alternatively, you can click Add to include the word in the User Dictionary, so that future occurrences will not be flagged as an error.

4　Repeat steps 2 and 3 until the spelling check is complete, and click Done.

Finding and Changing Content

 ACA Objective 4.5

InDesign's Find/Change command is a powerhouse that lets you search for content and replace it with something else in the document. This speeds up the process of making text changes throughout your project.

In addition to performing simple text changes throughout a document, such as replacing the word "captain" with "colonel," you can also use Find/Change to:

- Search for glyphs and replace them. Glyphs are special characters you can insert into text with the Type > Glyphs panel. Double-clicking a character in the panel inserts it at the text insertion point.

- Search for object formatting, such as stroke or fill colors, and change the settings.

- Search for text formatting, such as font and size, and replace the settings.

- Search for advanced pattern-based text strings with GREP, a language that codes the finding of patterns in text (for example, any text in brackets), and make changes.

To search and replace text:

1　Choose Edit > Find/Change (**Figure 6.11**).

2　Click the Text tab in the Find/Change dialog.

3　Enter the text to search for in the Find What field.

4　Enter the replacement text in the Change To field.

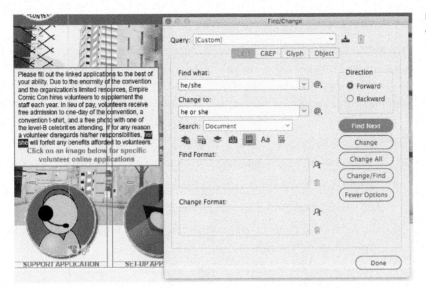

Figure 6.11 Finding and changing text

5   Under Direction, select Forward to search from the current page through to the following pages.

6   Click Find Next to find the first occurrence of the search word.

7   Click one of the change options:

  ▪ **Change:** Replaces only the found text.

  ▪ **Change All:** Replaces all occurrences of the found text.

  ▪ **Change/Find:** Replaces the found text and immediately moves forward to the next occurrence.

TIP

For common document cleanups, such as removing double paragraph returns or double spaces, select one of the preset searches from the Query menu at the very top of the Find/Change dialog. The Query menu contains GREP presets.

Embedding Media Files

★ *ACA Objective 4.7*

▶ *Video 6.9 Creating Controller Buttons for the Video*

You can use the Place command to easily add a video file from your computer to an interactive document you're creating in InDesign. You can set a video so that it automatically plays when the page appears, or you can provide a controller so that the reader can start and stop the video. When you use the Place command, the video becomes part of the document and will add to the total file size and download time.

Adding Video

▶ *Video 6.8* Adding a Video

Although you can import a number of different video file formats into InDesign, such as QuickTime (MOV), Flash Video (FLV, F4V), or SWF files, the one format that works for all digital media publication types is H.264-encoded MP4. This format also works on all operating systems (iOS, Android, Windows, macOS).

PLACING VIDEO

TIP

Video file sizes can be quite large. Consider keeping your embedded videos short and below about 10 to 15MB in file size, especially when your digital media publication is published through an online format that requires downloading.

To add a video file to your publication:

1 Choose File > Place and navigate to the location of the video file.

2 The pointer turns into a loaded video icon ().

3 Using the Pages panel or other navigation options, display the page on which you want to add the video.

4 Drag to create a new frame. The video will automatically resize to fit proportionally in the frame.

5 Choose Object > Fitting > Fit Frame to Content to reduce the size of the media frame so that it is the same size as the video (**Figure 6.12**).

Figure 6.12 Fitting the frame to the content resizes the media frame to match the size of the video.

TIP

You can also add a video file by clicking the Place a Video or Audio File button at the bottom of the Media panel.

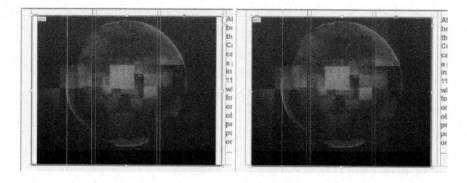

CONFIGURING THE VIDEO WITH THE MEDIA PANEL

A placed video file appears on the page like a static image. You can't access the video controller buttons, such as play, pause, or stop, from the media frame. Thankfully, the Media panel (Window > Interactive) comes to the rescue. You can use the Media panel to play the video and to set playback controls for the video.

To change the media settings for the video:

1 Using the Selection tool, click the media frame to select the video.

2 Choose Window > Interactive > Media to display the Media panel (**Figure 6.13**).

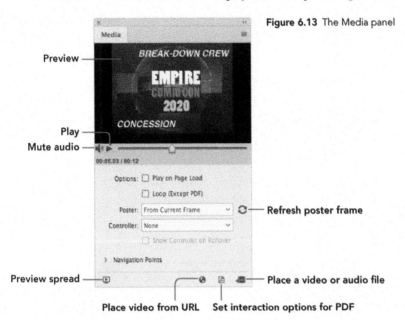

Figure 6.13 The Media panel

Preview

Play

Mute audio

Refresh poster frame

Preview spread

Place a video or audio file

Place video from URL   Set interaction options for PDF

3 To preview the video, click the Play button below the Media panel video preview area.

4 To mute or unmute the audio, click the Audio button below the preview.

5 Select Play on Page Load to automatically start playing the video when you get to the page with the video on it. Select Loop to play the video continuously.

6 To set the image that appears for the video when the page is first loaded, choose an option from the Poster menu. To use a frame from the video, move the controller to the frame you want, choose From Current Frame, and click the Refresh button ( ) next to the menu.

7 Select whether or not you want to add a controller to the video on the page.

If you choose not to add a controller and you deselected Play on Page Load, you'll need to add additional control buttons to the video page so that the reader is able to play and stop the video. This is the case if you're building the application form in Video 6.8.

TIP

If you want to add an audio file to a page, the steps are essentially the same as they are for placing a video file.

WARNING

Always test whether video controllers work as expected. They will work in Interactive PDF. However, EPUB export settings and Publish Online, for example, ignore the controller settings applied in the Media panel, and instead add a standard controller to the video. As a workaround, you could try hiding the controller by placing an object over the top of it.

ADDING CONTROL BUTTONS

▶ **Video 6.9**
Creating Controller Buttons for the Video

When the video controller is hidden from the reader, you can add custom-designed buttons to the page to play, pause, resume, or stop the video.

To add a play button for video:

1   Create and format objects to serve as the buttons.

2   Using the Selection tool, select the object or group that is the button design element on the page.

3   Select Video from the action menu (+) in the Buttons and Forms panel. The selected object or group is automatically converted into a button.

4   From the Video menu, select the video on the page. If there is only one video on the page, the video is automatically selected.

5   From the Options menu, select Play to create a button that will start video playback when clicked (**Figure 6.14**).

Figure 6.14 Adding custom-designed video controller buttons

TIP

If you want to use a file that isn't a supported format, you can convert it using Adobe Media Encoder, an application you can install using the Adobe Creative Cloud desktop application.

6   Enter a descriptive name for the button in the Name field.

To add a stop, pause, or resume button for the video, repeat steps 1 through 5, but for step 5, select Stop, Pause, or Resume from the Options menu, respectively.

★ ACA Objective 4.7

Creating a Slide Show

▶ **Video 6.10**
Adding a Slideshow

Slide shows are a series of images that are positioned in the same location on the page and displayed one after another. They are great to use in digital media publications, as they allow you to showcase a number of images without needing to insert more pages into your design.

You can create a slide show on an InDesign page using a multistate object (MSO). A multistate object behaves as a single page element but contains different "layers" of content, called states. Only one state within an MSO is visible at a time, and generally a button control is added to allow the reader to see each state within the MSO. For example, when you create an image slide show as a multistate object, the various images (slides) of the slide show are the individual states, and by clicking a "next slide" button you can see the different images one at a time.

To build an MSO-based slide show, you need to do the following:

- Place multiple images.
- Stack all the images exactly on top of each other.
- Convert the images into a multistate object.
- Set up the animation and interactivity for the slide show.

Given what you've learned so far, this won't take long. Let's go over those tasks in more detail.

Placing the Images

As you've learned, you can easily place multiple images simply by selecting more than one image in the Place dialog. And as demonstrated in Video 6.10, you can use the Gridify technique to place multiple images as a grid (press the arrow keys while dragging a loaded Place cursor on the layout). Combine these techniques and you'll be able to add all your slide show images onto the page in a few seconds.

Fitting the Images

The frame fitting options you learned about earlier, available on the Object > Fitting submenu and in the Control panel, help you present the slide show images at a consistent size.

If you want to avoid having to adjust images to frames, prepare the images in advance so that they are all the same dimensions (such as 600 x 400 pixels). That will let you simply apply the Fit Frame to Content option to them so that their frames exactly match the image dimensions, which are already the same.

If the images aren't all the same size, they might not consistently fit their frames. To address this, apply one of the fitting options:

- If you don't want gaps between an image and its frame, apply Fill Frame Proportionally. Some parts of the image may be hidden outside the frame. This can be an effective choice if all the images are the same orientation (all horizontal or all vertical).

- If you want to show entire images, apply Fit Content Proportionally. This will leave empty areas along one dimension when an image doesn't match the proportions of the frame. But it's a better choice if you are using both horizontal and vertical images.

Aligning the Images

The last thing to do is ensure that all the images are aligned. If they aren't aligned, the slide show may appear to jump around as it plays back. If the images are all the same size, you can align their centers horizontally and vertically. You can also choose to align the images by another side or corner.

To align the images:

1 Using the Selection tool, select all the images for the slide show. You can drag a selection marquee around them or Shift-click each of them.

2 In the Align panel (Window > Object & Layout > Align) or Control panel, click an icon to align the selected objects (**Figure 6.15**). Typically, you'll click one of the horizontal alignment options, and then one of the vertical alignment options.

Figure 6.15 Using the Align panel to ensure the images are perfectly stacked

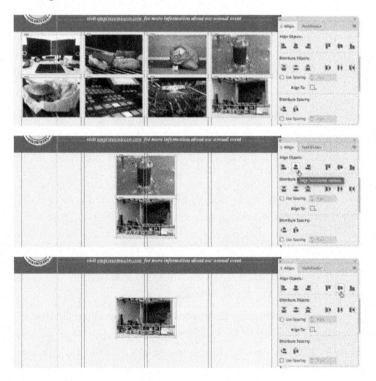

Creating a Multistate Object

With the images all stacked on top of each other, you're ready to convert the stack of images into a multistate object with different states for each image.

To create a multistate object:

1 With the Selection tool, drag a marquee around the images to select them.

2 Choose Window > Interactive > Object States.

3 Select New State from the Object States panel menu, or click the Convert Selection to Multistate Object button at the bottom of the Object States panel (**Figure 6.16**).

As with a button, the bounding box on the new multistate object changes to a dashed line. When you see the dashed line bounding box, the MSO is selected; if it isn't a dashed line, then one of the states is selected.

4 In the Object Name field, enter the object name for the slide show.

TIP

Multistate objects are not restricted to images only. You can also convert text frames to MSOs. When you want to combine text and images as part of a slide show, first group each state and then convert selected objects to an MSO.

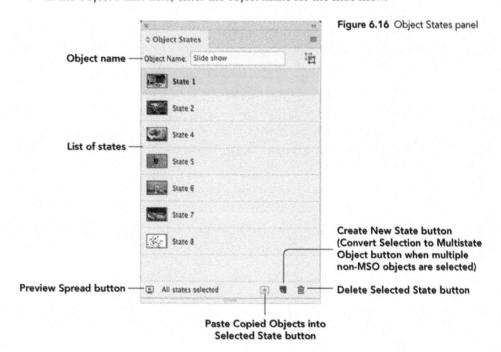

Figure 6.16 Object States panel

Object name

List of states

Create New State button (Convert Selection to Multistate Object button when multiple non-MSO objects are selected)

Preview Spread button

Delete Selected State button

Paste Copied Objects into Selected State button

The stack of images is combined into a single object. Within the Object States panel, you can click the individual states to see each image.

When you have several multistate objects on the same page, adding an object name for a slide show is helpful so that you can easily identify each one when you set up interactivity (such as a playback controller).

To edit the content of individual states—for example, to crop an image differently— do the following after you have created the multistate object (**Figure 6.17**):

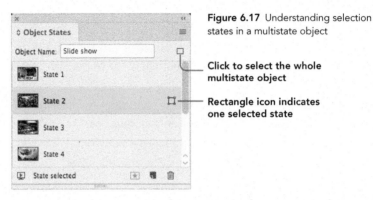

Figure 6.17 Understanding selection states in a multistate object

Click to select the whole multistate object

Rectangle icon indicates one selected state

1   Select the multistate object on the page.

2   In the Object States panel, click the state you want to edit. A small rectangle appears to the right of the state name to indicate that the state is selected.

3   With the Selection tool, click the Content Grabber to select the image, and resize or reposition it as needed. The icon to the right of the state changes to indicate that an object in the state is selected (in this case, the frame's content).

4   To select the multistate object again, click the icon to the right of the object name.

Changing the Stacking Order

The order in which the images will appear in the slide show is set by the order they appear in the Object States panel. The topmost object displays first.

To change the order in which images appear:

1   Select the multistate object on the page.

2   In the Object States panel, select a state and drag it to its new position.

3   Release the mouse button when you see a thick line appear at the insertion point.

Adding Control Buttons

To allow a reader of the fixed-layout EPUB or web version of the digital media publication to see the different slides in the slide show, you must add control buttons so that the reader can see the different states of the multistate object.

After you've prepared the multistate object for the slide show, you can add button graphics. As with the other button graphics you've worked with, you can create them in Photoshop or Illustrator, or using the drawing tools in InDesign.

To add a controller button to show the next slide in the slide show:

1 Using the Selection tool, select the object or group that will serve as the button.

2 Choose Object > Interactive > Convert to Button, or in the Buttons and Forms panel select Button from the Type menu.

3 Enter a name for the button.

4 Leave Event set to On Release or Tap.

5 From the action menu (+), select Go to Next State.

6 From the Object menu, select the multistate object. If there is only one multistate object on the page, InDesign automatically selects it (**Figure 6.18**).

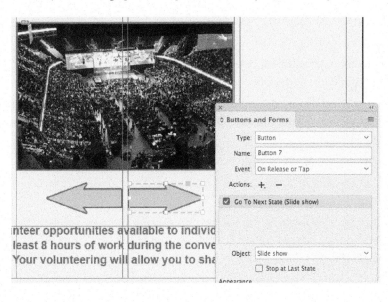

Figure 6.18 Setting up a controller button for the slide show multistate object

7   Deselect Stop at Last State if you want the slide show to loop back to the first state in the multistate object when the Next Slide button is clicked or tapped.

8   Click the Preview Spread button at the bottom of the Buttons and Forms panel to test the button in the EPUB Interactivity Preview panel.

To add a controller button that navigates to the previous slide in the slide show, repeat steps 1–6, but in step 5 select Go to Previous State from the action menu (+) instead.

★ *ACA Objective 4.7*

Inserting HTML

▶ *Video 6.11*
Adding a Map

You might wonder why you would ever want to insert HTML, the markup language used for the creation of web pages, in your InDesign publications. HTML allows you to embed content from the Internet into your digital media publications. For example, you can embed an online video from YouTube, or a Google Map.

The first step to take when embedding web-based content into a digital publication is to obtain the embed code. That sounds a little scary, but websites that allow their content to be embedded often provide a special Share button that helps you locate the embed code.

Let's look at Google Maps as an example:

1   Start by opening your default web browser.

2   Enter **maps.google.com** in the URL field at the top of the browser window, and press Enter (Windows) or Return (macOS).

3   In the Search Google Maps field at the top left of the screen, enter the address or location you want to locate. In the example, the location is Pioneer Park in San Francisco.

4   After the map updates, click Share (**Figure 6.19**).

5   Click Embed a Map. Select the preferred map size from the Size menu—for example, Medium.

TIP

To avoid issues with some e-readers, remove the **allowfullscreen** *text from the pasted embed code.*

6   Click the `<iframe>` code at the top of the screen and choose Edit > Copy to copy the text to the Clipboard.

7   Back in InDesign, navigate to the page on which the map belongs.

8   Choose Object > Insert HTML.

9   In the Edit HTML dialog, select the default text.

10 Choose Edit > Paste to insert the embed code, replacing the default text (**Figure 6.20**), and click OK.

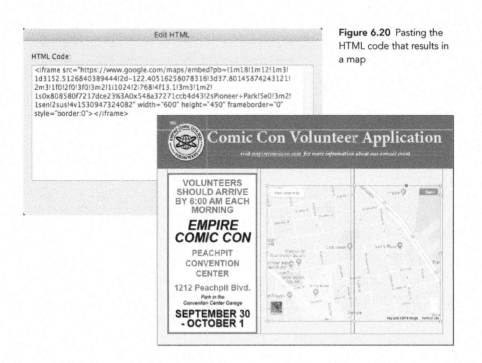

Figure 6.19 Copying the HTML embed code

Figure 6.20 Pasting the HTML code that results in a map

It might take a few seconds for the embed code to render on the page, but you'll see the map on the InDesign page. When your digital media publication is published using the Fixed Layout EPUB export or Publish Online options, an interactive Google Map will appear on the page.

★ ACA Objective 5.1

★ ACA Objective 5.2

Exporting the Project

 Video 6.12
Animating an Object on a Path and Exporting the EPUB

At the start of this chapter, we mentioned a number of different interactive digital media projects you could design with InDesign. As you have seen, many of the interactive features work across a number of publication types, from Interactive PDF to EPUBs to publishing online.

It's time to export your project and test the new interactive features in the finished publication.

Exporting to EPUB

You can create two types of EPUBs from InDesign: a reflowable EPUB and a fixed-layout EPUB. Only the fixed layout supports the interactive features, such as animations and slide shows.

To test your EPUB, you'll need access to an e-reader.

TIP
You can add metadata to any InDesign document. Choose File > File Info. Data in the File Information dialog is automatically used to populate the EPUB metadata.

If you work on Mac OS X 10.9 or higher, you'll be able to use the iBooks application for this. Adobe has also released an e-reader called Adobe Digital Editions. You can download it from the Adobe website, and it is available for Windows, macOS, and iOS (iPad). The latest version can display reflowable and fixed-layout EPUBs.

To export your publication as a fixed-layout EPUB:

1 Choose File > Export.

2 Select EPUB (Fixed Layout) from the Save as Type (Windows) or Format (macOS) menu.

3 Enter a name for the eBook in the File Name (Windows) or Save As (macOS) field.

4 Click Save. The EPUB – Fixed Layout Export Options dialog appears (**Figure 6.21**).

5 Click General in the scroll list at the left, and set the options you want (for this exercise you can simply leave the options at their default settings):

TIP
Continuous page ranges are separated by a hyphen; for example, 1-3 would include pages 1, 2, and 3. Noncontiguous page ranges are separated by a comma; for example, 1, 4 would include only pages 1 and 4.

   ■ **Export Range:** Select All Pages to export the complete document. You can also enter a page range.

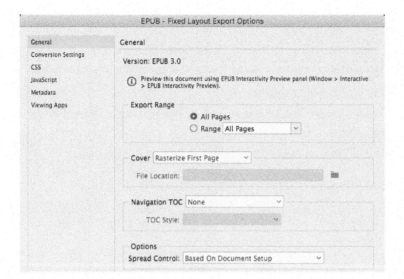

- **Cover:** Select Rasterize First Page to add a cover image based on the first page in your document. You can also select Choose Image and use a custom image file as the cover image for your book.

- **Navigation TOC:** Select None for short interactive publications such as the Comic Con volunteer application form.

  For longer digital media publications, you can select an option such as Multi Level (TOC Style), and select a table of contents style you created (Layout > Table of Contents Styles) in the document. This would build a table of contents similar to the one you created earlier for the print recipe book.

- **Spread Control:** The Spread Control menu lets you choose whether pages appear as single pages or as page spreads in the e-reader. For a document like the application form, you can leave it set to Based On Document Setup because the Mobile intent does not enable facing pages.

6 Set options as needed in the Conversion Settings, CSS, JavaScript, Metadata, and Viewing Apps panels; for the application form document, you can leave all of those panels at their default settings.

7 Click OK to export and view the EPUB.

With the EPUB published, you can now go through all the pages in an e-reader and test the many interactive features you added to the project.

NOTE

By rasterizing the first page for the cover image, the cover will appear twice when the eBook is viewed: first, the rasterized version, and second the converted InDesign page, which is converted to HTML.

NOTE

CSS stands for Cascading Style Sheets, which are used to control how HTML appears on the page. Under the hood, InDesign EPUBs are HTML based, so attaching CSS could overwrite any CSS formatting created by InDesign itself.

NOTE

JavaScript is a programming language that works with HTML and CSS; it can be used to add more interactive effects to your publication.

Publishing Online

Publish Online lets you publish your digital media design to the Internet and share it publicly. Most of the interactive features will work, including animations.

To publish your interactive project online:

1 Choose File > Publish Online or click the Publish Online button in the application bar.

   The Publish Your Document Online dialog opens (**Figure 6.22**).

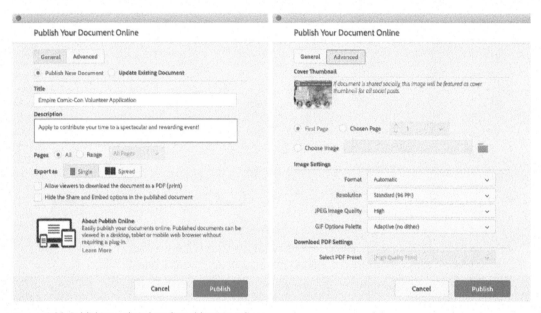

Figure 6.22 Publishing a digital media publication online

2 Select Publish New Document to create a new online publication. If you've previously published a project, you can select Update Existing Document to make a change to the online version.

3 Click General, at top left.

4 Enter the title for the project.

5 Enter a brief description of the project.

6 For Pages, select All so that all the pages of the application are published.

7 Select Single from the Export As section.

8   Optional: Select Allow Viewers to Download the Document as a PDF (Print) to allow readers to download a PDF copy of the published online version of the document. Keep in mind that this is a static version of the publication, without any interactivity.

9   Click Advanced to access additional export options.

   ■   For Cover Thumbnail, select the First Page option.

   ■   Select the image settings to use; you can leave the default settings as they are.

10 Click OK to start the file upload to the web.

When the document upload is completed, you can click View Document to view the project in your default web browser. You can also copy the web address (URL) so that you can share it with others, and you can share the project through social media networks such as Facebook and Twitter.

Managing Published Projects

The projects you published online can be managed and deleted as necessary.

To manage online publications:

Choose File > Publish Online Dashboard. A web page opens in your default web browser, and you might be prompted to sign in with your Adobe ID (email) and password.

Once logged in, you can access all of your online publications. Click the publication name to load the publication in the browser. To delete a publication, move the mouse over the publication name in the Publications list and click the Delete icon at right. The Overview tab lets you see viewing statistics for your Publish Online documents.

Conclusion

Congratulations! You have completed an interactive digital media publication to complement the printed publications you worked on earlier. These lessons, combined with the experience you'll gain from practicing with your own projects, help give you a solid foundation for publishing both print and digital media project with InDesign.

Success in the field of digital design doesn't depend solely on knowledge of the InDesign application, because InDesign expertise is part of a wider field of essential professional and team skills such as graphic design and project management. To help you develop those skills, Chapter 7, "Leveling Up with Design," and Chapter 8 "Working with Outsiders," are provided in the online version of this book, available when you sign into your account at peachpit.com.

ACA Objectives Covered

DOMAIN OBJECTIVES	CHAPTER	VIDEO
DOMAIN 1.0 Setting Project Requirements		
1.1 Identify the purpose, audience, and audience needs for a web authoring project.	**Ch 2** Introducing the Magazine Cover Project, 120 **Ch 2** Starting a Magazine Cover Design, 121 **Ch 8** Working with Outsiders, 8-1	**3.1** Introducing the Magazine Cover Project **3.2** Setting Up the Cover Design **8.3** Finding the Target Audience **8.4** The Golden Rule for Client Work
1.2 Communicate with colleagues and clients about design plans.	**Ch 8** Project Management, 8-14	**8.9** Project Management Intro **8.10** Project Management— Understand the Problem **8.11** Project Management—Think It Through **8.12** Project Management—Get It in Writing **8.13** Project Management—Avoiding Creep **8.14** Project Management—Make It So **8.15** The Advantages of Working at a Firm **8.16** Wrapping Up Project Planning
1.3 Determine the type of copyright, permissions, and licensing required to use specific content.	**Ch 8** Copyrights and Wrongs, 8-8	**8.6** Digital Tools for Tracking Copyright **8.7** Fair Use and Copyright **8.8** Licensing: Strict and Free
1.4 Demonstrate an understanding of key terminology related to publications.	**Ch 2** Adding Guides and Changing Preferences, 62 **Ch 2** Understanding Graphics Formats, 76	**2.4** Adding Guides to a Document and Changing Preferences **2.7** Assigning Objects to Layers

continues on next page

continued from previous page

DOMAIN OBJECTIVES	CHAPTER	VIDEO
DOMAIN 2.0 Project Setup and Interface		
2.1 Create a document with the appropriate settings for web, print, and mobile.	**Ch 2** Planning a New Document, 50 **Ch 3** Starting a Magazine Cover Design, 121 **Ch 4** Setting Up the New Document Dialog, 166 **Ch 4** Setting Up Master Pages, 167 **Ch 5** Setting Up the Recipe Book, 203 **Ch 6** Types of Digital Media, 240 **Ch 6** Setting Up for Digital Media, 241	**2.1** Introducing the Poster Project **2.2** Creating and Saving a New Document **3.2** Setting Up the Cover Design **4.2** Setting Up Master Pages **5.1** Introducing the Recipe Book Project **5.2** Setting Up the Project File **6.2** Setting Up the EPUB Document **6.1** Introducing the Interactive Digital Media Project
2.2 Navigate, organize, and customize the application workspace.	**Ch 1** Starting InDesign, 4 **Ch 1** Using the Start Workspace, 4 **Ch 1** Getting to Know the InDesign Workspace, 6 **Ch 1** Getting to Know the Tools Panel, 15 **Ch 1** Using Workspaces, 32 **Ch 1** Working Faster with Keyboard Shortcuts, 43	**1.4** The InDesign Workspace **1.5** The Tools Panel **1.2** Launching the Application **1.3** Understanding the Start Workspace **1.7** Creating a Custom Workspace **1.10** Learning Keyboard Shortcuts
2.3 Use nonprinting design tools in the interface to aid in design or workflow.	**Ch 1** Getting Around in a Document, 4 **Ch 1** Getting Around on a Page, 34 **Ch 2** Adding Guides and Changing Preferences, 62 **Ch 2** Changing the Unit of Measure, 64 **Ch 2** Adding Objects to a Document, 65	**1.9** Choosing Options for Displaying a Document **1.8** Using Zoom to View a Document **2.4** Adding Guides to a Document and Changing Preferences **2.5** Adding Objects to a Document
2.4 Import assets into a project.	**Ch 1** Getting Around on a Page, 34 **Ch 3** Placing the Featured Image on the Cover, 124 **Ch 5** Adding Text from Other Applications, 221 **Ch 5** Importing Text and Tables, 222 **Ch 6** Working with Libraries, 242	**1.8** Using Zoom to View a Document **3.3** Placing an Image as the Background **5.7** Adding Master Pages, Images, and Object Styles (part 2) **6.3** Creating a Logo

continues on next page

continued from previous page

DOMAIN OBJECTIVES	CHAPTER	VIDEO
4.1 *(continued)*	**Ch 4** Adding Master Pages, 170 **Ch 4** Working with Text Frames and Columns, 175 **Ch 4** Placing a Graphic Without a Placeholder, 189	
4.2 Add and manipulate text using appropriate typographic settings.	**Ch 2** Adding Text, 95 **Ch 2** Moving and Sizing Text, 103 **Ch 3** Adding Teaser Text, 128 **Ch 3** Creating the Title Masthead, 132 **Ch 3** Finishing the Title Masthead, 146 **Ch 3** Adding the Main Coverline, 153 **Ch 3** Applying an Inset to a Text Frame, 156 **Ch 4** Working with Text Frames and Columns, 175 **Ch 4** Creating a Drop Cap, 176 **Ch 4** Adjusting Space Between Paragraphs, 177 **Ch 4** Setting Indents, 178 **Ch 4** Setting Tabs, 179 **Ch 4** Adjusting Hyphenation, 180 **Ch 4** Wrapping Text Around Objects, 181 **Ch 4** Creating Bulleted and Numbered Lists, 183 **Ch 4** Threading Stories Through Text Frames, 185 **Ch 4** Adding a Pull Quote, 190 **Ch 5** Aligning Text Vertically in a Frame, 206 **Ch 5** Creating a Table of Contents, 234	**2.13** Defining Swatches and Coloring Text **2.14** Moving and Sizing Text **3.4** Adding a Teaser **3.5** Creating the Title Masthead **3.7** Finishing the Title Masthead **3.9** Adding the Main Coverline **3.10** Working with Text Frame Options **4.5** Adding Text Frames **4.7** Applying Text Wrap **4.6** Adding Body Copy to a Document **4.8** Formatting Text **4.9** Designing a Sidebar with Lists and an Image **4.10** Threading Text from One Page to the Next **4.11** Adding Page Jumps to a Story **4.14** Adding a Pull Quote **5.5** Finishing the Front Cover **5.13** Creating a Table of Contents
4.3 Make, manage, and edit selections.	**Ch 2** Creating a Shape with the Pathfinder Tools, 82	**2.9** Introducing the Pathfinder Tools

DOMAIN OBJECTIVES	CHAPTER	VIDEO
4.4 Transform digital graphics and media within a publication.	**Ch 2** Understanding Graphics Formats, 76 **Ch 2** Moving, Scaling, and Locking Objects, 85 **Ch 3** Adding to the Title Masthead, 138 **Ch 4** Wrapping Text Around Objects, 181 **Ch 4** Converting Text into a Graphic, 188 **Ch 4** Adding a Pull Quote, 190 **Ch 5** Styling Corners, 207 **Ch 5** Designing Page 5 On Your Own, 232	**2.7** Assigning Objects to Layers **2.11** Moving, Scaling, and Locking Objects **3.6** Adding to the Title Masthead **4.7** Applying Text Wrap **4.12** Replacing Spot Colors with Process Colors **4.14** Adding a Pull Quote **5.6** Adding Master Pages, Images, and Object Styles **5.12** Designing Page 5 on Your Own
4.5 Use basic reconstructing and editing techniques to manipulate document content.	**Ch 2** Creating a Color Swatch, 67 **Ch 2** Creating a Shape with the Pathfinder Tools, 82 **Ch 4** Working with Text Frames and Columns, 175 **Ch 6** Checking Spelling, 253 **Ch 6** Finding and Changing Content, 254	**2.5** Adding Objects to a Document **2.9** Introducing the Pathfinder Tools **2.10** Using the Pathfinder Tools to Create a Globe **4.6** Adding Body Copy to a Document **6.7** Adding Interactivity to the Buttons
4.6 Modify the appearance of design elements by using effects and styles.	**Ch 3** Creating the Title Masthead, 132 **Ch 3** Adding a Coverline, 147 **Ch 3** Adding the Main Coverline, 153 **Ch 4** Adding Buttons, 196 **Ch 5** Formatting Faster with Styles, 208	**3.5** Creating the Title Masthead **3.8** Adding Teaser Text **3.9** Adding the Main Coverline **4.19** Continue Making the Form Interactive & Animating Buttons **5.7** Adding Master Pages, Images, and Object Styles (part 2) **5.8** Using Character and Paragraph Styles to Refine the Layout **5.9** Applying Character and Paragraph Styles

continues on next page

continued from previous page

DOMAIN OBJECTIVES	CHAPTER	VIDEO
4.7 Add interactive or dynamic content or media to a project.	**Ch 4** Creating an Interactive Form, 193 **Ch 4** Adding Page Transitions, 199 **Ch 4** Creating an Interactive PDF, 200 **Ch 6** Working with Animations and Timing, 246 **Ch 6** Embedding Media Files, 255 **Ch 6** Creating a Slide Show, 258 **Ch 6** Inserting HTML, 264	**4.15** Adding a Foldout Subscription Form **4.20** Adding Transitions & Exporting as Animated PDF **6.6** Animating the Buttons **6.9** Creating Controller Buttons for the Video **6.10** Adding a Slide Show **6.11** Adding a Map
4.8 Create and edit tables.	**Ch 5** Using Tables, 225	**5.10** Adding and Styling a Table **5.11** Guided Page Layout
DOMAIN 5.0 Publishing Documents		
5.1 Prepare documents for publishing to web, print, and other digital devices.	**Ch 3** Preflighting the Document, 162 **Ch 6** Exporting the Project, 266	**3.12** Preflighting the Document **6.12** Animating an Object on a Path and Exporting the EPUB
5.2 Export or save documents to various file formats.	**Ch 2** Packaging Your Finished Project for Output, 109 **Ch 4** Creating an Interactive PDF, 200 **Ch 6** Exporting the Project, 266	**2.15** Packaging Your Finished Project for Output **4.20** Adding Transitions & Exporting as Animated PDF **6.12** Animating an Object on a Path and Exporting the EPUB

Glossary

additive color Created by combining light.

alignment Controls how the text is positioned horizontally within the text frame—for example, left, centered, or right.

all caps Using uppercase letterforms for each letter. All letters are the same size.

alpha channel An image channel that indicates which areas of the image should be transparent; used to create a transparent background for the image.

analogous colors Colors that are side by side on the color wheel.

anchor point A point on a path that connects to a line segment.

animation Transforming objects over time.

asymmetrical balance Achieves balance with different elements with different weights on each side (or the top and bottom) of a page.

attribution Creative Commons licensing indicated with "BY." Requires that you credit the original author when using work; you are allowed to tweak the work as long as proper credit is given to the author.

auto-size Automatic growth in depth or width of a text frame dependent on the amount of text it contains.

balance Evenly distributed, but not necessarily centered or mirrored.

baseline An imaginary line used to organize text along a horizontal plane.

blackletter fonts Fonts that feature an overly ornate style and that convey a feeling of rich and sophisticated gravitas. Also known as Old English, gothic, or textura.

cast shadow The shadow cast on any objects that are in the shadow of a form. Shadows fade as they get farther from the form casting the shadow.

chaotic lines Look like scribbles and feel unpredictable and frantic. Convey a sense of urgency, fear, or explosive energy.

character formatting Text formatting for selected text—for example, font choice, font style (bold, italic), and size.

character styles Styles used to format words or phrases within a paragraph differently from the rest of the paragraph.

clipping path A vector path saved with an image, indicating which areas should be transparent; used to create a transparent background for the image.

color The perceived hue, lightness, and saturation of an object or light.

color harmonies Color rules that are named for their relative locations on the color wheel.

color stop A color that is a starting color for a gradient blend.

complementary colors Colors that are opposite each other on the color wheel.

contrast Creates visual interest and a focal point in a composition. It is what draws the eye to the focal point.

corporate colors Colors that are part of a company's branding.

Creative Commons Ways that artists can release their works for limited use and still choose the way the works are used and shared: Public Domain, Attribution, ShareAlike, NoDerivs, and NonCommercial.

curved (lines) Expresses fluidity, beauty, and grace.

date line Text on a magazine cover that indicates the issue's date of publication.

decorative fonts Also known as ornamental, novelty, or display fonts, these fonts don't fall into any of the other categories.

deliverables A predetermined list of items that will be delivered to the customer.

design elements The building blocks of art defined by artists to provide a framework for creating art.

design principles Essential rules or assembly instructions of art.

diagonal (lines) Lines traveling on neither a vertical nor a horizontal path. Express growth or decline and imply movement or change.

dingbat fonts Also known as wingdings, they consist of a collection of objects and shapes instead of letters, numerals, and punctuation.

direction A common way to describe lines, such as vertical, horizontal, or diagonal.

direction line Line attached to an anchor point that controls the curvature of a path.

docked panels Panels that snap to the side of the document window.

elements of art The building blocks of creative works. They are the "nouns" of design, such as space, line, shape, form, texture, value, color, and type.

emphasis Describes the focal point to which the eye is naturally and initially drawn in a design.

EPUB A digital media format for e-books, compatible with a wide range of devices, including reading devices, tablets, and smartphones.

fair use A set of rules that specify how and when copyrighted material can be used and that make sure copyright protection doesn't come at the cost of creativity, study, and freedom.

feathering Blurring the edge of an object or effect to create a smoother transition.

feedback loop A system set up to continually encourage and require input and approval from a client on a project's direction.

flow A category related to the energy conveyed by lines and shapes.

focal point What the design is all about. The call to action or the primary message you are trying to get across.

font The whole collection of the typeface in each of its sizes and styles.

footer Area below the bottom margin of a page.

footer row Bottom row of a table.

form Describes three-dimensional objects, such as spheres, cubes, and pyramids.

frame Objects of varying shapes (rectangles, ellipses, and so on) that contain content (such as text or images) or simply have a stroke color, a fill color, or both.

geometric (lines) Tend to be straight and have sharp angles. Look manmade and intentional. Communicate strength, power, and precision.

geometric shapes Predictable and consistent shapes, such as circles, squares, triangles, and stars. They are rarely found in nature and convey mechanical and manufactured impressions.

glyph Each character of a font, whether it is a letter, number, symbol, or swash.

gradient Blends between different colors or between different shades of color.

gradient ramp Preview for a gradient that shows the color blend and color stops.

gutter The spacing between columns.

handwritten fonts Also known as hand fonts, they simulate handwriting.

hanging indent Paragraph formatting in which the first line is indented less than the rest of the paragraph. Useful for creating bulleted and numbered lists.

header Area above the top margin of a page.

header row Top row of a table.

highlight The area of a form that is directly facing the light and that appears lightest.

horizontal Moving from left to right; expresses calmness and balance.

horizontal scale Describes the function of stretching letters and distorting the typeface geometry.

hyperlinks Interactive links that take you from a source point you click (or tap) to a destination somewhere else.

hyphenation Determines if and when words should be split with hyphens when wrapping to the next line.

ideographs (ideograms) Images that represent an idea, such as a heart representing love.

IDML InDesign Markup Language, a file format that provides backward compatibility with earlier versions of InDesign.

implied lines Lines that don't really exist but that are implied by shapes, such as dotted or dashed lines, people waiting in lines, or the margins of a block of text.

in port A control on a text frame that receives text flowing in from the previous threaded text frame.

indent Settings that determine how far an entire paragraph or its first line is indented from the edges of the text frame's columns.

index A list of topics, also referred to as index entries, that includes page number references and "see also" references.

index entries Topics listed in the index.

index markers Hidden characters that provide a page reference for the topics listed in the index.

iterations New versions of a design that successively become closer to the desired result.

iterative work Work that is shared as it is completed, allowing the customer to chime in with comments while it is still easy to make changes.

justified Aligns text to a straight edge on both the right and left edges of a paragraph.

kerning The space between specific character pairs.

leading (line spacing) The amount of space between the baselines of two lines of text. In InDesign, leading is set as a character attribute.

library A way to store objects independently of a document so that you have access to them from any document. CC libraries are integrated with Creative Cloud across devices and can also store formatting.

ligatures Special characters used to represent letter combinations, such as "fi."

licensing A way to legally use copyrighted material for a certain time and in a certain way, usually associated with paying a fee established by the copyright holder.

light source The perceived location of the lighting in relation to the form.

line A mark with a beginning and an end point.

line segment Part of a path that joins two anchor points.

line spacing *See* Leading.

lowercase Small letters; the opposite of uppercase.

margins Define the image area on the page. Headers and footers are positioned in the top and bottom margin area between the page edge and the margins.

master items Design elements placed on a master page.

master pages Pages that add common design elements to document pages, such as page numbers, headers, and footers.

masthead Headline or title for a magazine. Can also refer to a page containing business information about a publication, such as the staff, contact information, advertising rates, and so on.

metadata Information that is included in a document but is hidden, such as copyright, lens information, location via GPS, camera settings, and more.

metric kerning Kerns letter pairs based on information specified in the font; kerning adjusts space between characters.

model releases The permission that is required when a person's face is identifiable in a photo and the image will be used to promote something—whether it's a product or an idea.

monochromatic Different shades and tints of the same color. Communicates a relaxed and peaceful feeling.

monospaced font Fixed-width or nonproportional fonts that use the same amount of horizontal space for each letter.

motion path Line that an object follows as part of a animation.

movement Visual movement within a design, such as the natural tracking of the eye across a page as the eye moves from focal point to focal point.

multistate object Object that contains multiple appearances, such as a button that appears to highlight when clicked or tapped.

negative space Empty areas in a design; also known as white space.

nested styles Combining character and paragraph styles so that a single paragraph can contain character ranges with different formatting.

NoDerivs (ND) Creative Commons licensing. Requires that you not change material when you incorporate it into your own work. It can be used freely, but you must pass it along without change.

NonCommercial (NC) Creative Commons licensing. Means you can use work in your own creative work as long as you don't charge for it.

object shadow The area of the form that is facing away from the light source and that appears darkest.

object styles Styles that apply basic formatting attributes (such as fill, stroke, corner options, and text frame options) to selected objects.

opacity Level by which an object is transparent or see-through; 100% opacity is nontransparent.

optical kerning More even kerning applied by InDesign that overrides metric kerning; kerning adjusts the space between characters.

organic lines Lines that are usually irregular and imperfect. Found in nature.

organic shapes Shapes that are random or generated by something natural. They are usually asymmetrical and convey natural, homemade, or relaxed feelings.

out port A control on a text frame that flows text out to the next threaded text frame.

overset text Text that does not fit inside a text frame.

page reference A page number for topics listed in an index that points the reader to the location in a publication where the topic is covered.

paragraph formatting *See* Paragraph settings.

paragraph settings Affect an entire paragraph rather than selected words. These settings include alignment, hyphenation, and so on.

paragraph spacing Similar to leading, but applies to an entire paragraph instead of lines of type within them. Also includes the spacing above or below paragraphs.

paragraph style Style that applies text formatting to a paragraph.

pasteboard Area surrounding the document pages; used to store design elements that don't appear on a page.

path Shape assembled from anchor points and line segments.

pattern A repetitive sequence of different colors, shapes, or values.

photoshop path *See* Clipping path.

pica Old typographical unit of measurement. One pica is made up of 12 points.

pictograph (pictogram) Graphic symbol that represents something in the real world. Computer icons are pictographs that suggest the function they represent, such as a trash can icon to delete a file.

points Unit of measurement used for type size.

poster (poster frame) The preview image that appears when a media element is first viewed in a digital media publication.

preflighting Reviewing a document for output issues to avoid costly mistakes on final output. Named after the preflight checklist used by airplane pilots.

primary color Red, blue, or green. These can be combined to create every other color in the visible spectrum.

principles of design Essential rules or assembly instructions of art.

process color Color made up of multiple color components; generally refers to mixing Cyan, Magenta, Yellow, and Black for offset printing.

project creep Unplanned changes that increase the amount of work (scope) that a project requires. When the project loses focus and spins out of control, it eats up more and more time and effort.

project deadlines Dictate when work needs to be completed.

project scope Outlines the amount and type of work to be completed.

proportion (scale) Describes the relative size and scale of elements.

Public Domain When copyright is expired or released and no longer applies to the content, or when an artist releases his or her work. It can be used without worrying about infringement.

pull quote A short, provocative excerpt from a story, typically set in larger type; intended to draw interest to the story.

radial balance Circular type of balance that radiates from the center instead of the middle of a design.

reflected highlight Area of a form that is lit by reflections from the ground or other objects in a scene.

repetition Repeating an element in a design.

representative shapes Shapes used to represent information. They are helpful in communicating with multicultural and multilingual audiences.

rhythm Creative and expressive, rather than a consistent pattern or repetition in a design.

Rule of Thirds A technique for laying out the space of your page to provide a focal point. Two vertical and two horizontal lines evenly divide the space into nine equal boxes, as in a tic-tac-toe board.

run-in head A heading that is part of the paragraph text itself, rather than a paragraph on its own.

runt A single word that appears on the last line of a paragraph; is considered typographically undesirable.

sans serif fonts Font without serifs (the small lines extending from the strokes of a character). Often used for headlines and titles for their strong, stable, modern feel.

script fonts (formal) Mimic handwriting. They convey a feeling of beauty, grace, or feminine dignity.

secondary colors Created when you combine primary colors.

sepia tones Images in which the shades of gray appear as shades of a reddish-brown color.

serif fonts Fonts that feature small lines extending from the strokes of the characters. Serif fonts are associated with typewriters, and they convey tradition, intelligence, and class.

shape An area enclosed or defined by an outline, such as circles, squares, triangles, and even clouds.

ShareAlike Creative Commons licensing. Allows you to use an item in any way you want as long as your creation is shared under the same license as the original work.

shuffling (pages) When InDesign moves pages to the left or right side of a spread because other pages were added or removed.

sketches Representative drawings of how to lay out a document or web page. These are sometimes one of the deliverables of a project.

slab serif fonts Squared-off versions of a typical serif font. Also known as Egyptian, block serif, or square serif, they convey a machine-built feel.

skyline Teaser text across the top of a magazine cover, written to draw attention to the publication.

small caps Uses only uppercase letterforms for each letter, with lowercase letters appearing in a smaller size.

space The canvas or working area. Its dimensions are determined by the resolution of the page you are creating.

specifications Detailed written goals and limits for a project. These are sometimes one of the deliverables of a project.

spot color Premixed ink created specifically for use in print production.

spread Page layout in which pages face each other.

stock photo Images for which the author retains copyright but for which a license for use is available.

story A single continuous text object; may be threaded through multiple text frames.

style (line) An effect applied to a line, such as varying width.

style A named preset of formatting options applied to a character, a paragraph, an object, a table, or a table cell.

style groups Styles, such as paragraph or object styles, organized in folders.

style override Extra formatting applied in addition to a style's formatting. For example, an object may have a stroke applied in addition to the formatting specified in its object style.

subtractive color Created by subtracting light. Printing uses subtractive color, whereas digital devices use additive color.

swashes Special characters with flowing and elegant endings for the ascenders and descenders.

symmetrical balance Occurs when you can divide a page along its middle, and the left side of the page is a mirror image of the right (or the top reflects the bottom). Conveys an intentional, formal, and mechanical feeling.

tertiary color Created by mixing primary and secondary colors.

text frame Box-like element that contains text.

texture The actual, tactile texture in real objects or the appearance of texture in a two-dimensional image.

threaded text (frames) A single text story continued through multiple text frames so that edits ripple through the threaded frames.

tracking Uniform spacing applied to two or more selected characters.

typeface Specific letterform set, such as Helvetica, Arial, Garamond, and so on. It is the "look" of the characters.

type size A font's height from the highest ascender to the lowest descender.

unity (harmony) Sharing similar traits. Low contrast. Things that go together should look like they belong together. The opposite of variety.

uppercase Words typed in capital letters.

value Describes the lightness or darkness of an object. Together with color, value represents the visible spectrum, such as a gradient.

variable width lines Expresses flow and grace.

variety High contrast. The opposite of unity.

vertical Moving from top to bottom. Vertical lines tend to express power and elevation.

vertical scale Describes the function of stretching letters and distorting the typeface geometry.

weight (line) The thickness of a line.

wireframe Rough, representative sketch of how to lay out a document.

workspace Everything you see onscreen in InDesign, such as the application with its Tools panel, Control panel, and document window containing pages and pasteboard.

Index